Also by Mike Gray

The Death Game
Drug Crazy
Angle of Attack
The Warning
The China Syndrome (screenplay)

BUSTED

STONE COWBOYS, NARCO-LORDS AND WASHINGTON'S WAR ON DRUGS

EDITED BY MIKE GRAY

Thunder's Mouth Press / Nation Books
New York

BUSTED: Stone Cowboys, Narco-Lords, and Washington's War on Drugs

© 2002 by Mike Gray

Published by
Thunder's Mouth Press/Nation Books
An Imprint of Avalon Publishing Group Incorporated
161 William St., 16th Floor
New York, NY 10038

Nation Books is a co-publishing venture of the Nation Institute and Avalon Publishing Group Incorporated.

Library of Congress Cataloging-in-Publication Data

Busted : stone cowboys, narco-lords, and Washington's war on drugs / edited by Mike Gray
            p. cm.
      ISBN 1-56025-432-7 (trade paper)
         1. Narcotics, Control of–United States. 2. Drug abuse–Government policy–United States. 3. Drug traffic–United States. !. Gray, Mike

HV5825 .B89 2002
363.45'0973–dc21
2002072435

9 8 7 6 5 4 3 2 1

Designed by Sue Canavan
Printed in the United States of America
Distributed by Publishers Group West

CONTENTS

THE BUSINESS

FOREIGN AFFAIRS

CRIMINAL JUSTICE

THE VIEW FROM THE FORTIETH FLOOR

CONSERVATIVE COMPASSION

THANKS . . .

To Ruth Baldwin, who shepherded this project from beginning to end with speed, precision, and sound advice. And thanks to Carol Gray for guidance along the way.

Finally, my deep appreciation to Robert Field, Kevin Zeese, and Doug McVay of Common Sense for Drug Policy for their ongoing support and assistance.

Introduction

The village of Darlington is on the Indiana film board's list of movie locations if you happen to be looking for Small Town America. On the bluffs above Sugar Creek, surrounded by some of the country's most fertile farmland, its white clap-board houses and brick sidewalks seem so timeless and unassailable that the cit-izens still leave their doors unlocked. So I was surprised last spring when my cousin told me that the sheriff had just found a meth lab across the road from the high school. Some time earlier, she said, they had arrested a couple of the locals for dealing cocaine.

For a town of 740 people in the middle of the Indiana corn fields to be sup-porting a meth lab and a couple of coke dealers is impressive. It's clearly not what the government intended when drug prohibition was launched in 1914, but 90 years and $1 trillion later, this is the tragic payoff in the tree-lined Mid-western sanctuary where I grew up.

Almost every neighborhood in the country has a similar tale and that prob-ably accounts for the fact that three out of four Americans think the drug war has failed. The drug warriors, however, remain steadfast. Asa Hutchinson, head of the U.S. Drug Enforcement Administration, is adamantine. "You do not win in these efforts by giving in."

A few years back that would have been the end of the argument. The gov-ernment effectively controlled the discussion and any deviation from the official policy was strictly out of order. As former Los Angles police chief Willie Williams said when asked about legalization, "It should not be even discussed here in America."

All that changed abruptly over the last decade when two unexpected players came onstage. First was the canny Hungarian-American billionaire, George Soros. Then there was the Internet. Before Soros showed up, scientists and aca-demics who deviated from the drug war orthodoxy simply couldn't get any funding. Over the last thirty years the federal government spent tens of millions of dollars in largely unsuccessful research efforts to establish the harmfulness of mar-ijuana, but they have yet to complete a single study into its possible usefulness.

When George Soros dropped several million dollars into the hands of a few cash-starved researchers and reform organizations, he managed to kick-start a vigorous national academic debate. And when this debate was hooked up to the Internet it went mainstream at light speed. Suddenly obscure documents that had previously been available only through university or government libraries were on-screen for anyone at the click of a mouse. A student debating the success or failure of Dutch drug policy could find the actual data at the Dutch government's official Web site and compare it with the U.S. numbers from the Department of Justice—no middleman required.

Watching this electronic town meeting evolve was an insight into the politics of the future. Drug policy reformers all over the country began to realize they were not lone voices howling in the wind. And instant access to hard numbers proved to be an argument terminator. When a controversy erupted and facts were in dispute, the electronic dialogue would soon be joined by leading authorities with numbers and citations.

As these virtual seminars gained momentum, it became clear that a lot of the underlying assumptions about the war on drugs were not supported by any scientific evidence. And a close examination of the history revealed that the whole thing had come about more or less by accident. The conventional wisdom— that drug prohibition was triggered by a terrible opium problem after the Civil War—turned out to be myth.

When these contrarian opinions began showing up on the op-ed pages, the prohibitionists found themselves playing defense for the first time in years. It was not their strong suit. Accustomed to the luxury of making unchallenged sweeping statements, they stuck with their traditional set of slogans and suddenly found themselves in a factual minefield.

Quite by accident, I happened into one of these public confrontations myself. Shortly after *Drug Crazy* was published in 1998 I got a call from a young CNN producer in Atlanta. She said Gen. Barry McCaffrey, the Clinton White House drug czar, would be on "Talkback Live" that afternoon and one of the other guests had just cancelled. Would I step in? "It's time for people to hear the other side," she said.

The General was probably as surprised as I was. He had gone to Atlanta with the president to kick off the new White House anti-drug TV campaign. When they cut to me in Los Angeles for a reaction to the spots, I said that broadcasting messages of abstinence to teenagers was a good idea but that these ads wouldn't work. They lumped all drugs together as equally dangerous. And as one kid told me, "You lied to us about marijuana, I figured you were lying to us about heroin." Unfortunately we weren't lying about heroin but how was he to know?

I said, "The Dutch don't do it this way, General. They have a much more tolerant policy and their results are better than ours across the board."

McCaffrey said, "The Dutch drug experience is not something we want to model. It's an unmitigated disaster."

This is provably false—marijuana use among Dutch teenagers is half that of the U.S.—and since I'd heard him say this before, I had tipped off the Dutch Embassy in Washington just before I went on the air. I told the General that the Dutch Government was distressed about his misrepresentations and that he would be receiving a formal diplomatic protest. Later, a Dutch official told me that the foreign office not only sent the protest, but briefly considered barring McCaffrey from the country.

Officials in the Bush administration, to their credit, are much more likely to engage in open debate. Unfortunately, they're still insisting that the only answer is full steam ahead. Defending the drug war record, DEA chief Asa Hutchinson told ABC's John Stossel, "Overall drug use in the United States has been reduced by 50 percent over the last 20 years."

When Stossel reminded him that the major drop was years ago with no improvement in the last decade, Hutchinson admitted, "We have flat-lined. I believe we lost our focus to a certain extent."

It's hard to imagine how Mr. Hutchinson hopes to tighten the screws. The annual drug war budget is already over $40 billion, we're arresting nearly a million people a year, and the prisons are packed to the rafters. Despite these fairly staggering social costs, you can now buy high quality cocaine and methamphetamine in small Indiana farm towns.

Today, the drug war establishment finds itself confronting a couple of major threats. The first is medical marijuana, and here again, the government is digging in. The official position is that marijuana has no therapeutic value whatsoever. In fact its history as a medicinal herb stretches back 3000 years and it was widely prescribed in the U.S. for a variety of aches and pains until 1937.

Anyone who has any doubts about the potential life-saving qualities of cannabis should take a look at the remarkable case of Steve Kubby, the sometime Libertarian candidate for Governor of California. Kubby also campaigned for Proposition 215, the first state initiative to make it legal for qualified patients to grow their own marijuana, but he was arrested nonetheless.

Since his case would be plowing new terrain, I went up to the trial in the tiny gold rush town of Auburn to find out what lengths the government would go to in defending its position that marijuana is useless. This trial would be definitive in one sense. If anyone on the planet qualifies as a medical marijuana patient it is Steve Kubby.

Diagnosed back in the 1970s with a rare form of adrenal cancer, Kubby was treated by Dr. Vincent DeQuattro of U.S.C., a leading authority on the disease. At the time DeQuattro did what he could—surgery, chemo, radiation—but it was a delaying action. The cancer—malignant pheochromocytoma—is not fatal in itself but it causes the adrenal glands to work overtime, dramatically boosting blood pressure. You can drop dead of a stroke at any minute. Nobody lives longer than five years.

Dr. DeQuattro assumed Kubby had passed on long ago, then he opened the 1998 California voter's guide and there was his former patient running for governor. Astounded, the doctor tracked him down and asked him what miracle had granted him this reprieve.

"Marijuana," said Kubby. It seems he had abandoned the traditional treatment and switched to cannabis, smoking some 10 grams a day for the last 15 years.

Dr. DeQuattro's first reaction was to put Steve Kubby under a microscope. At the U.S.C. medical center he ran Kubby through an exhaustive two-week workup. While the doctor is no fan of marijuana—he had never recommended it—the results convinced him that marijuana was somehow keeping Kubby alive.

The day I went up to Auburn, Dr. DeQuattro was scheduled to testify. In the cramped little courtroom, DeQuattro told the jury that Kubby's tumors are clearly visible on the X rays but, for reasons he can't explain, the disease is apparently stabilized. What's more, the side effects of smoking marijuana day and night for 15 years appear to be zero.

DeQuattro said his team tested Kubby for cognitive function before and after smoking and found his mind, memory, and motor skills unimpaired. But the discovery that really jolted them was the lungs. Here they had a subject who admittedly smoked a couple hundred joints a month for 15 years—a perfect opportunity to measure the damage from chronic high-level consumption—but they couldn't find any. "His respiratory functions are the same as for someone who never smoked at all."

When the prosecutor suggested that Kubby might be faking it—that he was really just smoking the Devil Weed for pleasure, Dr. DeQuattro disabused him. He said that if the adrenaline in Mr. Kubby's bloodstream were injected into the prosecutor's veins, he would have a heart attack.

After deliberating for several days, the jury hung 11-to-1 in favor of acquittal and the prosecutor threw in the towel. But that did not clear the field. U.S. officials wanted Kubby to serve a four-month sentence for possession of a mushroom stem. That would probably have been a death sentence since Kubby wouldn't be allowed access to marijuana in jail, so he's now a fugitive in Canada.

Which brings us to the second crisis looming for the drug warriors. In addition to apostasy of medical marijuana, they are increasingly confronted with desertion in the ranks. One after another our former allies are abandoning the U.S. zero-tolerance battle plan. The Canadian government just established regulations to expand the use of medical marijuana and the Journal of the Canadian Medical Association called it, "a step in the right direction," then added, "but a bolder stride is needed. The possession of small quantities for personal use should be decriminalized."

This was hardly music to Washington's ears but it was just the latest voice in the chorus. The U.S. has always been the driving force behind this campaign. We more or less forced the rest of the world to go along with drug prohibition in the early 1900s, but by 1974 Holland had decided to go its own way. Now other countries are gauging the Dutch results against those of the U.S. and deciding that the Dutch experience is a lot more appealing. The UK is conducting the first government-sponsored scientific tests of medical marijuana, and the British Parliament is inching closer to full decriminalization. Italy, Spain, Portugal, and Luxembourg have already decriminalized possession of marijuana—and all other drugs as well.

It is in the arena of hard drugs where the boldest moves are being made, and the boldest of all are the Swiss. Here the government is providing virtually cost-free heroin to serious addicts. The dramatic results—major savings in health costs, overdose deaths cut in half, AIDS deaths down by a third, crime among the addicts down 85 percent—with many addicts actually holding jobs—these startling facts are beginning to undermine the whole concept of drug prohibition. Martin Hosek, the Swiss health official in charge of the project, says, "We see some interest from countries like Britain and the Netherlands. . . . A German trial started in February . . . Spain wants to start trials in November."

Critics of the Swiss heroin prescription program rightly point out that it doesn't wean addicts off drugs. Says DEA chief Asa Hutchinson, "Maintaining addictions will never bring down demand. . . . The only way to end the many devastating effects of drug abuse is to overcome addiction and stop using drugs."

While this is certainly a self-satisfying moral posture, there has never been a drug-free society anywhere, least of all in the United States where the dividing line between legal and illegal seems almost whimsical. Now we have former

Senator Bob Dole on TV pushing Viagra to help aging lovers get it up, but if their mates take a puff of marijuana to get in the mood, they're looking at jail time. If our real objective is a safer, healthier society, we must demand a drug policy based on scientific fact instead of wishful thinking.

We've tried in this collection to give you a broad cross section of recent writings on the drug war at home and abroad. What follows is almost totally critical of current drug policy, and while that may seem unbalanced, there has been little change in the historic position of the prohibitionists. Their traditional arguments are effectively summarized in "The Myth of 'Harmless' Marijuana," by White House Drug Czar John Walters in Chapter six.

Though you won't find much support for the drug war here, you will find a wide political spectrum aligned against it, from Bill Buckley to Christopher Hitchens, and everything in between. We've got the view from the street and the view from on high, from big city mayors to recovering addicts, and the common thread is that it's long past time for another approach. As former Kansas City police chief Joe McNamara says in Chapter six, "About $500 worth of heroin or cocaine in a source country will bring in as much as $100,000 on the streets of an American city. All the cops, armies, prisons, and executions in the world cannot impede a market with that kind of tax-free profit margin."

MIKE GRAY
Los Angeles

[SOUTH OF THE BORDER]

BLOW BACK

T. D. Allman

An earlier version of this article appeared in *Rolling Stone*, May 9, 2002

Two nations that had always brought out the worst in each other's natures were now going to bring out the best. Bill Clinton, nearing the end of his White House tenure, knew that he had to be seen doing something to help end drug abuse in America. And Colombia's incoming president, Andres Pastrana, knew that Colombia would not win the world's respect unless he could transform his nation into something other than the most agile and productive drug exporter in the global marketplace.

Pastrana had a master plan—or at least a name for one: "Plan Colombia." And the U.S., supposedly, had the know-how, money, and resolve to help make it work. The payoff for Colombia would be a new economic and social foundation for a future free of drugs and civil violence. The payoff for the U.S. would be meaningful and measurable progress in the War on Drugs.

Today, nearly four years later, Plan Colombia is dead. According to CIA findings, Colombian coca cultivation is up by nearly 25 percent since the U.S. first launched its effort to eradicate coca production by aerial chemical spraying. The administration's reaction is even more revealing: When the CIA's statistics on soaring coca culitivation contradicted the official line, the State Department censored the statistics. "U.S. omits Colombian coca figure from drug report," announced a little-noticed Reuters story. The article began, "The United States omitted a Colombian coca-production figure—the most important single statistic—from its 2001 drug-trade report."

A short time later, the CIA released its findings. And then? Nothing. The White House did no re-evaluation. There was no reaction in Congress and the press. In a reality-based situation, a drug report without drug statistics would be startling, an intelligence finding that drug cultivation was increasing, not disappearing, grounds for a policy reappraisal.

But that's not how U.S. drug policy gets made. No matter who is president, drug policy trundles along, divorced from reality, so this latest indication that Plan Colombia is a tissue of illusion was scarcely noticed. Instead, before our eyes, a failed "war on drugs" is turning into an open-ended "war on terrorism."

Last year, I spent nearly two months traveling to every part of Colombia. While I was there, I talked with human-rights heroes and I supped with murderers. I talked with peasants, guerrilla leaders, and billionaires. I flew with President Pastrana in his official jet and wound up in a no-blinking contest with "Ivan"—the guerrilla commander, and drug warlord, of the Putumayo region.

Everywhere I went, I found a country that simply wasn't like the one we imagine Colombia to be. The first discovery was simply how big it is. Colombia looks so manageable on our maps, so compact in comparison with gigantic neighboring Brazil, but it's bigger than California and Texas combined. Of all the people I met, no one made better sense of Colombia than Lee Miles, an American chandler and emerald trader, who has lived there for decades. "There's the Colombia with roads. And the Colombia with no roads," he told me one afternoon, sailing in Cartagena's harbor. "Once the Colombia without roads counted for nothing. But drugs and the airplane have revolutionized Colombia. Go out beyond the roads. Grow some coca. Make some cocaine. You don't even have to get it to market. Just clear a landing strip—and they fly right in for it with suitcases full of money." He goes on: "Drugs and airplanes have revolutionized power relationships because the Colombia without roads now can get ahold of lots of money, and with money you can buy anything: guns, equipment, people."

In the rough little city of Puerto Asis, in the Putumayo region of southern Colombia, the two Colombias meet. Amazonian near-wilderness encroaches from every direction. But Puerto Asis has its soccer stadium, its ATMs and its passenger-jet airport where, almost since dawn, high-ranking local Colombians have been waiting for the American congressional delegation to fly in.

Back when Plan Colombia was being slammed together in sealed offices in Washington, D.C., Putumayo and the rest of southern Colombia were thought to account for as much as 80 percent of the coca produced in Colombia. That figure was never anything more than a guess. Even so, Putumayo has become the scene of the biggest U.S. attempt to eradicate Colombian cocaine production by spraying chemical defoliants on coca fields from airplanes. There are a number of reasons for this—chief among them is the fact that much of Putumayo and its expanding drug business wound up under the control of the Revolutionary Armed Forces of Colombia (FARC), the larger of Colombia's two main insurgent groups (the other is called the National Liberation Army, or ELN). So right from the beginning, a war against drugs in Putumayo was also a campaign to expand the influence of the Colombian government and deprive the guerrillas of land and narco-profits.

According to the State Department, in the initial fumigation campaign, begun more than a year ago, defoliants—a compound of herbicidal chemicals sold commercially in the U.S. under the brand name Roundup—were sprayed on more than thirty thousand hectares in Putumayo (and ninety-four thousand hectares in the entire country in 2001). That explains why, on this breezy morning, the U.S. ambassador to Colombia, two members of Congress, and a score or so of congressional staffers, embassy aides and representatives of American nongovernmental organizations are exiting the plastic cool of the charter jet that flew them down here from Bogotá and are descending into the hot glare and vegetal damp of the Puerto Asis airport tarmac.

Reps. Jim McGovern of Massachusetts and Jan Schakowsky of Illinois, the closest that Plan Colombia has in Congress to critics, are trying to find an answer to a question that often gets obscured in the debates over drug policy: Will U.S. efforts here do anything to stop Colombian drugs from coming into the U.S.? In addition to the members of Congress, two other Americans getting off the plane need to be identified from the start. One is David Becker, who, at the time of our visit, was Deputy Director of the Narcotics Affairs Section of the U.S. Embassy in Bogotá. Standing nearby is a young American woman named Winifred Tate, who, as of this trip, worked for an NGO called the Washington Office on Latin America, or WOLA.

Dave Becker, in his forties, looks like he's a car-pool commuter, not a frontline veteran of low-intensity conflicts in places such as Honduras, El Salvador, Burkina Faso, and Guatemala. As for Winnie Tate, she could be just another perpetual grad student in third-world studies, but Becker and Tate together merit a closer look, for they embody an old, deep split in our American national personality.

Except for Vietnam, we tend to forget how frequently our country's foreign crusades have divided us. Is it our duty to police the world or to redeem it? Back in 1849, Henry David Thoreau wrote "Civil Disobedience," his account of how he was imprisoned for protesting the U.S. war of aggression against Mexico. Yet supporters of that war against Mexico called it a war to "extend the area of freedom," in this case an extension of freedom to practice slavery in the conquered territories.

A war to extend freedom: That's how Dave Becker still remembers U.S. involvement in the slaughter in Central America, which, among other things, launched his own State Department career in counterinsurgency. "We were really there to ensure that violent change—at the point of a gun—did not win," Becker told his college-alumni magazine just as Plan Colombia was beginning.

Becker was educated at Reed College, in Portland, Oregon. In one of our talks, Becker said that he got into counterinsurgency because he wanted to do something in the world. As he tells his story, it's clear Becker doesn't consider it odd or questionable that his origins should entitle him to decide what democracy is in El Salvador, or whose crops get defoliated in Colombia. So sure is he of his own virtue, he tends to assume that those opposing him are bad as well as wrong, as becomes evident during our visit to Puerto Asis.

And Tate? If Becker looks like a 4-H alumnus, Tate calls to mind one of those classic marble effigies of "Justice" or "Agriculture" you find adorning state capitols all over the U.S. She is statuesque and belongs to that school of thought which holds that the wretched of the earth are by definition virtuous and that being American in itself is almost invariably a sin.

The Drug War is Becker's war, but today's meeting turns out to be Tate's teach-in. The two visiting members of Congress wanted something more than the usual embassy briefings, so they asked Tate and WOLA, not the embassy handlers who normally arrange such visits, to organize this trip. It turns out to have been a smart move. This will be the first time that U.S. officials involved in the anti-drug campaign in Colombia willl actually meet face-to-face with people directly affected by aerial defoliation.

After getting off the plane, the American delegation is bused to the nearby municipal meeting hall. There is no tour of the area, no attempt to acquaint the visitors with local landmarks.

Inside, there is no presiding officer. One by one, the Colombians get up to talk. It is, from the start, like the committee of blind men assessing an elephant. From the official U.S. perspective, raining down chemical defoliants on these people and their crops has something to do with trying to stop Americans from snuffling coke in distant U.S. suburbs and cities. It is all, indeed, part of a plan. For these Colombian farmers and community leaders, however, it all seems less of a plan and more of a plot: an impulsive, futile gringo plot to deprive them of all the good things of modern life—boomboxes, motorbikes, antibiotics, VCRs—and push them back into pre-Reeboks subsistence agriculture.

A teacher speaks. "Since the defoliation," she says, "some parents have stopped sending their children to school because they can't buy the textbooks."

She looks at the Americans and says, "Don't you understand? The coca crops are just going to move to another place."

Now a man stands, addresses the visitors and politely says, "Unless you stop abusing it, coca will always be produced."

As they talk, the coca farmers make no effort to pretend they weren't growing coca. As one woman puts it, "How else can I support my family?" It's a question I hear repeated many times across Colombia. It is a question to which I never get an answer, because no one has an answer to it—certainly not the creators and implementers of Plan Colombia.

As the Colombians bombard them with realities that do not comport with policy, the embassy Americans begin to zone out. Only two of the embassy officials remain engaged. One is Ambassador Anne Patterson, a professional diplomat of a certain age. While others flag, she keeps chugging along in her American-accented, though fluent, Spanish and her by now wrinkled and somewhat sweaty pastel linen suit. All day long she sits there, listening and taking notes.

The other U.S. official who continues to pay close attention is Dave Becker, who gradually becomes a portrait of agitated and, in the end, uncontainable vexation.

"You destroyed my chili peppers," one man says, while Becker stares back with a flinty look in his eyes.

A government official says, "Our pineapple project was fumigated." A community leader says, "We had a fence around our alternative-crop demonstration project and signs at the gate. There was no coca there, as anyone could see with his own eyes."

A farmer is describing how the defoliants destroyed his crops even though he was not growing any coca. He does this at great length, because describing things at length is what Colombians—ranging from this farmer to Gabriel Garcia Marquez, Colombia's Nobel laureate in literature—do. It isn't the man's orotundity that vexes Becker, however; it is his version of reality. It contradicts Becker's reality and, therefore, in Becker's view, the man must be lying.

So Becker breaks in. "That's not right," he announces.

The man directs a confused look at Becker. After all, they were his crops. He saw the planes appear overhead. He saw his crops die.

Ambassador Patterson glances at Becker and gives him a downstroke wave of her hand. Becker simmers down, but he does not let go of it. He periodically shakes his head in dismay and punches his palm in frustration.

Later on in the meeting, a Colombian community leader tries to explain that it would be more effective to rely on manual eradication—to use people, instead of spy satellites, to find the coca and then to use people's hands and hoes, instead of airplanes and defoliants, to remove it.

Uprooting the coca plants by hand, he's trying to explain, would avoid the errors built into aerial defoliation. It would also create work and put money into the pockets of the people who need it most. "Millions of dollars could be saved . . ." the man is saying, but no one pays much attention, because at this potentially illuminating point the Americans can't take their eyes off a giant dark-brown spider. The spider, having emerged from under the chairs of the two members of Congress, starts heading toward the ambassador.

The Colombians no more notice the spider's intrusion than the Americans, in Washington, would let the wail of a car alarm distract them, but the Americans can't take their eyes off it. So no one explains to the community leader the reason why there's so little American enthusiasm for manual eradication, which is that while manual eradication may make sense here in Putumayo, it makes no political sense whatsoever in Washington.

Moments after the spider retreats to its hiding place, a man steps to the microphone and says, "My name is Roger Hernandez. We are victims of the drug consumers. We need help to break the circle." An old man is eager to speak. "I am from the Farmers' Association," he says. "We need social investment!"

Since anyone is free to speak, I raise my hand and ask, "Who in this meeting hall would like to get out of the coca business?" The farmers all raise their hands and cry out, "Yes!"

Then I ask, "Have any of you received aid of any kind to help you stop growing coca under Plan Colombia?"

They all shake their heads: No! They all say, Nada! Many of these people have traveled for up to thirteen hours to get here. Several have tried to learn enough English so they can be understood in the visitors' language. One man, referring to the aerial defoliation, speaks in an English he clearly has been practicing for this occasion. He says, "We never opposed eradication, but this is not the correct means. The peasants are keeping their side of the bargain, but they are caught. They can't see their coca or nothing to replace it."

Finally, Becker can't stand it anymore.

In a you-have-only-yourself-to-blame tone of voice, he interrupts one of the campesinos and says, "We offered you geosatellite equipment, but you wouldn't take it. You were afraid the guerrillas would kill you!"

It takes a moment for the meaning of what Becker has just said to sink in. Then I realize: Yes, I heard right. As part of America's anti-drug technowar, scrub farmers in equatorial Colombia have been offered satellite beacons so they can beam up to U.S. spy satellites in outer space the information that, yes, we have no coca, we have no coca today.

THE REALM OF LITTLE GREEN DOTS

The theory behind the high-tech targeting of coca cultivation—which the U.S. does from outer space—is simple. Everything that lives, including coca plants, emits radiation. Coca, therefore, has its own unique radiation signature.

This telltale radiation can be recognized by orbiting satellites and then converted into data. Next, the data are represented visually or mathematically using the Multiple Digital Imaging System.

Up in Bogotá, during the standard Plan Colombia briefings at the U.S. Embassy, the visual representations of the coca radiation data take the form of computer-generated little green dots. Each tiny square symbolizes an area of more than fifty acres where the radiation signature of the coca plant has been detected.

The little green dots are very important when it comes to marshaling congressional support for Plan Colombia because when most U.S. senators and members of Congress visit Colombia on a "fact-finding" mission, they never get as far as the meeting hall in Puerto Asis. Many stay in Colombia for only a few hours, and the closest they get to reality is the darkened embassy briefing room in Bogotá.

The visiting dignitaries enter this room, as I did the day I attended the Plan Colombia briefing, through the building's gigantic front door, a lofty, multithon, bombproof portal already turned bronze-green by the Colombian climate. The day I was there, deli sandwiches were served as the little green dots swarmed onto the map. Ambassador Patterson herself, holding a pointer, gave the signal for them to appear.

These bright-green dots produce a powerful psychological effect when projected onto the mural-size screen in the darkened room. They suggest that real-life coca cultivation can be eliminated the same way these computer images were generated in the first place: through the use of American technology. The little green dots are the problem? We'll delete them! This kind of imaging makes coca cultivation seem a dramatic problem but also one within the ambit of American know-how—a danger to our national well-being that is also like a video game.

The problem is that Colombia is actually a messy human reality.

"See? The satellite imaging doesn't lie," Becker tells me a few weeks later, on another excursion in southern Colombia. First from a light aircraft, then leaning out open-door combat helicopters, we overfly the coca fields of Putumayo and neighboring Caqueta.

Thousands of acres below us have been defoliated, but as Becker himself points out, "Look! There's new coca everywhere." Every time he looks outside the plane's window, Becker sees a target and—he tells me he really believes this—if only we hit enough of those targets, life will change for the better all over the U.S. "We'll gain time to do something good," he says, "as we dry up the supply of drugs in the projects and ghettos."

Also onboard is the State Department's chief official in managing the Drug War, Assistant Secretary of State R. Rand Beers. The next stop has been designed to show him how Plan Colombia is helping former coca farmers build new lives. However, the showcase project proves to be nothing more than some palm nuts hastily thrown onto an abandoned field of diseased coca plants. "My coca plants were already dying," the farmer tells me, "so this money is a help." Are there any healthy coca plants nearby, and is anything being done to help those farmers shift to legal crops?

"We're all growing coca," answers one woman in the crowd of Colombians who have gathered to watch the Americans disgorge from their helicopters and stand in this field, "to help our children."

On the way back to Bogotá, Beers sits in his seat with his eyes closed during the entire flight. Seated across from him is President Pastrana's chief official in charge of drug-crop substitution programs. She gives me her card, so I recognize her name a while later, when her son is arrested and charged with being part of a heroin-smuggling ring.

Since the U.S. aerial-defoliation campaign began in Colombia, at least three pilots have been killed. On the ground, churches, soccer fields, flowers, and schoolchildren have been "defoliated."

Coca cultivation and subsistence agriculture in Colombia traditionally occur cheek by jowl. And you have to fly low and close-in if these messy chemicals are actually going to hit their targets. But the hired crews aren't flying these missions out of some altruistic urge to rid America of drugs. They do it for money. Once upon a time, these pilots and crews were called mercenaries. Today they're known as contract personnel. Many of these contract personnel come from countries with histories of heavy U.S. involvement in clandestine warfare, including Cuba and the nations of Central America.

I met one of these defoliation pilots at Larandia, a former plantation in Caqueta, which the U.S. Embassy has transformed into a military training base. The pilot, a Guatemalan, told me he had flown for the Contras in Honduras back in the 1980s, as part of the operations that produced the Iran-Contra scandal during the Reagan administration.

In the past, operations such as the Colombia defoliation might also have been run by the CIA. But in the current age of downsizing and outsourcing, the U.S. has subcontracted a lot of the War on Drugs to DynCorp, a "consulting" firm with Virginia headquarters convenient to the CIA and the Pentagon. DynCorp in turn subcontracts many of the Colombia defoliation flights to Eagle Aviation Services and Technology Inc., another U.S.-incorporated company, usually known by its acronym,

EAST. During the Iran-Contra affair, EAST was used extensively for secret operations in Central America. It's convenient for the State Department to use such outfits as DynCorp and EAST today for the same reason they were useful in clandestine operations earlier. These private subcontractors are harder to scrutinize than government agencies; if there are casualties or foul-ups, they make smaller headlines.

So, technically speaking, the State Department doesn't pay the defoliation crews. The State Department pays DynCorp, which pays EAST to pay the defoliation crews. Whatever the accounting devices, the pilots defoliate coca for exactly the same reason the campesinos grow it: to get the yanqui dollar.

CO-OPTING A PLAN

Back in 1998, when Colombia's newly elected President Pastrana first took his idea of Plan Colombia to Washington, targeting coca plants with spy satellites was not what he had in mind. He wanted the emphasis to be on economic development. He also wanted to fight drug production by increasing Colombia's legal exports to the U.S.—products such as textiles and flowers that face high tariffs and strict regulation, even as cocaine and heroin from the roadless Colombia flow into the U.S. uncontrolled and untaxed. "The original Plan Colombia was a beautiful vision," says Pastrana's ambassador in Washington, Luis Moreno.

His vision was never realized. "Pastrana's idealism ran into U.S. political reality," says Professor Peter Reuter of the University of Maryland, a leading expert on America's drug consumption and our fitful attempts to control it. "Bill Clinton warned me," Pastrana himself said, the first time I met him in the presidential palace in Bogotá. "When I told him I wanted U.S. help for human development, President Clinton said, 'I can't help you on that. What I can get for you out of Congress is weapons and military supplies.' "

The result, once it was fed into the Washington policy mill, was a makeover of Plan Colombia suitable to various Washington power groups. First, the State Department—which tends to be even more compulsive about such things than the Pentagon—transformed Plan Colombia from a development concept into a military-assistance program. Then Congress, as it habitually does, transformed the program into pork. That is, the senators and representatives directed the money away from Colombia, and into their own home states and districts. Authorizing more than one billion in high-tech appropriations for Plan Colombia, as that farmer in Puerto Asis tried to explain, made no sense in Colombia, but it made a lot of political sense in Washington. In fact, the high-tech weapons were essential to getting Plan Colombia through Congress. For if the plan had been a low-tech, barrios-up approach — if it hadn't contained hundreds of millions of dollars in contracts for their home states and districts — who in Congress would have carried the flag for Plan Colombia?

Perhaps not Sen. Chris Dodd of Connecticut, a former Peace Corps volunteer who speaks fluent Spanish. Dodd is generally considered a careful scrutinizer when it comes to U.S. involvement in places like Putumayo — except, it would appear, when the military equipment is manufactured in Connecticut.

Dodd, a liberal Democrat, along with Dennis Hastert, the Republican Speaker of the House, was one of the biggest flagwavers for Plan Colombia. So were moderate Republicans such as New York Rep. Benjamin Gilman, a fervent backer of the Colombian National Police. Plan Colombia, as it rolled triumphantly through Congress, had something in it for practically everyone except the Colombians.

By the time the folks up in Washington had finished, at least 80 percent of the U.S. aid was going for military, police, and other expenditures ostensibly necessary to make drug suppression in general, and aerial defoliation in particular, a resounding success down there in Colombia. Simultaneously, they had jiggered this "aid" so as to ensure that scarcely any of the actual money ever gets to Colombia — but instead gets spent right here in the U.S.

Even then, out of the money Congress voted for Plan Colombia, hundreds of millions weren't for Colombia at all. More than a third of the money was allotted for such "Plan Colombia" activities as improving airports on the Caribbean resort islands of Aruba and Curaçao. Once the non-Colombian appropriations are edited out, only about $860 million appears to be left, but even that is an exaggeration. For out of that remaining sum, yet more hundreds of millions go for such items as "secure communications," "intelligence" support, and "force protection."

That is, roughly half of what remains in Plan Colombia for Colombia actually goes to pay for "Made in USA" high-tech military toys, and for the salaries and creature comforts of the Americans, Colombians, and contract personnel who use them, and to provide security for them. A lot of this is super-expensive, hush-hush technology, but we're also talking microwave ovens for popcorn and satellite TVs for hometown news. At the U.S. training base in Larandia, I find a lively debate has erupted on how to spend the Plan Colombia money: It is over the size of the bedrooms being built as part of the U.S. contribution to Plan Colombia.

"The Colombians like big rooms where they can entertain their wives, kids, friends, and mistresses," a DynCorp executive tells me. "Our guys want small rooms that can be air-conditioned."

Only $68.5 million, just under 8 percent, stands any chance of actually making a positive difference in the life decisions of the people whom the U.S. wants to stop growing coca. That's the total amount slotted for alternative-crop development—to encourage Colombia's farmers to switch to crops like chili peppers, in the whole country of Colombia, not just in Putumayo.

In comparison, $234 million goes for just eighteen U.S.-manufactured Black Hawk helicopters, produced in Dodd's home state of Connecticut. Everyone agrees on three things: The Black Hawks are technological marvels. They are hideously expensive. And, considering their firepower and mobility, using them for anti-drug purposes is a curious allocation of very costly military resources— like assigning Maseratis to meter-maid patrol. So why are these high-strung machines—which cost $13 million each—part of Plan Colombia?

The Black Hawks are there, it turns out, simply to discourage disgruntled farmers, drug dealers, and guerrillas from taking potshots at the DynCorp's sub-contract personnel when they appear overhead in their crop-dusters. That's the theory: In reality, the Black Hawks provide ideal guerrilla targets. With a single lucky hit, lightly armed insurgents can inflict dozens of fatalities and cost Colombia or the U.S. tens of millions of dollars.

As if nearly a quarter-billion for Black Hawks weren't enough, Plan Colombia allocates an additional $120 million for even more helicopters. This brings the total for helicopters up to $354 million, or 41 percent of the total. In comparison to the money spent on the Black Hawks, however, this is an example of fiscal rationality. The additional 20 million pays for no less than forty-two reconditioned Vietnam-era Super Huey helicopters, plus operating costs for them, and eighteen more choppers, for a year. If helicopters really are the key to winning the drug war in Colombia, and if the choice of which helicopters to use were practical, not political, these proven workhorses of air warfare would be the first choice for the low-intensity conflict in Colombia—not the enormously expensive Black Hawks, two of which already have been shot down during Colombian military operations.

So, thanks to the Plan, we now have (or to be precise, soon will have) a total of seventy-eight helicopters buzzing through the skies of Colombia, making sure that no one will dare open fire on the little spray planes when they appear over-head to zap the coca.

The results? As I overfly the burgeoning coca fields of southern Colombia, listening to Dave Becker tell me how effective U.S. technology is, there is a sense of history—and of the American capacity for self-delusion—repeating itself.

Aerial defoliation has in fact already been tried, and has failed, in Colombia.

During the 1990s, nearly seven hundred thousand acres of coca were defoliated. Consequently, Colombia went from producing less than 15 percent of the world's coca to producing more than three-quarters of the world supply. It is also the number-one supplier of heroin to the United States.

NO RIGHT TO COMPLAIN

At that meeting in Puerto Asís, Dave Becker said something that stuck in my mind. One farmer was complaining about the defoliation when Becker interrupted him, saying something that, I later discovered, put Plan Colombia into even clearer perspective.

"You have no right to complain," Becker told him. "You shouldn't even be speaking. You refused to sign the social pact."

What is the social pact? A U.S. Embassy-generated briefing paper titled "The Results of Plan Colombia" and published last year explains, "The pact is a written agreement by which the peasants commit themselves to manually eradicate their coca crops in twelve months or less, from the moment they get the first government aid. In exchange for that, the government provides assistance in alternative development, subsidizes agricultural supplies and funds the design, development, and implementation of productive projects."

Curious as to what "productive projects" had been designed, developed, and implemented since Plan Colombia was launched, I read the report from cover to cover. Not a single such completed project was mentioned.

"In terms of education, twelve new schoolrooms are presently being built in Putumayo, of a total of twenty-four that will be built under Plan Colombia," the report states.

Notice that those are new rooms, not new schools—that they're "being built," not "have been built." That's the educational component under Plan Colombia for the entire department of Putumayo, which has a population of nearly three hundred thousand. "Total investment," the report states, "for education infrastructure at a national level is $289,000."

So $234 million for eighteen Black Hawk helicopters, $289,000 for the millions of Colombian children of school age. As the U.S. was about to launch its defoliation flights, farmers around Puerto Asis were presented with an ultimatum. Sign this paper or we'll drop defoliants on you. Of course, it wasn't phrased that way. Villages were also invited to sign "alternative development agreements" or "pacts."

Many farmers did not sign the pacts because they are indeed guerrillas or drug profiteers, or are at least under their control. But there was another reason.

"There wasn't time to build democratic consent," Luis Martinez, the acting mayor of Puerto Asis, told me.

Democratic consent was necessary, first of all, because Colombia is a democracy. But why couldn't those farmers who wanted to simply have signed the pact, leaving those who didn't to risk the consequences?

The technological margins of error in U.S. high-tech warfare, again. The satellites and spray planes—even with the helicopters hovering nearby—can't reliably avoid hitting targets as small as an individual farm. Whole communities have to be targeted or not targeted, unless—as in Afghanistan—we insert U.S. ground forces to do the dirty work.

So it wasn't enough for individuals to sign the pact. Whole municipalities had to agree, and there was no time to organize democratic consent, because, by then, the Americans couldn't wait.

In the end, it came down to this: a lot of coca in Colombia; a lot of technology in the U.S. And in between? A void—a void of honest inquiry in Washington, a void of administrative capacity in Colombia.

So Plan Colombia wound up vindicating a law that also operates at the strip mall. When a retailer finds himself with too much technostuff on his hands, you get a discount sale. And when the Pentagon, the CIA, and the White House find themselves with too many military video games on their hands, you get a free-fire zone.

That's what all the money, all the technology—all the rhetoric about Plan Colombia being "a comprehensive strategy"—ultimately produced: a free-fire zone for plants, along with whatever else, and whomever else, happens to be there when the spray planes, escorted by the helicopters, show up.

And as spraying anything in the way becomes standard operating procedure, an even more significant metamorphosis occurs. The perpetrator becomes his victims' moral superior. Or, as Becker put it to that farmer, "You have no right to complain."

Since September 11, it has become commonplace for policymakers to announce that everything has changed forever, and that America can't and won't go on dealing with its problems in the old, outdated ways.

But when it comes to Plan Colombia and U.S. drug policy, it's as though 9/11 never happened. Just before Christmas, Congress was finally able to take a break from anthrax and Afghanistan and get back to the once hot-button, now back-burner, issue of Plan Colombia and the Drug War.

The Senate and the House together voted an additional $625 million in aid for Plan Colombia, though there has been one change. It isn't called Plan Colombia any more but rather President Bush's Andean Counterdrug Initiative.

Plan Colombia has become what the war on terrorism already is in danger of becoming: another entitlement program for the Washington policy-spinners—grabbing appropriations and generating comforting press releases year after year. "It's a colossal waste of money," says Rep. Jim McGovern, who attempted last year to shift $100 million in spending from military aid to child development. "The ignorance among U.S. officials is astounding when it comes to Colombia, and yet we're trudging ahead."

Before leaving for Colombia, I visited the headquarters of the Drug Enforcement Administration, located not in downtown Washington, D.C., but in suburban Arlington, Virginia. Here at the DEA, as much as in the coca fields of Colombia, there was no real sense that the War on Drugs was something that might actually be lost or won, and end someday. Instead, the War on Drugs has become an institutionalized part of the American government, much like the Department of the Interior.

The DEA budget, which accounts for only a fraction of the money the U.S. spends "fighting drugs" annually, is more than six billion a year. This means that over the decades, billions and billions more dollars appropriated to fight drugs will be spent in suburban Virginia than will ever be spent in drug-producing countries, and it shows. Right near the DEA headquarters is a beautiful shopping mall with deluxe department stores, including a Saks as well as an exclusive Four Seasons Hotel.

The pleasant, unhurried appearance of the people you see in the elevators at the DEA building complements this sense of recession-proof suburban ease, as does the landscaping surrounding the headquarters. At the time I visited, some of our "anti-drug" tax dollars were being spent on a major upgrade of the shrubbery surrounding the DEA building.

After completing my interviews with DEA officials and going outside, I spent some time observing the landscape work. Almost all the gardeners were Hispanic—most of them recent arrivals from Latin America. How had they gotten here, I wondered, and had any arrived carrying drugs?

In a way that the U.S. government never intended, the DEA headquarters tells you everything you need to know about America's War on Drugs. Inside a sealed, air-conditioned sanctuary, U.S. officials send one another memos, oblivious to the world outside.

A TALK WITH MANUEL NORIEGA

Oliver Stone

From *The Nation*, January 24, 1994

The 1989 invasion of Panama and the capture of Gen. Manual Noriega marked a bizarre moment between the end of cold war Realpolitik and the beginning of new-world-order fantasy. Other U.S. interventions during the Reagan/Bush years were devised to roll back what might be perceived—even at an aching stretch—as Soviet power in foreign lands. Grenada, El Salvador, Nicaragua, Afghanistan: Washington's rationale for the money, the massacres, and the military deployments was essentially the same as it had been for forty years.

Bush's putsch into Panama had a somewhat different odor. No one ever said definitively why we were there, but the reigning reason always seemed to be drugs. Someone had the idea that Noriega had become the paramount drug "kingping," on a par with the leaders of the Colombia cartels, just a heartbeat away from selling crack to little kids in American schoolyards. (That made it an important, early example of the exploitation of children for political purposes and their protection by the state as the primary goal of public policy.) The proximate cause of the hunt for Noriega was his 1988 indictment, by Federal grand juries in southern Florida, for facilitating the flow of drugs from Colombia through Panama, a charge made before the grand jury by one of his closest aides, Jose Blandon, who turned against him in return for legal protection and untold riches. By the way, the drug tide seems to have been utterly unaffected by Noriega's apprehension.

The plot in which Noriega plays the leading role is so dense and deep that it could easily take Oliver Stone another trilogy of films simply to skim the surface, if he had the inclination. Stone spent part of a day in prison with Noriega not long ago in pursuit of material for a film he is planning about the peculiar prisoner, and which he described on Charlie Rose as a political "satire" in the Stanley Kubrick mode. The interview is thus by a filmmaker, not an investigative reporter, and except in two places, we have not flagged in the text arguable deviations from the historical record—a checkered one indeed.

Noriega's contacts with U.S. intelligence services and the military go back many decades and cover so many conspiracies, scandals, covert actions, and unsolved mysteries that only a satirist's eye could make the story credible. He may have been picked out by the C.I.A. as a nemesis (and possible successor) to Gen. Omar Torrijos, a problematic populist-nationalist who negotiated the giveback of the Panama Canal from Jimmy Carter and then was killed (along with everybody else) when his plane exploded in midair in 1981. How con-veeeenient!

Noriega was up to his ears in Iran/contra and other scandal "gates" that involved the triangular trade of U.S., Israeli, and Middle Eastern interests. He met with George Bush on two occasions and with several others in the White House entourage. According to journalists and government officials, he facilitated narcotrafficking for the Colombian cartels. He spied on Fidel Castro for the United States and vice versa. He gave covert aid to the contras and discussed expanding Panama's involvement in that sordid enterprise with Oliver North. There is no end to his multiple-dealing, double-agentry, and value-free treachery. Many of the most intriguing revelations about Noriega were made in 1987 by a retired Panamanian colonel, Robert Diaz Herrera. Diaz accused Noriega of conspiring with the C.I.A. and U.S. Army in the death of Torrijos. Diaz also charged that Noriega ordered the 1985 murder of Hugo Spadafora, a prominent critic (Diaz recanted after he was imprisoned for treason).

At the end, Noriega may have angered the White House by backing off from full support of Bush's war in Nicaragua, but with so many foul deeds in play at the same time, it's hard to say what precipitated his persecution. The U.S. military in Panama was known to be nervous about his continued compliance with U.S. strategic demands. In any case, a grotesque campaign was waged against him, with loud rock music to force him from the Nunciatura (Vatican Embassy) in Panama City, ludicrous disinformation bulletins (remember the "cocaine stash" that turned out to be tamales?), the bounty on his head, the bumbling U.S. airborne soldiers—and with disastrous results from Panamanians, who were slaughtered by the hundreds, whose neighborhoods were razed, and who were once again made to kneel before the Yanqui invader.

OLIVER STONE

Metropolitan Correctional Center, Miami. Morning, November 22, 1993. I am in a conference room with Gen. Manuel Noriega, now P.O.W. #38699-079; his daughter Sandria; and a paralegal, who is interpreting. The deputy warden waits at the other end of the table. The interview lasts three hours. What follows is a con-

densation of our conversation. The general declined to be quoted regarding his legal appeal and any new evidence he may present.

As we begin the formal interview, the general is showing me a book of personal photographs and map of his country, dotted with more than a dozen U.S. military bases.

MN: It's always important to know the strategy of the United States, when there are points to view contrary to your politics. It's as Kissinger said, "You first have to create the problem in order to solve the problem," and that's what's been done with my position. From 1970 until 1988, plus six more years before that when I was a student, I was a friend of the United States. In everything related to intelligence [and] to military assistance. I fought as a Panamanian patriot, and when I opposed their point of view regarding the Panama Canal, when I began to say, "No, no" to the violation of the Canal Treaty, after twenty-four years of friendship suddenly I become a devil. They needed to create a devil in order to get rid of the devil. That's what happened.

OS: Is this your mother?

MN: (peruses the pictures): I never met her. She died when I was very young.

OS: And your father? . . . He was an alcoholic?

MN: No. No! Who said? My father never touched a drop of alcohol.

OS: Why did he ignore you?

MN: He didn't ignore me. . . . I didn't live with him, but I've carried his name since I was born. And he provided support from the moment I was born.

OS: But you lived with an aunt?

MN: No, with—yes, with an aunt, yes.

OS: Because your father couldn't support you?

MN: No, no, no. My father could. But when my mother died she gave me to my aunt so she would raise me. And she raised me. My father always respected my mother's final wishes.

(He points to the map.) These are the American bases from the Atlantic to the Pacific. So the struggle is for permanent stay of the United States on Panamanian territory. They want to control strategic territory. This is where they intercept all the codes and phone calls toward the south, toward Patagonia. It was here that during the Falklands War all the Argentine war plans were detected, and this is where the United States can exert control over the Caribbean, Cuba. Panama is unique. So that was the struggle, when they didn't want to comply with the treaty. In other words, it was a nationalist struggle that lasted twenty-four hours. Then they wanted concessions, bases, military bases. And I was opposed because it wasn't legal within the Torrijos-Carter Treaty. And that's why my position was so unyielding.

This (pointing to a picture of himself jogging) speaks a thousands words—a man who worked twenty-four hours a day. From Monday to Friday, I'd get up at 5 in the morning and I'd run with my instructor. I think you met him; he was Chinese.

os: Yes, Chu Yee. But I hear you drank a lot? You drank Old Parr?

mn: Saturday and Sunday, yes. At home.

os: No, people say you drank a lot—two bottles of Scotch a night.

mn: Nobody who drinks two bottles—

os: (looking at photograph): That's Caspar Weinberger . . . Caspar the Ghost.

mn: Close friend . . . Bush pardoned him. Irangate problem and Mr. Bush . . . (trails off)

os: I'd like to talk about that. . . . Is that the Shah of Iran's wife water-skiing?

mn: (laughing): Yes, yes. You have the eyes of a hawk. Without—

interpreter: Without a bra [laughter].

mn: I helped them solve their problem with the Shah. When the Shah didn't have anyplace to go, no country wanted to help him. . . . This is me in Sweden.

os: I heard it cost him a lot of money, too. It seems to me that many of your present difficulties began when the United States, when Poindexter, Reagan, Bush, Elliott Abrams, Oliver North—these people put pressure on you to participate in la guerra contra los Sandinistas. I would like you to describe as much as you can about that period and your impressions, your participation in the war.

mn: Well, when the contras had failed in their program of sabotage against the Sandinista government, the United States thought that Panama could be a support. First they requested several places in Panama for training and provisioning. I said no.

os: Was this in the meeting with National Security Adviser Poindexter in '85?

mn: No, before. Poindexter came later. He said he was coming on Reagan and Shultz's behalf. In that meeting he didn't say "please." He ordered me. He said, "Panama must go against Nicaragua. Panama must get out of the Contadora Group." We had a strong argument, then Poindexter left, and he made a threat: From here to December 1985, if President [Nicolas Ardito] Barletta [fired as President of Panama] isn't back in his old position and you don't help in this war then you are going to see the consequences. And he left.

os: Jose Blandon described a meeting to me where you were with Oliver

North and he was saying that there were 20,000 contras and either Jose or you said, "Colonel North, they're not an army, they are joke." North thought they could attack and win from the Southern Front [Costa Rica], but they didn't have leadership, so you were asked to train the leaders—

MN: There were three stages. The first when they asked for training bases. Then when Poindexter came, and later when Oliver North invited me to meet him in London [September 1986], at the Victoria Hotel. North was coming from Israel. He was with Secord and another general. The contras' problems were very bad. And there was the Iran problem. Then he asked me for the last time. And I explained to him, "You're defeated."

OS: North asked specifically for what, though?

MN: They lacked the combat capability. They needed trained men. The United States had failed with the contras, with their leaders; they were no good. They wanted us, our people, to go into Nicaragua.

MN: Is it true that in the meeting you said you would assassinate the entire leadership of the Sandinistas?

MN: Nunca.

OS: You never said that?

MN: Never; it's as we say, ridiculous. My point of view was that the Sandinistas were our friends.[1]

OS: Borge and Ortega? I met them in Nicaragua—

MN: Ortega, yes, Ortega. Borge—because we had trained the Sandinistas when they fought against Somoza.

OS: But you had to play the game. You had to give the United States something.

MN: Yes, yes, yes.

OS: So what did you give them?

MN: Oh, no. I explained to them the mistake they were making. I told them they were thinking the Sandinistas were the old, ignorant armed civilians that fought against Somoza. But the Sandinistas had learned strategy from the Soviets. They had Soviet training, Soviet technology, and they were applying it. So the contras couldn't compete with them.

OS: Were the U.S.-supplied Russian arms for the contras coming through the Panama then at some point?

MN: The Americans supplied the contras, but not from Panama. Panama was too far away. They had a military base in Honduras.

OS: So what did they use Panama for? Money laundering, banks?

MN: No, no, no. Remember, the Canal Zone is United States territory. So they could have meetings here, small-scale training, small ones. Training—not practical but theoretical.

os: Is Jose Blandon's story accurate about Fidel Castro being angry with you for busting the Darien coke laboratory [a Medellin cartel drug base in the Panamanian jungle]?

mn: No. That's not true. Blandon was the witness that they took to Congress, and that they used for the indictment. But Blandon didn't testify. He didn't ratify his accusations.

os: But in the past few years, you know, the Castro connection to the drug trade seems to have been proved. As has the Sandinistas' involvement.

mn: It's very confusing. I would suggest that you look for more information. They don't have any proof.

os: Castro shot his top military guy, Gen. Arnaldo Ochoa, for drug dealing in 1989. Many people think that was a way to take the blame away from—

mn: Yes, that's part of like you do in the Kennedy movie (laughs). Who killed him? The same thing. Why did he kill him?

os: What were your personal relations with Castro?

mn: We never talked about drugs or anything. We spoke about international politics. The United States always sought me out as a special conduit to solve small problems. When they invaded Grenada they make mistakes, and they were attacking a military position, but behind it was a dormitory of American students, so they asked Castro not to fight.

os: So you called Castro to make sure these students were protected?

mn: Yes, I called Castro, telling him the United States wanted the Cubans not to return fire. That they didn't want any of the students killed. The call was Bush, Mr. Casey, and me on one phone and on another phone was me with Castro.

os: Did you ever discuss the John Kennedy assassination with Castro?

mn: He had been sorry about it. He said, "Of course, the C.I.A."

os: What do you think?

mn: That the large economic interests of petroleum and all that [were involved]. Kennedy's liberal policies weren't advantageous to them.

os: We know oil is big in this world and in comparison, the drug trade is not as big as oil, but you must be aware that the Medellin cartel was very powerful in Latin America in the early 1980s, and they must have contacted you at some point? Pablo Escobar came to Panama in 1984.

mn: The D.E.A. [Drug Enforcement Administration] worked in Panama full time. I never, never, never met Escobar, ever. I was never in Medellin. When I went to Colombia, I'd be invited officially by the government, the army. I didn't go in a clandestine way. I'd go normally, with bodyguards. And there were signed agreements for a joint U.S./Panama fight against drugs. We hit the Medellin cartel hard. We confiscated banks. We destroyed their product. Boy, did we ever confiscate money from them.

os: Why do you think the problem is continuing in Panama?

MN: The problem will continue because it's the law of supply and demand at work. While the United States had a demand, there will be a supply in the Andean countries.

os: Did you give permission to Escobar to enter the country?

MN: I had a very high position to be dealing with who entered and who left the country. Escobar went to Washington, too, took a picture in front of the White House with his children.

os: What was your relationship with Hugo Spadafora [a doctor and romantic revolutionary figure in Panamanian politics]?

MN: Well, he, Eden Pastora, myself—we were all friends. Afterward Hugo had a fight with Pastora. Hugo had a fight with the Sandinistas, and Hugo began to work with the people who transported arms, with the drug-arms group that would take arms and bring back drugs from Costa Rica. In Costa Rica there is a large airport that they built and used to support the contras. Hugo was working alone. He didn't fight anymore. He had dedicated himself to getting arms. Commercial.

os: Are you saying that Hugo was involved in the drug trade with the contras?

MN: There's a connection, which came out in the trial a little. An arms shipment gets lost. Hugo has to deliver them. Then—

os: So you think that he was not killed by the P.D.F. [Panamanian Defense Force]?

MN: Do you know Fernandez in Costa Rica? Do you know a Dulce? John Dulce?

os: John Hull, you mean?

MN: John Hull and Joe Fernandez [former C.I.A. station chief in Costa Rica]. In Costa Rica they were his contact in the job of helping the contras.

os: So you think that Hull and Fernandez were responsible for his death? And the torture?

MN: No. They were the brains of the operation. The people that killed him, killed him because they were paid to.[2]

os: The C.I.A and the U.S. Army have admitted paying you $322,000 over thirty-one years—is that about right?

MN: Not much, huh? (laughs)

OS: Is that about right? Muy poco. So not yes or no.

MN: That's what they wrote down.

OS: That's what they wrote down. You received more? [laughs].

MN: That's their books.

OS: Did you spy on the American military, diplomats, or government officials in Panama? To protect yourself?

MN: To protect myself, no. In every military system of every country in the world, including the Vatican, espionage between nations of the world, spying, it's a case of self-defense. So Panamanian espionage is for the defense of Panama. It was more like counterintelligence.

OS: But everyone says you had many sapos [informants], friends in the C.I.A., people like Nestor Sanchez who tell you things. I get the impression that you have many friends and enemies in the American government. And you have people who were telling you that maybe you were in trouble with the American press.

MN: Yes. It's just that my relationship, my main relationship, was with the Central Intelligence Agency and the Army. So then I had no relationship with the political part—there was an imbalance.

OS: There you are in 1988. You have Vice President Bush running for office. He's making the war on drugs a big issue. Is there somebody in the agency who tells you to be careful? Oliver North, somebody like this? That the press in America is attacking you? What John Kerry is doing and Jesse Helms and the indictment in Miami—all this is in progress. Do you have friends who tell you—

MN: Well, all that was public.

OS: Yes, but with all this pressure I don't understand; why do you renege—do you know the word "renege"?—on the deal you made with Roberto Diaz Herrera? I don't know what happened, but I'm told you had promised Diaz that he would be an ambassador in—I don't know—Japan, Taiwan. But then you changed the deal, and Diaz got very angry and went public with many accusations that were very damaging.

MN: Yes, they were damaging, but it's not true. Diaz was retired.

OS: He was retired?

MN: Yes, I ordered it. I ordered him to leave. Because of his mental capacity, he became very difficult. Yes, he was not a mentally sane person at the time. And there was never any promise about him going to Japan. He wanted to go to Japan, but there was never any promise on my part.

os: Did you see it coming that he would go on television and make those charges?

MN: Well, that was madness on his part. His madness. Because a reasoning and normal person wouldn't have done it.

os: So, in hindsight, if you could do it again, if you could go back in time, what would you have done with Diaz?

MN: I'd have him arrested. I'd leave him in jail.

os: On what charge?

MN: On the charges of lying. Also of going against the state. He hurt the country of Panama.

os: You did say that you had Bush "by the balls." That you had information.

MN: A lot of those things were exaggerations by the press. Since there was a fight between us, they would say things.

os: Are you aware of the new book coming out by Billy St. Malo? In the book he says that in 1987 he and Michael Kozak [a State Department official] was in the middle trying to make a deal between you and the Americans to get you out of Panama. He says, interestingly, that Reagan and Shultz wanted to make a deal but that Bush and Baker did not want to make the deal because Bush was running for President. He did not want to be perceived as being "soft on drugs." And at the last time it was Bush and Baker that subverted the potential agreement.

MN: Bush didn't carry any weight. The one who carried all the weight was Reagan. But let me say this: First, if I had been guilty on charges of drug trafficking brought by the U.S. Attorney in Miami they wouldn't have wanted to make a deal with me. Second, I didn't accept their offer because a group from the military staff told me not to accept it.

os: Why? What was it?

MN: It was an insult to Panama. Because the United States was setting conditions. The conditions were that I leave the country but before leaving that I hand over the government to the opposition, that I eliminate the trade unions and the P.R.D. [Democratic Revolutionary Party], the parties, a series of conditions. That we eliminate the courts of justice. So that they could change the whole government.

I made the decision not to accept it. There was the sovereignty of my country. And it was violating my right as a Panamanian. It was blackmail. They were telling me to leave. How much money do you want? Do you want to be decorated? How many friends do you want to take with you? We'll send you to Spain. Go. So that's blackmail. They were doing the same thing they did to Duvalier.

os: So in negotiating this agreement, were you buying time?

MN: Negotiate? I heard them out. I wanted to see what the points were to be able to see what the—I had my lawyers in Panama and the politicians to discuss it with them.

os: O.K., but you did say some things about Bush after you were arrested. You were very angry with Bush.

MN: Whatever I said was not important. But I didn't make any strong or damaging statements against Bush.

os: Didn't you make some reference to having documents or audio or video or your meetings with Poindexter, North, Abrams?

SANDRA: You told CNN that you had proof that he had met with you.

MN: Well, it's one thing to meet—

os: In your meetings with Poindexter or North, did you tape the meetings?

MN: No, tape, no. I fight cleanly.

os: So you have no bad feelings about Bush? About the invasion?

MN: Not today, not today. I forgave him as a Christian.

os: You are a Catholic?

MN: Yes, I am a Christian.

os: I thought Buddhist.

MN: I have some understanding of it because I went to Japan. . . . They invited me to the temples and I learned about the philosophy of the Soka Gia Nishen Reshoshu, an international organization that seeks world peace.

os: You know Oliver North might be a senator in Virginia next year. Good chance. [Noriega laughs.] You laugh. Do you ever talk to him?

MN: No, no, no.

os: He won't talk to you. He doesn't like you anymore?

MN: We were never friends.

os: Never friends?

MN: In life and in politics there is no friendship. There is only convenience, political or friendly. But friends? The Mexicans have a saying that goes like this, "Friends—"

SANDRA: Dad—oh, my God.

MN: "My balls are friends and when I run, they bump into each other."

os: (laughs): When you said recently that "the last chapter in the Noriega story has not been written," what realistically do you see for your future?

MN: I learned that life is in God's hands. You're here now and you can go out, and find you won the lottery, a new contract or an event that you didn't expect.

Who did it? You didn't plan it. You didn't see it coming. There is a higher power that's God which places things in your path.

os: God loves you?

mn: Eh . . . God. Yes, God protected my life. There were ten thousand American soldiers looking for me in Panama. With my picture. House to house.

sandra: And civilians promised a million dollars.

mn: I survived. Ten thousand! And who did it? God.

os: If you had had to have left Panama, which country would you have picked?

mn: If I had to? Ah . . . Eh . . . [laughs.] There were so many, so many . . .

os: Japan? [laughs].

mn: China.

os: China or Taiwan?

mn: Taiwan. No, I don't know China.

os: [laughing]: Ambassador to Taiwan. When you were in the Nunciatura during the invasion, were you scared of the Americans outside?

mn: The Americans were planning to kill me there. They were planning to storm the Nunciatua. But the moment arrives in which you are no longer afraid. You face the situation. The human organism is chemical. Chemical. They took away my weapons in the Nunciatura. They left me with no means of defending myself.

os: Did you think you were going to stay there for a while?

mn: I thought I would, for months. The important thing is that I wasn't originally going to the Nunciatura. I was told that the Nuncio wanted to speak to me. And he sent me his car.

os: How did the Nuncio find you?

mn: Well, I had a liaison on the outside, a person. The telephones were out, there was no communication, everything was blocked off. Remember that American troops were in control of the roads. But I had a person who could communicate, and I was in touch with that person.

os: What were you thinking about in the Nunciatura?

mn: I was thinking about the impotence of the weak before the strong.

os: If you were writing a movie of your life, what would be the principal theme?

mn: The main theme is the chapter about the nation, of Panama. Because that was my downfall. I was free of worry before I was head of state. And then when I became—I took the problems of Panama on me.

os: But when you look back at your whole life, and coming from poverty you wanted to be a medical student at one point but you didn't qualify. And here you became one of the most powerful men in the region. Do you believe that you were destined?

mn: Yes, yes. Yes, yes. I believe that—it's not that I didn't qualify, it's just that the medical scholarships were only given to the rich.

os: But so many changes in your life . . . what are the lessons you personally have learned?

mn: I have learned not to be stubborn. I have learned that you have to negotiate. That life is not all or nothing. And that it's better to submit than to defy. Confront things, confront things. I have learned that the fight for ideals carries a high cost.

os: And certainly the Buddhist law that life is change?

mn: Yes. Scientifically speaking, life is an evolution.

os: What music do you listen to in prison?

mn: Every kind of music.

os: Opera?

mn: No, I don't like opera. I like Rachmaninoff.

os: What books do you read?

mn: I like science fiction very much.

os: Any favorites?

mn: No, whatever, whatever.

os: How does the time pass in prison? It's a long time.

mn: I speak to God. No, that's . . . time passes . . . I look for—I read something. I look for something to invest my time in. I write.

os: What do you write?

mn: I write about the Canal, the projections for the Canal. The mistakes of Panama. I am also a poet. A minor poet.

os: Like Mao, Mao Ze-dong. Sometimes great poetry comes from prison.

mn: Yes. I have always written.

os: Who is the political hero you admire most?

mn: Well, if we go into the past, Simon Bolivar; later Juan Domingo Pero; and of my people, I have many.

os: I'm going to ask you a question again, to maybe deepen your response. What was the one thing that you believe caused the change in your relationship with the United States? When did this happen? Did Bush turn against you? And start demonizing you? Or did he warn you?

MN: What turned the United States against me was my refusal to accept their political conditions that violated the Canal Treaty. They first wanted to keep the school at Fort Gulick. They wanted an extension. And I didn't accept it. Here's a letter of General Gorman requesting that—

OS: Run this by me again, what is Gulick?

SANDRA: It was a training school, for military. It was called School of the Americas, and everybody from Latin America comes to Panama to this school to take training from the American Army. So it said in the treaty that they had to give it back to Panama in '84. But when 1984 arrived they tried to negotiate. It is very important to them to keep the Americas school because that way they were training Latin American armies.

OS: You feel that this is the main reason that the situation turned against you?

MN: That's one of them. After having said "no, no" to supporting the contras against the Sandinistas. The United States understood that Noriega is not the same man that was lieutenant colonel. Now he is commander in chief and said "no" to our interests. And he is not our man.

OS: So your theory is that America does not really want to give up the Canal? And that America wanted to destroy the P.D.F. so that there would be no Panamanian security force to protect the Canal, and that would be a reason to abrogate the treaty? That's what you think?

MN: The treaty signed by Carter indicates that Panama has to have an armed force so that the United States can turn over the defense of the Canal to Panama. That's why they destroyed the defense forces, the P.D.F., in the invasion.

OS: I've asked several American military people about this, and they say that this is not true. Because with present-day technology it is not necessary to keep American soldiers there. The Canal can be monitored with satellite technology from Florida.

MN: It's not the Canal itself. It's the strategic location. It's not in Costa Rica, not in Colombia. It's only in the Galeta Island [off Panama's Pacific coast] that the detector exists, the point of detection to all of South America and North America and the Caribbean. It is the only point in the world. They say they're not interested in the bases in Panama anymore. But they are going to demand in the year 2000 a base on the Atlantic and another base in the Pacific.

OS: So you are saying that the technology will be such that they can monitor Latin America better from Panama than from Florida, or is it psychological?

MN: No, it's specific. Listening posts, from Panama. You can't monitor from Florida.

OS: Is there anything else you would like to speak about?

MN: I understand that the nature of your profession is sensationalist. I don't seek to change what you believe. But I want to tell you that there is another truth in this situation. Not the truth that the apparatus, the establishment, hurled at me. I hope that within your professionalism, and your poetic roots, that you will find that the ones that fight for their country against injustice, run the risk of my situation. I could have died. There was a plan in place to do as they did to Maurice Bishop in Grenada. That was the plan, that I would die there. That's why when I arrived at places where they said I was hiding, they'd shoot. Because they were looking to kill me, not capture me. And since they didn't kill me, they sentenced me. As the Spanish did with the Venezuelan patriot Miranda in the nineteenth century. The Spanish took him as a captive during the wars for independence. I have all the details for you, of how the conspiracy against me was carried out [gives notes].

OS: I appreciate this. I want to tell you that I like you very much . . . and I can't paint you as a white knight either—

MN: I'm not [laughs].

After farewells and whispered partings with his daughter, the general, about five feet six inches, is walked back to his cell by two large federal guards, his gait springy and defiant as his small frame recedes across the lawn. He smiles at his guards, makes small talk.

NOTES

1. According to North's notes of the London meeting, the two discussed developing a commando training program in Panama for contras and sabotaging major economic targets in Nicaragua.

2. In *Our Man in Panama* John Dinges writes that U.S. Ambassador Everett Briggs concluded that P.D.F. personnel killed Spadafora, but Noriega's involvement could not be proved. Dinges writes that "once Noriega found out about the killing he actively participated in covering it up," and he opposed President Barletta's decision to create a commission to investigate the murder. Spadafora was inquiring about drug trafficking within the government when he was killed.

TEACHINGS OF DON FERNANDO: A Life and Death in the Narcotics Trade

Charles Bowden

From *Harper's Magazine*, June 2002

The man in the coffin wears a gray Western suit and white cowboy shirt, and his large hands clutch a rosary. I look hard at the hands, and I can see them as they were three years ago, hoisting a rock for a wall he was building, then pausing as a jolt in his chest marked the revolt of his body. He did not tolerate revolt. He was that thing most unnerving for us: a finished man, complete and at ease with his private universe. A fine Stetson rests on the box, and just over his head gleams a color photograph of him astride his horse. Off to the side on a table, he looks up as a young man in a suit, as an older man getting married, and as an old man dancing with his wife. About four hundred people file past to pay their respects. Most are wearing freshly pressed jeans, clean shirts, and cowboy hats. The parking lot is full of pickups. A newspaper death notice sums it up neatly: "Terrazas, Fernando, 83, miner."

Vases of mums, azaleas, and red roses dot the front of the sanctuary while a mariachi band plays off to the side. I sit next to a young woman who knew Fernando. When she was in college, he would suddenly show up at her door with fresh fruit for her father. He was always courtly, she recalls. But she found out about his real life only last night.

After the rosary and mass, in the soft light of February that washes over the desert, the men stand outside, smoking and talking. A guy in his late forties ambles over to one cluster of men wearing suits. He is a former Customs agent and spent a part of his career undercover buying dope on the border. He knew Fernando for over fifteen years. They spent time in each other's houses, drinking coffee and talking about life and horses, the usual patter of rural Arizona. He knew Fernando as a miner, a gentleman, a guy who always asked the same question: "You need anything?" But he recognizes this cluster of suits as D.E.A. and so he figures he'll say hello. One agent is up from Guadalajara, evacuated because a cartel has put out a contract on him. Another ran D.E.A. intelligence. He hears them talking of big scores, of multiton busts, of back pages. And on each of these pages looms Fernando.

He suddenly realizes that the man he'd known for years he did not know at all. But then maybe ten people of the four hundred at the funeral mass knew the truth about Fernando Terrazas's life. Hundreds of people in prisons have dreamed for years of seeing him in a coffin and tried for years to put him there. He was that man, the double, trusted but always unknown.

I can hear him making me an offer at this moment. His voice courtly, his face calm, his body singing of ease, I will trust him completely. And he will destroy me.

I have learned a simple lesson: You can trust no one. But in the end, you must trust someone. And when you are betrayed, and you will be betrayed, the ruin will come from the person you trusted. Fernando always warned me that when a man is saying one thing he is thinking another, and that I must also hear this other thought.

Fernando came into my life because of my hunger to know informants. He lived a few hours from my house, and so from 1999 until his death in February I'd drop in on him from time to time. I was attracted to the solo nature of the work, to the fact that informants floated free of both the law and the drug merchants. The drug industry had become my prison, in a way: I had set out to do a simple magazine story, which became a book, and the book devoured seven years of my life. For a time, I was obsessed with one figure, Amado Carrillo Fuentes, head of the Juarez cartel. I'd had to trust people, knowing that only the people I trusted could betray me. Fernando was an independent who lived in a realm of self-created freedom. Unlike most informants, he was successful and survived for decades, a black hole moving through the drug galaxy and disappearing loads and people into his vortex, all the while remaining undetected.

I have never had a candid conversation with a D.E.A. agent when a third party, even another agent, was present. Never. Distrust is a growth industry in our culture, as the tiny microphones and cameras multiply and the strange hands paw through cyberspace, reading our lives. For decades, Fernando would leave his blue-collar job in the mines at least once a month and disappear into the drug world. He hurled hundreds if not thousands into the gulag of our prisons, and his deals without question sent countless others to secret graves along the border. And yet he remained unknown, his name always missing from the newspaper stories about his deals. The drug merchants he ruined were seldom if ever sure Fernando was the traitor who blew up the transaction. He lived the history of our future.

It's May of 1999. The fresh green of spring licks the Sierras, and I've been on the road for over a week with Julian Cardona, a Mexican friend. We've plunged down the eastern slope of the Sierra Madre, a green roll of hills, oak, pine, and narcotraficantes. More than thirty times we are stopped by armed men, some in uniform, some not, and always they ask: Why are you here? Where are you going? Just north of the city of Durango, around midnight, in the rain, the army pulls us over and searches. We are at the turnoff to a town against the mountains that is functionally a gated community for drug merchants. I remember sitting in a Texas prison with a convict as he circled the place on the map and said, "Go there. You won't believe it, they've got shops like on Rodeo Drive."

A contract on Fernando's life has come from this area, and as I drive people are probing Phoenix trying to pick up the old man's scent. About an hour north of Zacatecas, the federal police pull us over at a checkpoint. They tear my truck apart. A crowd gathers, and Julian drifts away, and I am alone.

A fat federale with a .45 thumps me in the chest and asks, "You mad at me?" He does this again and again as the minutes tick past. I think: They want the truck, they will plant something if I turn my back.

I know if I react, I will lose. I know if they have access to a computer, I will lose. There is a list, I've been told, and my name is on that list. Julian is standing at the back of the crowd now, and still he is drifting away. All the while big semis pull over for the check and are automatically waved through to the border with a laugh between the cops and the drivers.

Finally, after half an hour or so, they let us go.

Ten minutes down the road, Julian says, "They will call ahead. We are in trouble."

About this time, a retired D.E.A. agent named Phil Jordan calls my home looking for me. He's a friend, but I have not told him about my trip. When he hears where I am, he explodes to the person who's answered the phone: "Doesn't he know he can't do that anymore? Doesn't he know how fucking dangerous it is? It's not safe for him down there. That's over."

What I think as I drive the eight hundred miles of highway north to the line is this: Julian. He is my friend.

But that's how you go down. That is the velvet wrapped around the betrayal when it comes for you.

I take comfort from the fear in Julian's face. And then I stare through the windshield and wonder if the fear is feigned.

He comes out of the house for that first visit in July of 1999 and I feel the iron of his hand as we shake. He's eighty, but his big frame still intimidates. He's tall and moves like a horseman, body erect, gut tight. The face is warm, inviting, and yet closed. Meeting his eyes is like staring into a mask. Seven doctors keep track of his body, a thing busted up from a lifetime of horses, mines, and heavy equipment. His bones bear the mark of a Caterpillar tractor that rolled over onto him. We sit on the porch, his wife of fifty years serving cold drinks, his grandchildren underfoot. He has raised two sons and three daughters, and they have given him nine grandchildren and now a great-grandchild. He built the house with his own hands.

"I'm a lying son of a bitch," Fernando says, and beams.

He leans toward me and asks, "You are not going to use my name, are you? Or tell where I live?"

"No. No one will know where you live."

As the afternoon crawls along, clouds begin to spew off the peaks and hint at rain in the valley. Fernando tries to teach me the work.

He would meet a stranger in a town where he himself was unknown. Fernando would talk, then he would listen, and bit by bit an atmosphere of trust would fill the air. Sometimes this trust would take time. Once, a perfect stranger told Fernando to get into the driver's seat of a car, and then the man climbed into the passenger seat and thrust a gun into Fernando's ribs and said, "I'm going to find out if you're for fucking real." Fernando had no gun. He is of the belief that guns cause trouble.

He tells me, "Assholes never kill you. Anybody who shows you a gun won't kill you, because he is a coward." As he felt the cold metal of the pistol against his side, Fernando decided. He got out of the car and sat on the ground.

He told the stranger, "Shoot me and I'll keep my fucking money and you keep your fucking shit."

Fernando notes, "I got pretty damn cold blood."

"What happened?" I ask.

He looks at me with mild surprise.

"He did the deal."

The late Amado Carrillo Fuentes, head of what was then the biggest drug combine in the world, had a simple rule: to root out all the Fernandos of the world. If a load was lost, everyone connected with the load was killed to ensure that the traitor died. He also often ordered "a dose of milk," some quicklime to be tossed on the corpse to hasten its decomposition.

Fernando speaks English with the formality and cadence of a man whose first language was Spanish. He hands me a heap of clippings and I read, over and over: HEROIN DEALERS TO JAIL.

"All you gotta be," he calmly explains, "is be quiet. Don't tell. It's not the business of anyone else. My children didn't know. My wife knew, I had no secrets from my wife. To do this kind of job you have to be a liar and don't forget what you say. It's easy, it's easy: Don't tell.

"The only way you can do the big cases is: I'm the dumb one. I don't know anything about drugs. I buy, you sell, we make money. That's it. Never be smarter than the other guy, even if you're just selling a pickup. When you talk, don't tell them anything you don't know or anything they don't need to know. Don't open your mouth if you're not supposed to. Be nice, buy drinks, go out to eat. Never lose control."

It begins in the early days of the Great Society, in 1964, and feels as casual as having a cold beer after a hard day in the mines. In his mid-forties, Fernando thinks he'd like to own a bar. At a joint in rural Arizona he sees someone plant a bag of marijuana in the car of the man who owns the place. He and the owner are friends, so Fernando tells him what he has seen. Later, they pitch the bag into the river. Fernando goes to the state police and offers to inform on drug guys if the cops will help him get a liquor license. They turn him down, as do Federal agents.

But he becomes a phone number in a file, and a year later the feds call him up. There is an old man peddling heroin near Phoenix whom they can never nail. After making a deal, the buyer must walk alone eight miles into the desert to a tree where the product is waiting. The old man stays clear of the stuff. Fernando talks and talks with the old man, draws him in until finally he is offered a partnership. The trap is set. The old man goes away for what is the rest of his life.

Fernando discovers he is a natural and that he loves the work.

A man tells me to check the back room at the restaurant. And he tells me about the parties at the mansion. This is in 1992, before the drug business seriously entered my life, a time when I still trusted without thought. The guy, who owned the restaurant and the mansion, did big real-estate deals and got big loans without a blink. He was rumored to hire whores and have coke parties in the back room. They were secretly videotaped. The same for the parties at his house. I'm deep into a book on Charles Keating, the poster boy for the savings-and-loan crisis of the eighties. The tip has nothing to do with Keating himself but does connect with people involved in his deals. Soon I find a man who had been to such a party.

In the midst of this research, I get a call. A woman I visited six hundred miles away has been hounded by guys pounding at her door late at night, demanding to know about me. So have her neighbors.

I start moving, buy a gun, use pay phones, travel to unknown addresses.

But first I warn the guy who told me of the parties. Then I tell a lawyer looking into the financial case. The lawyer blows me off. A few weeks later the F.B.I. intercepts a contract coming out of Miami aimed at the lawyer's children.

I never found out who was doing it, though I'm certain Keating himself was not involved. Nor could I figure out where I had slipped up, or if I had simply been betrayed. You always have to trust someone.

I became very close to the man who first told me about the coke parties and whores. Then we drifted apart. I was busy, things to do. One Father's Day, about two years later, he sat alone and put a round through his skull. The bone and flesh must have taken a toll on the bullet because when it hit the window, its force was spent, and it fell to the floor like a pebble.

I thought, I should have called. I thought I had betrayed something I could not quite name. I put that suicide behind me but still I would think about it, a memory floating like lace, so delicate in still air, a memory with a savage rent in it where I had clumsily torn it with my hand. He had trusted me, told me things I'm sure he never told his wife. I had won his trust slowly but surely. I had made my sale. But I'd been busy. He was part of a story I had finished, and now I'd moved on to new stuff. I'm a writer. I listen, I win trust, I pour coffee and cook dinners. I lean close until I disappear inside their hearts and fears and dreams. And then I tell. It was a small thing, a sliver really of the world in which Fernando lived and thrived. To this day I picture that bullet spilling off the glass and falling to the floor. I remember the man telling me the lessons of his youth, how in the summer of his fifteenth year he broke horses in Kentucky and created the bankroll that got him out into the greater world. I know that I lack what it takes to close the deal, to really do people. But I wear a feeling of betrayal.

"If you really want to buy something," Fernando advises, "you need good jewelry." He goes to the back room and returns with a small cloth bag. He shows me his $1,800 gold bracelet, the gold watch swaddled in what look like diamonds, $400 cowboy boots, the finely stitched cowboy shirts, gold rings with rubies, a $350 Stetson. His wife forbids him to wear these things where they live. She thinks they make him look like a criminal.

I handle the heavy bracelet while he watches to make sure I understand the importance of its weight. A small pile of rings grows as he empties his sack. One by one he holds them up to the light with his big hand. He fingers the fabrics of his drug wardrobe and outlines the cut and quality. The closet in his home is lined with boots of the very finest leather. A man without pride cannot do the deal.

And then he plunges again into the life. He tells me about entering a cantina in San Luis, Sonora, across the border. At the time, this little town of dust was a major crossing point for drugs. The stranger is beside him and Fernando says, "I need something good."

The man delivers a sampler of kilos so they can be tested for quality. In the beginning Fernando did kilo deals, but soon he sought greater weight and deals had to be in tons. The samples prove to be low-grade.

Fernando returns to the cantina and snaps at the man, "You give me shit. You embarrass me before my people."

Apologies fill the air. The real shipment is high-grade. The stranger wants to win over this new soul in his life named Fernando. The man goes down.

In almost three decades Fernando never fails, not once. In the mid-sixties, Fernando teams up with Phil Jordan, a Mexican-American out of El Paso, who became a federal agent in 1965. Jordan is in his early twenties and fresh off a university basketball career. He treats Fernando as an equal. This is rare in the work, since most Cooperating Individuals, C.I.s (typically, flipped felons nabbed doing drug deals), are disdained as snitches. Fernando is an independent operator, and when anyone treats him like a doper or a lesser being he bridles. He has more street smarts than most of the agents, and so, in his reserved way, he holds them in contempt as clumsy instruments he must use for his special work. Jordan is a product of the barrio and knows how to treat a man with proper respect. Fernando becomes his mentor, and their work makes Jordan's career. They make three to four hundred cases over the years. Their families socialize. The woman at Fernando's funeral who has just learned what Fernando really did, she is Phil Jordan's daughter and has known Fernando since childhood.

In the early seventies, Fernando returns to San Luis. He crosses the border and within four hours makes a deal in a cantina. His probing has brought him inside a cell that will become the school for almost all the major cartel leaders of the eighties and nineties. Pedro Aviles Perez heads the organization, and his young underlings include Rafael Caro Quintero, who will later torture and slaughter D.E.A. agent Enrique "Kiki" Camarena; Amado Carrillo Fuentes, who will become the biggest drug merchant on earth; Amado's uncle Don Neto Carrillo and Felix Gallardo, both of whom will help to create the Guadalajara cartel; and many other drug dealers who in a few years will be handling hundreds of millions and then billions of dollars' worth of dope.

Some of Aviles's lieutenants are lured to the United States in 1973 and taken down right next door, as it happens, to a fund-raiser for Senator Barry Goldwater. A joint raid with Mexicans in Sonora bags ten tons of marijuana. One of the raiders, a young Mexican federale, rises in the ranks through the years. He becomes the federale that the U.S. agents lean on, the one who is different. Years later he kills a cartel leader and becomes a kind of hero in the F.B.I. And years after that the U.S. agencies discover he did the killing only because Amado Carrillo paid him $1 million for the hit. Carrillo had been very close to the dead man and used to freebase with him. When the dead man was cut down he was wearing a fine gold watch given to him by Carrillo. You have to trust, in the end.

Fernando leans toward me as he recounts this episode and says, "The only reason you are here is because of Phil."

He asks again if I am going to use his name, reveal his location. And then he smiles, because he already knows.

I am in his home because another man gave his word. And that is all that is necessary. If I am a traitor, the other man is responsible.

Fernando tells me with pride of his marksmanship with a .45.

"I trust Phil like a brother," he continues.

I remember the feel of the cartel's breath on my neck. I'd been looking into a murder in Juarez in August of 1995. It was officially listed as a drowning, but I had asked questions. I was naive. I remember drinking in a bar with a Mexican and asking about Amado Carrillo. The man winced, instantly crouched down, and searched the room for faces and ears. Later, I learned Carrillo drank in that bar.

On the U.S. side I'd been dealing with the D.E.A. at EPIC (El Paso Intelligence Center), and that is where I met Phil Jordan, who headed it. He gave me leads. Then one day, one of the Juarez dailies came out with a story about an American writer looking into a drowning and claiming it was murder. The story gave the city where I lived. I knew the paper was controlled by the cartel.

I called up the D.E.A. and asked why they had burned me. They denied it. Jordan's aide said, "We would never do that."

I slowly calmed down. It is so much easier to trust. It is a beckoning drug.

I kept looking, coming and going unannounced, changing where I stayed. In the fall of 1996, I found out that someone very close to Phil Jordan and his family, someone he trusted, had partied with the cartel leaders in Juarez. And knew Carrillo.

So I disappeared with a .9mm, boxes of notes, and some black coffee. Later, I learned Phil Jordan had been calling, trying to find me. Eventually, we became friends.

He told me he would never do that, put me in play.

But I'd had a taste. You think betrayal is something covered by those cheatin' songs in the country bars. You think it is the coworker who burns you with the boss, or even that business partner who tries to sell you out. I've had all of those and more. But they are something else, they call for some weaker word. They lack the surprise of the knife going into your guts. The floor falls away, you are spinning, and you are absolutely alone. And no one can hear you, no one can help you. And the only trace of trust you have is acid on your tongue. Phil Jordan had that person close to him who was dirty. There was that story in the Mexican newspaper that came out of nowhere and bothered to mention where I lived.

But still I came in from the cold after a few weeks. You have to trust someone. That is the rub. You have to make your deals. It is a fact of life.

"When I see a drunkard," Fernando says, "I turn away." Those who use drugs are also to be despised. Fernando lives off control. His childhood in southern Chihuahua meant almost no schooling—he made it to maybe the second grade—and endless hours of ranch work. Toiling alone at age fourteen, he planted and brought in, with the help of horses, an eighty-ton crop of pinto beans.

At fifteen, someone shot at him. He walked home to the ranch, got a rifle, walked back, and shot his assailant in the neck.

He leans forward and asks, "Could you kill someone?"

I answer, "I don't know."

He waits a minute and says, "I can."

He falls silent for a moment and adds, "I did pretty good. I'm alive."

"What protected you?" I ask.

He smiles and points toward the sky.

There is a tiny window into Fernando's soul. It's the early eighties, and Fernando is in Dallas. The D.E.A. puts him and a bodyguard up in a business hotel while they wait for the pieces to fall into place.

The bodyguard is a young cop, on the edge of his undercover career. He picks Fernando up at the airport, and he's stunned at first because he thinks this old man shouldn't be doing this work. After an hour or so in the hotel room, Fernando asks the guy to get him a bottle of Jack Daniel's. He tells him he does not smoke but to get him some cigarettes also.

They sit up that night drinking the whiskey straight, the butts growing in the ashtray. And Fernando shifts into that voice he uses with me, that voice that teaches the facts of a different level of life.

Fernando explains, "I don't need to do this for the money. I don't need the money."

The cop listens. Fernando tells him that at the heart of the deal, what the other person senses is strength. That is the key, that they smell the strength in you. They want you because they want your strength. They have money and they have power, but it is not enough. That is their weakness. Nothing is enough, because they do not really know what they want. They do not really know who they are. And so they must keep doing deals, expanding, reaching out, Fernando continues, for this thing they cannot name.

But you, if you have strength, you know who you are and what you need, and so you pull them into you, and then you are in control.

Years later, the cop, now seasoned, now a man living undercover, still remembers one thing Fernando pounded into his head that night as they drank the whiskey and the man who did not drink and did not smoke lit cigarette after cigarette.

Fernando put it this way: "No matter what you do, never forget, you are always alone. No one can save you or help you. Alone."

In the late sixties one of Fernando's sons comes out into the yard and sees his father's pink Cadillac gleaming in the sunlight. The boy is about eight, and he goes around to the driver's side and finds seven bullet holes in the door. He looks at his father, who smiles, but the boy says nothing. Finally, years later when he is in college, he figures out what his father has been up to all those years. He comes to him and asks, "Did you get caught with a load? Did they turn you? Is that why you are doing this?"

Fernando looks at his boy and says, "No, son, it is not like that."

He tells his son that drugs are a cancer, and they are killing their people and that his son must stay "on the right side of the law."

Nothing more is explained. The work stays in a sealed world. Because there are fresh holes waiting in the desert, gray masking tape across the mouth, bullets through the head, a splash of quicklime. And so Fernando's life goes on, unexplained even to his sons and daughters.

Once, in 1971, he followed up on an invitation to visit a drug laboratory in Chihuahua. A ton of heroin was in the offing, but the D.E.A. would not put up the money for the visit. So he and Jordan went in with no backup, no communications system, no permission from the agency, and, of course, no money. Fernando pulled the car off into the desert of Chihuahua, opened the trunk, and brought out an arsenal. He gave Jordan a .357 magnum and kept a .44 magnum for himself. He said to Jordan, "We must now practice. They will fear such guns." And Jordan complied, because he realized that he was in Fernando's house, in the culture and throb of Chihuahua.

"Phil was nervous," Fernando remembers with a smile. They were packing guns in violation of Mexican law and U.S. agency regulations. And Jordan had another good reason to be nervous, since in Mexico a D.E.A. agent is despised by every man, woman, and child as a foreign police agent operating on their soil.

They kept in touch with the agency by using Mexican pay phones. At the drug lab there were pistoleros, huge black dogs, and, of course, lots of dope. At such places in the sierra a man dies and no one cares or even hears the cries. The deal collapsed because it eventually meant tons of heroin, and the D.E.A. balked at fronting the necessary money.

Fernando received good chunks of money for his work, with one payment over a hundred thousand dollars, but he waited until he turned sixty-five to leave his brutal job at the mines. He did not understand life without work. He came from a world of toil and never let the D.E.A. money or the gold chains of the drug merchants he ruined touch his own rock-hard core.

Once he went to Los Angeles and took down ten tons of hashish. The agency gagged on the percentage he deserved for such a haul. Finally, they cut a check for a piddling amount, a few hundred dollars. Jordan came to Fernando's house and gave him the check. Fernando looked at it and said, "Give it back to them and tell them to shove it up their ass."

But he did not quit. He said, "I would work for Phil for nothing." And sometimes he did just that. He wasn't doing it for the money, or at least not only for the money. Nor do I think he did it because of a deep hatred of drugs. I think he did it because he could, and the rest of us cannot.

I've known Fernando for about a year, and we are sitting on the porch. A storm is growing off the mountains, and black clouds start to float over the hills around his home. His old frame comes alive as he tells me how to cut the deal. Never, he tells me, taste the product. Tell them it is a business and you don't want to mess up your mind. You have to drink, but don't drink much, just some beer and water.

I ask about the contract killers looking for him. Just a few months earlier, they had been stirring in a nearby city, sniffing the wind for him. One had called his son asking for him.

He offers this thought: "When they come, there will be only two of us. And one will be dead."

I ask him to explain. But there is no more detail: When the man comes, either he will die or Fernando will die.

He enters the El Camino Real, the old hotel in El Paso near the bridge into

Juarez. It is 1989 and Fernando, seventy, has come to test himself against a legend. The Herreras operate a drug business that stretches from the Mexican state of Durango to Chicago. The organization is the family—around 3,000 blood members and several thousand more associates. They hail from a village in the Sierra Madre called Las Herreras, their own company town surrounded by their own fields lush with their own dope. Starting right after World War II, the founder, Don Jaime Herrera Nevares, set up heroin labs. No one can penetrate deeply into their organization except by marriage. And no one can cross them without facing 3,000 blood-related enemies scattered from Mexico to the American heartland. The Herreras often carry badges of various Mexican police agencies, a commonplace in the drug world. They spend money on parks, streetlights, and other Robin Hood touches to buy the complicity of the poor.

At the El Paso hotel, a father and son, one sixty-three, the other thirty-four, await Fernando. This is a coup in itself, this wooing of the Herreras to cross the line and discuss business in the United States. The D.E.A. has gotten the deal this far but can go no further without Fernando. The Herreras and Fernando go to the coffee shop, and they talk for three hours. His talks with the Herreras go on for two to three weeks, as he slowly reels in his prey. Years later, when he recounts this last deal—the big one—he relishes each little moment of their conversations.

The older Herrera is very bright and asks many questions of Fernando.

"What do you do?"

"Oh, I buy things and then sell things."

"Where do you live?"

"Oh, that hardly matters. I am here to buy something good, not to talk about my house."

The older Herrera keeps trying to get Fernando off balance. "Pancho," the older Herrera will say, or "Arturo," or "Paco," or "Chuy." He keeps talking and then tossing out these different names to see if Fernando will react, to see if he can catch him off guard.

Fernando is at ease. This is the part he loves, the reeling in of the stranger. He talks of horses, thoroughbred horses, of how he loves to race his horses in Baltimore. The old man listens: the Herreras with their millions are into thoroughbred stock.

And then suddenly another name pops out. Fernando does not flinch and continues to ignore the probe. He is feeling better and better, but the older Herrera is the smartest stranger he has ever met.

They get into real matters, money. Fernando says he is looking at, say, a $2 million deal as a way of launching their relationship and testing its future. He represents some very large people, and they do not wish to do little things.

"Ah, that is no problem," the older Herrera replies. "We can get any amount of goods and deliver it. Where do you live? We will fly it to you, our planes will go right under the American radar, it is no problem."

"No, no," Fernando says, "my people prefer to handle their own shipments."

"No, senor," the older man replies, "let us. It is easy. We have tons warehoused right here, just across the river in Juarez."

"That is very kind," Fernando says, "but we handle our own deliveries. You just get it to El Paso."

"But the money," he says, "we want you to bring the money to Juarez."

"No, senor," Fernando says, smiling, "I am not going into Juarez with my money. That would not be the act of a wise man."

This goes on for hours, this probing, this testing.

And they agree to talk some more later.

Fernando has become the closer, the man they bring in on deals that are there, right there, but just out of reach, cases that the D.E.A. has been building but cannot finish because there the agency leaves its own scent in the air. So Fernando flies to San Francisco, Dallas, Los Angeles, wherever. He is never Mr. Big, he is the man who represents Mr. Big. And he has lots of money. He will be there for an hour, a day, a week, and then the deal goes down. He never fails, not once. And when the deal goes down, he wants out. He insists, always, on being taken immediately to the airport and returned to his family.

The Herreras try to find him. They call a dummy number he has given them, a line controlled by the D.E.A. When he comes to the second meeting at the El Camino Real hotel, they sit in the bar, a place legend says was once visited by Pancho Villa. The bar has a Tiffany-style dome above its circular black marble top. Splashes of green and blue play across the faces as the sun streams through the stained glass overhead. The room is full of soft chairs and sofas. They sit there for hours.

"Where were you?" the older Herrera asks. "We called and you were not there."

"Oh, I had some business in Las Vegas."

"How did it go?"

"Very well, senor."

Fernando can feel him relaxing, feel it getting closer. Fernando tells jokes, many jokes, and the older Herrera never laughs, but Fernando can sense he is rising to the bait.

The older Herrera says, "Look, why don't you come to Mexico with me, we will go to Durango, to my village, Las Herreras. We have just built a public park there for the people, everyone there works for us. It will be easy. We will send a plane for you."

"No, senor, I cannot do that. This is business, and I do not mix pleasure with business. Surely you understand."

Hours of this, hours. And then the older Herrera says, "We will do a deal. For over two million. No problem."

And they go into the fine restaurant of the hotel and eat thick steaks.

"He was ready to go. It was already made," Fernando says.

There are always surprises. That is part of the art of the deal. Sure, control—control is necessary, and being alert and careful and at ease. But no matter how much planning and thought go into the work, there will be surprises. Once, in the eighties, Fernando is at a family funeral in an isolated hamlet deep in Chihuahua when a man walks in. Years before, Fernando did a deal, and the man went down hard and spent years in prison.

He sees Fernando and comes over. Fernando turns to the man and says, "You fool, remember that deal? I told you not to come to the meeting, I could sense something, no? But you came and look what happened to you, you fool." The man is cowed, he is on the defensive. Control. That is what it takes if you are to come out of these deals alive.

The final meeting is in the hotel coffee shop. Here is the arrangement: The older Herrera sits with Fernando, and they talk. Across the street is a parking lot where the car with the kilos of heroin is to be delivered right before their eyes. Then one of Fernando's men will take the car away and test the load for quality. At the same moment, the younger Herrera will be in a nearby bar where he will be paid for the load. Fernando and the older Herrera will not get near the load.

So they sit and drink coffee and wait.

They look out the window and see a man approach the car and then drive it away. Perfecto. Fernando, full of coffee, tells the older Herrera that he must use the bathroom. As he leaves, the agents move in and take the man down. When Fernando comes back from the bathroom, the waiter comes over and says, "What is going on? The police came and took your friend away."

Fernando shakes his head and says, "I don't know, I hardly know the guy."

And then the police come and handcuff Fernando to give him cover. They take him to the D.E.A. office, and then he goes to the airport and home.

The Herreras get twelve to twenty years, and this time Fernando testifies. He likes the experience of testifying. Normally, a deal is structured so that no one can be certain who was the traitor. The matter is further clouded by bringing in several agents toward the end to give cover to the Fernandos of the world. But when you testify, then they know.

As he recounts the trial to me, he pauses and says with a smile, "I wanted him to know I did him."

In this case, Fernando's last big case, there is a special satisfaction. The Herreras have been stung, and this is something that never happens, and it feels good. The heroin, it turns out, is Colombian, from the Medellin cartel, and that gives even more satisfaction. But there is an extra bonus: the man brokering the heroin for the Colombians is a baron, the infamous Frog One, who escapes at the end of the film *The French Connection*. This time he does not escape.

In the thieves' market of Tepito, men come up to me and ask if I want heroin. I can feel eyes pawing my back as I walk through this fabled warren of Mexico City. I have come here tracking Amado Carrillo, the head of the Juarez cartel, for a project of mine. It is the spring of 1997. I have not let Phil Jordan know of my journey.

I stay in a hotel owned by the Juarez cartel. I look at a cartel bank when I drink at the rooftop bar. I visit with Mexican reporters who spread word that I am C.I.A. or D.E.A. I go to the restaurant where a hit was attempted on Amado Carrillo, and when I leave, after drinking and making notes, men from the restaurant follow me. I have been living this way for months, and I feel a clock ticking, and I do not believe time is on my side.

When I finally get home, I learn from a friend that he dined at the American embassy in Mexico City while I was down there looking for traces of Amado Carrillo. He sat next to the D.E.A. head of station, and when he mentioned where he lived in the States the man asked if he knew me. He said, "Tell him there is a contract on him." I will never know if this was true or if the information was ever shared with Phil Jordan. Or if he knew and for his own reasons did not tell me. But it's not what you can or cannot know; it's that you cannot ever completely trust anyone. I will know only one thing for certain, what Fernando taught that bodyguard, and me: You are always alone.

What I knew as I looked for these details was that my story on Amado Carrillo was in type, that I was only phoning in little changes, and that no matter what happened to me nothing could stop this story. I knew I had won. I had done him, I would make him famous, and in the drug industry fame leads to death. He had kept his name out of the Mexican media, he had managed to be almost entirely ignored by the U.S. media. In Juarez, a city he virtually ran, his name never appeared in print. Even the corridos, the folk songs of Mexican popular music that commonly celebrate major drug figures, never mentioned his name. And I think I felt exactly what Fernando felt again and again as the stranger finally said yes and gave Fernando that trust that made the stranger's doom possible.

About ninety days after my story on Carrillo ran in GQ, and after I appeared on the "Today" show, publicizing his power, he was dead.

Fernando tells me, you have to hug. Always hug. Embrace the stranger, pull him to you, say, "Amigo," and hug him. That way you can feel if he is armed.

I like Fernando. I respect him. But I cannot be him. Not because I am better than he or even believe I am as moral as he. But because I lack something he possesses. In *The Shootist,* John Wayne's last film, a boy asks him why he is a famous gunfighter when he has just demonstrated in target practice that he is only an average shot. "Because I was willing," Wayne says, "and most men are not."

I ask Fernando if he were ever frightened.

He smiles and looks at me and is silent.

I ask him if he worries about the men who still hunt him.

He remains silent. And serene. My questions are beneath contempt. They hail from a world he left long ago, shortly after birth, somewhere in that hard childhood.

As he eats his chili and beans, the Herreras are still hunting him; he knows this, the D.E.A. has picked up their probes. No matter. He himself has fielded phone calls from hunters. Once he picked up the phone and a voice asked, "Does Fernando Terrazas live there?" and he calmly answered, "No, no one of that name lives here. I'm sorry but you have the wrong number." He keeps a .45 loaded and he practices with it. There will be two men, he knows, him and the other man. One man will die.

I ask his wife if she worried about him when he would go off to do deals.

"Yes," she says. "I wondered if he would come back alive."

So I ask him once again, Why did you risk your life? And he gives the same answers: He hates drugs, he liked the money, he liked the work. But this time he keeps talking, talking about a long time ago. He came up as a teenager from Mexico, he rode the rails, worked the fields—damn hard work for little money.

Once his two sons came to him and said they did not want to go to college. He thought about it. Then he took them to California for the summer, put them in a tent, and had them work in the fields. They said the work was too hard. He said, "You better get used to it. Because if you do not go to college, you will work like this the rest of your life." They went to college. Years later, one of his sons had a chance at a bigger and better job. He told his father he did not know if he would take it. His father said, "You can go up there. If you don't like it, you can always come back down. But you have the chance to go up there." So his son went up there.

Fernando went up there, up with the big guys and their gold chains and millions, up there with the agents and their college degrees and badges. He did not come back down. Theoretically, of course, Fernando has his Achilles' heel: he trusted me. While he was alive, he had to trust that I would hide his home and change his name. What intrigues me is that he had to trust someone. I know the feeling, the unease later when I sit there and wonder if I am being set up. I know what it is like to drive from a meeting and watch the rearview mirror because, well, because I have trusted and could be betrayed and in some instances betrayal would mean no one would ever know what happened to me. Still, knowing all this, I trust. It is a need. This need made Fernando's career. And this need has now placed his safety in my hands.

We are all, I believe, prisoners of this desire.

Phil Jordan has flown in from Dallas for Fernando's rosary and funeral. He has come for the burial of the other half of his own identity. He sees the same flock of four hundred mourners I see and knows they do not know. He has felt the blows of Fernando's world. He has a murdered brother, the subject of the book that had dragged me for seven years into the drug world. The case has never been solved. He once talked to Fernando about it, and the old man listened and said, "There, there is the traitor." And he pointed to a person close to the core of Jordan's own blood. But the murder is filed away in Jordan's head at the moment and kept safe for a while from his thoughts.

He has come here to close the books on a friend and to keep things wrapped up and tidy. Fernando Terrazas was the partner that made his career, the friend who taught him rules in a world free of rules. He was the liar who was always the honorable man. I would have trusted Fernando with my life without a second's thought.

I look out at the full church, scan the faces of his children and their children. I talk to a son who is now a Federal agent, the same son who as a boy found the bullet holes in Fernando's car, and I ask him if he ever saw his father have too much to drink. He thinks and says, yes, once or twice he saw him kind of light up from alcohol. I remember years ago meeting this son in a border bar. He sat with his back to the corner of the room, a black bag with his gun on the table between us. I did not mention his father, and he never mentioned such a father existed. This silence is part of that world. Never trust. And yet you wind up trusting, just as the son did when he met me in the bar with his pistol and his back to the wall. The son asks me not to mention where his father lived. When I ask why, he says, "It never stops."

Phil Jordan comes over to the son and asks if he can pin a D.E.A. badge on his father's lapel. The son nods agreement. I watch Jordan delicately pin on the badge, then stand back and look almost with love into Fernando's cold face.

I want to say more. I want to say that Fernando Terrazas was a very fine man. And he was. I want to say, Never forget you are alone, always alone, that there is no backup. And you are. But I want to live somewhere else, someplace safe from the cold truths of Fernando.

Now the old man has been properly filed. Now he has been made safe for all of us. And we can feel comfortable in our worlds and our words. We can forget what we have learned.

$$\left[\text{THINKING OUTSIDE} \atop \text{THE BOX} \right]$$

GEORGE SOROS'S LONG STRANGE TRIP:
A Philanthropist Defies Drug War Orthodoxy

Russ Baker

From *The Nation*, September 20, 1999

One thing about George Soros everyone can agree on: He isn't worried what people think of him. Malaysian Prime Minister Mahathir Mohamad blamed the American billionaire for nearly ruining Malaysia's economy with massive currency speculation. Hard-core Russian nationalists decried as "meddling" his funding of progressive newspapers and institutions in post-Soviet Russia. Now, it's a prickly domestic cause—drug policy—that has folks taking aim at this hard-nosed financier and controversial philanthropist.

Soros is the "Daddy Warbucks of drug legalization," says Joseph Califano Jr. of Columbia University's National Center on Addiction and Substance Abuse. Clinton Administration drug czar Gen. Barry McCaffrey won't speak directly about Soros, but McCaffrey's spokesman, Bob Weiner, was typically biting in his assessment of the Lindesmith Center, a Soros-backed institution that serves as a leading voice for Americans who want to decriminalize drug use: "I'm sure Lindesmith's desire to take us into nihilism and chaos and to jam our hospital emergency rooms with more users has some valid purpose." Out on the lunatic fringe, anti-Semitic cult leader Lyndon LaRouche has labeled Soros, a Hungarian-born Jew, the mastermind behind a global drug cartel.

As a creative philanthropist, Soros is perhaps best known for his largesse to causes in Central and Eastern Europe (last year alone he gave away half a billion in places like Bosnia and Kazakhstan). When in 1994 he chose, as one of his first domestic programs, to fund efforts to challenge the efficacy of America's $37-billion-a-year war on drugs, he seemed intent on proving that he was either a fool or a visionary. It's still too early for a final judgment. But one thing is clear: He's touched a lot of raw nerves in challenging a long-entrenched view that the best way to fight drug abuse is through the criminal justice system.

That tendency was vividly apparent when in June 1998, at the United Nations' second conference on drugs, General McCaffrey was handed a perfectly timed two-page advertisement that had just run in the *New York Times*. The banner headline read: the global war on drugs is now causing more harm than drug abuse itself. Eyewitnesses recall the general fuming. And no wonder: The ad, brainchild of Lindesmith's director, Ethan Nadelmann, was an open letter signed by a spectacular array of opinion-makers, including numerous Nobel Prize laureates, former presidents, prime ministers and former UN Secretary General Javier Pérez de Cuéllar.

Soros's efforts to change the terms of the drug dialogue in America—from exhortation and punishment to treatment and rehabilitation—have ranged from such grand PR gestures as the *Times* open letter to the less glamorous tasks of research and grassroots advocacy. He has funded methadone-treatment and needle-exchange programs, supported a spate of successful medical-marijuana ballot initiatives and provided an institutional home in Lindesmith for Nadelmann, a man whom opponents tag as America's most unabashed proselytizer for legalization of drugs. Over the past six years Soros has given some $30 million to drug reform—just 7 percent of his overall domestic giving, but nonetheless a significant sum in the circumscribed world of drug policy advocacy.

In an interview with *The Nation*, Soros argued that his interest in shaking up the conventional wisdom about the war on drugs—and challenging political leaders to look beyond the zero-tolerance military model—is entirely consistent with his vision of an "open society." The parent organization of his worldwide philanthropic operation, the Open Society Institute (OSI), is founded upon the philosophical premise that nobody has a monopoly on the truth and that originally well-intentioned government efforts often turn repressive. "When I started looking to do something in the United States, [I saw that] one of the areas where policy has unintended adverse consequences is drug policy," Soros says. "That was the insight that got me involved." It's hard to argue with the facts he cites: Back in 1980 the federal government spent $1 billion on drug control and approximately 50,000 Americans were incarcerated for drug-law violations. Today Washington spends $18 billion annually, 400,000 people are in jail for nonviolent drug-related offenses and drugs are still widely available to anyone who wants them.

Yet Soros is remarkably frank about the fact that he hasn't got all the answers. "I don't know what the right thing to do is," he said, "but I do have a very strong conviction that what we are doing [now] is doing an awful lot of harm." In the name of reducing that harm and learning more about the problem, Soros is backing a range of organizations and initiatives that are testing out new ground, without subjecting them to a rigid ideological litmus test. Still, organizations using Soros money share certain core principles. Whether they lobby against harsh determinate sentencing for first-time drug offenders, run needle-exchange programs for addicts or promote methadone and other drug treatment programs, they reject the notion that drug users should be treated as criminals. "Criminalization," says Aryeh Neier, OSI's president (formerly executive director of Human Rights Watch and of the ACLU), "is a strategy that buys into the notion that if you lock up enough young black males—for whatever reason—you will promote public safety."

By far the most conspicuous part of Soros's empire is the Lindesmith Center. That's largely because it is directed by Nadelmann, who has a knack for saying things that others can't—or won't—say. Lindesmith is so integral a part of the Open Society Institute that its offices are mixed in right along with other Soros ventures like the Soros Documentary Fund and the Project on Death in America in the midtown Manhattan building that also houses Soros's business interests.

The two men met in 1992, when Soros was looking to extend his philanthropic efforts to the United States. Nadelmann was a Princeton professor and one of the most visible—and provocative—critics of US drug policy. (In 1993 Nadelmann declared, "It's nice to think that in another five or ten years . . . the right to possess and consume drugs may be as powerfully and as widely understood as the other rights of Americans.") Soros invited Nadelmann to lunch. After further discussions, in 1994 Soros agreed to create the Lindesmith Center and put Nadelmann at the helm. The center (named for the late Professor Alfred Lindesmith of Indiana University, the first prominent US academic to challenge the war on drugs approach) became the first of what are now dozens of domestic programs run out of OSI. Today, it has eighteen employees in New York and San Francisco and a modest budget of $1.7 million.

Although he's still actively managing billions in investments, Soros gives major face time to the drug reform effort. "My impression of Soros: extremely smart guy," says Kevin Zeese, a leading drug reform campaigner. "He can look at situations and be very helpful in figuring out strategies that make sense." When Zeese was a staffer at the Washington-based Drug Policy Foundation (DPF), which was, before Lindesmith, the leading pro-decriminalization advocacy group in the country, he sent Soros a grant proposal asking him to support lobbying and other advocacy activities. Soros invited Zeese to breakfast and confessed he didn't know enough about the policy issues to feel comfortable funding advocacy per se. But if Zeese was willing to tackle projects such as needle exchange and AIDS prevention—hands-on treatment as opposed to efforts to change laws—Soros was in. Zeese later moved on to form his own group, Common Sense for Drug Policy, which combines advocacy work with support for service-oriented programs. Last year Soros gave the organization $125,000, a quarter of its $500,000 budget.

As an alternative to locking people up, most Soros-backed groups advocate what they call "harm reduction"—a common-sense approach to drug policy that would nonetheless represent a radical departure from current practice. "The basic idea," Nadelmann says, "is that you have a fallback strategy for dealing with people who are engaged in behavior that can be risky or dangerous. So if you're smoking cigarettes, smoke less or don't smoke around kids or don't throw your ashes in dry timber. If you're drinking alcohol, don't drink and drive. You ride a bicycle—use a helmet. That's harm reduction."

In other words, harm reduction is about accepting certain realities about substance abuse and then trying to minimize the related harm to everyone. It accepts that some people will use drugs regardless of the consequences or penalties. Therefore, the key is to educate the public with accurate information—not hysterics—and, where that doesn't work, follow up with treatment. It involves containing and controlling drug use and therefore its harmful consequences to both the users and others who may be affected by the abuse—spouses and children, crime victims and so on.

Lindesmith is perhaps the foremost practitioner of this approach, but Soros's drug reform philanthropy is by no means limited to Lindesmith, and Nadelmann has played a key role in helping him decide what else to support. Since 1993, Soros's OSI has committed roughly $11 million to the DPF, which makes its own grants for needle exchange, women's treatment, drug education and methadone programs. Other recipients of Soros money include the Harm Reduction Coalition, an advocacy group with leadership largely made up of recovering drug abusers; the Research and Policy Reform Center, an OSI affiliate that works to affect the political process directly, coordinating medical-marijuana ballot initiatives and pushing for state-level legislation (such as revising the drastic Rockefeller laws in New York and expanding access to methadone in Vermont); Drug Strategies, a mom-and-apple-pie group that promotes treatment, education and prevention; and the Tides Foundation, a progressive San Francisco-based grant-making institution that supports needle exchange. Soros has also taken the issue abroad, giving $3.8 million over the past four years to support harm-reduction programs in Central and Eastern Europe.

An immediate goal of many organizations devoted to harm reduction is expanding access to methadone treatment—a program that is seen by skeptics as just substituting one addiction for another. In response, writing in *Foreign Affairs* last year, Nadelmann noted that the "addiction" to methadone is "more like a diabetic's 'addiction' to insulin than a heroin addict's to product bought on the street." While methadone has been shown in scores of studies to be an effective treatment for heroin addiction—and findings by the National Institute on Drug Abuse show that an intravenous drug user enrolled in a methadone treatment program is seven times less likely to become infected with HIV than a person not enrolled in one—it remains acutely underfunded, with at most 180,000 of the nation's estimated 800,000 heroin users able to get it. Closing this gap has been a top priority of OSI-funded drug reform organizations, which have pursued it by lobbying for legislation on methadone maintenance treatment in the eight states where it is still illegal, participating in conferences and spearheading public education drives to counter perceptions that methadone treatment is just drug abuse by another name.

Harm-reduction groups are also fighting to expand needle-exchange programs, bolstered by research by the federal Centers for Disease Control, which estimates that half of all new HIV cases stem from use of infected syringes. No more than an estimated 10 percent of injection drug users have access to clean-needle programs. (Contaminated needles have created a new AIDS generation: A 1995 National Academy of Sciences report, which called for the Surgeon General to lift the federal ban on funding needle-exchange programs, stated that "more than half of all pediatric AIDS cases reported in 1993 can be linked to the HIV epidemic among injection drug users.") Soros has made major grants for needle exchange through the DPF, the Tides Foundation and the George Williams Fund, which is the principal source of private funding for needle exchange in the United States as well as in Central and Eastern Europe.

Critics charge that while harm reduction sounds reasonable, it will only lead to increased drug use, with all its attendant social ills. "Anything that becomes more accessible to adults will become more accessible to young people," notes Dr. Jerome Jaffe, who served as director of the Special Action Office for Drug Abuse Prevention in the Nixon Administration. "Coming out with a sensible and workable policy is simply avoided in these very interesting flights of rhetoric Ethan is capable of. He can be an effective speaker to people who are not fully cognizant of all the problems we face."

Perhaps the most controversial element of Soros's drug-reform portfolio—and the one most frequently associated with a pro-legalization agenda—is the medical-marijuana movement. All told, Soros-backed ballot initiatives related to marijuana have gone to the people in seven states, beginning with California's Proposition 215 (where Soros donated $550,000) and Arizona's Proposition 200 in 1996, where Soros plopped down $430,000 and later tacked on $366,000 to help fortify the initiative, which also introduced probation and treatment for nonviolent first- and second-time offenders instead of prison. The California initiative has yet to take effect because of foot-dragging by conservative state officials. But in Arizona, since Prop 200 passed, jail rolls have been lightened of hundreds of drug users and the state has saved more than $2.5 million in prison costs, according to a recent report by Arizona's Administrative Office of the Courts.

Moving from grant-making and policy-working to passing laws has proven to be a productive step, but one requiring delicacy. "We are very cautious not to mix tax deductibles with non-tax deductibles, where you are trying to influence legislation," Soros says. "We live in a glass bowl, and people look at you very carefully, so we look at everything very carefully. If anything, we err on the side of caution." Soros has used his own money to back these legislative ventures, but it has nevertheless been Nadelmann brokering many of the crucial deals, bringing in two other businessmen, Peter Lewis (an insurance magnate from Cleveland) and John Sperling (founder of the for-profit University of Phoenix), each of whom ponied up approximately a third of a million dollars.

Nadelmann, 42, is the son of a rabbi. Lean and pale-freckled, with close-cropped auburn hair and a gray-tinged beard, he speaks with studied fervor, his voice ringing with conviction, his hands punctuating his arguments as he parcels out his words. At a typical gathering, Nadelmann might begin by acknowledging the widespread and often legitimate panic sparked by drugs: parents' fear of losing their children, the public's alarm over rampant drug-related crime, the spread of HIV. Quickly, though, he's challenging his audience to look more closely at positions they have probably never heard defended with such winning reasonableness: Throughout history and in all manner of societies, drugs have been present; like it or not, drugs will always be present. Drug abuse is self-directed behavior, and you cannot legislate such behavior. ("You shouldn't be arresting people and taking away their freedom and engaging them in the criminal justice system unless they really cause some harm to somebody else.") He argues that the drug war has devastated civil liberties, given police unprecedented new powers and penalized unevenly the preferred vices of various ethnic, racial and social groups. He complains that the massive rise in drug-related incarceration has decimated communities, destroyed families and put society's most vulnerable people not in a therapeutic environment but in one that actually fosters long-term drug use and related violence.

Nadelmann argues that the right of people to self-administer whatever they want is consonant with the objective of all libertarians, civil and otherwise. But he dislikes the word "legalize," which he finds needlessly divisive and somewhat misleading. The use of this term to disparage reformers reminds Nadelmann of the days when all trade unionists were labeled Marxists: "It's a pretty systematic effort by the drug warriors to really ghettoize us and portray us as one extreme," he says. Craig Reinarman, an OSI drug policy board member and professor of sociology at the University of California, Santa Cruz, agrees: "The way you hear it from the drug warriors, you get the vision of vending machines—you go to the supermarket and ask, 'Where's the crack aisle? Where's the heroin aisle?'"

As a result of attacks like these, Nadelmann has become somewhat of a pariah to the drug-policy establishment—signaling his effectiveness as a critic but also the hurdles he must overcome. "The drug czar has refused to be at any public event where Nadelmann is," says Reinarman. "[McCaffrey] is probably smart enough to avoid embarrassment." Calvina Fay, deputy executive director at the Drug Free America Foundation, who has never been on a panel with Nadelmann, says, "We don't think debating is a very good idea."

In his florid presentations, Nadelmann occasionally pushes the analogy envelope, noting, for example, our unwillingness to ban cars, which kill more people than drugs do. The hyperbole makes academic drug-policy analysts—generally the middle-grounders of a continuum on which Lindesmith is seen as extreme—shake their heads. "Advocacy groups like the Lindesmith Center benefit in terms of charging up the people who are affiliated with them by seeing this in a sort of good-versus-evil conflict setting...[but] I'm frustrated to the extent that the whole debate has been polarized," says Jonathan Caulkins, a Carnegie Mellon public policy professor and researcher at RAND's Drug Policy Research Center. "Lindesmith has, in some cases, blocked practical, incremental improvement because it allows politicians to posture and to make outrageous statements . . . in place of serious thinking."

Critics point out that Nadelmann openly supported legalization in his pre-Lindesmith days. But he has since had a change of heart (or tactics) that Soros himself has no trouble accepting as genuine. Nadelmann's discomfort with prohibition is still apparent, but his language has softened, and he acknowledges and even promotes the more moderate positions of other reformers. "Ethan started out with a more radical position than the one he stands for today," says Soros. "There has been an evolution in his thinking. Partly because of his role at the Lindesmith Center, he has evolved and is now looking for more consensual and less ideological ways of dealing with things." Despite criticism of Nadelmann's approach, Soros has no intention of backing away from him. "I believe in substance and not image," says Soros. "If Ethan has an image problem, I think I can live with it. At the same time, we have constituted an advisory board that represents a broader range of views, so I want to make sure that I am striking a balance." Other OSI drug policy advisory board members include three sociology professors and a professor of public health—and one other figure as out-front as Nadelmann, Baltimore Mayor Kurt Schmoke, famed for his early advocacy of decriminalization.

If Nadelmann and Soros are going to build any sort of popular movement around drug policy reform, one challenge they must face is the tension that persists between the legalization camp and black activists. Rev. Calvin Butts of Harlem's Abyssinian Baptist Church, for example, says he is for moving away from harsh penalties for possession, but against legalization. "There's a sharp debate in the black community regarding legalization," says Butts. "Those of us who deal with drug users and see the effects are opposed to legalization. Often white liberals just don't get it." Deborah Small, Lindesmith's director of public policy and community outreach, who is black and Latino, has a similar view. "To the extent there's tension in the drug-reform movement, it has a lot to do with the fact that the movement is dominated by white liberals whose principal issue has to do with legalization, particularly of marijuana," says Small, who was formerly legislative director at the New York Civil Liberties Union, where she worked with Nadelmann on changes in New York's harsh Rockefeller drug laws. "That doesn't have resonance in the African-American community, [where] the principal issues have to do with incarceration and punitive policies.... Legalization is not considered a legitimate option in the African-American community. With the alcohol and tobacco problems we face, legalization is seen as another form of genocide against communities of color. It is not enough to say you should be against the war on drugs. Removing that is not going to make the situation better unless you're talking about taking money from the war on drugs and using it for services so people don't return to drugs or drug-selling."

Small notes that Soros is, by definition, removed from some of the practical effects of the drug problem. "A month ago, we had a meeting at his estate—it was nice being up there; he has a beautiful home," she recalls. "That night—I live in Brooklyn near the projects—I heard gunshots. One of the things I couldn't help thinking about is that [Soros] doesn't have that experience. He doesn't have to hear gunshots. The drug war has a different meaning for me. . . . And yet I think he's a lot more sensitive than a lot of people who are disconnected from those consequences." Lindesmith itself, she says, is perhaps the strongest advocate on issues that matter to communities of color, such as the way felony convictions (many of which are drug related) have effectively disfranchised 13 percent of all black men.

Most drug-policy experts agree that Soros and his associates have affected the national dialogue on drugs but see only one or two areas of concrete advances. "Ethan Nadelmann is a major figure in the drug-reform area, but I don't detect any movement on the issues coming from anything other than medical-marijuana initiatives," says Philip Heymann, who served as Deputy Attorney General under Clinton, where he was a key Justice Department figure with regard to drug issues. And those initiatives draw credible criticism that Soros and his associates are using a medical issue to advance the broader political agenda of drug decriminalization.

The harm-reduction approach has achieved other, less spectacular victories. After years of inaction, the House finally passed what had been a perennially doomed bill to soften the punitive forfeiture of civil assets by those arrested for drug offenses [see Eric Blumenson and Eva Nilsen, "The Drug War's Hidden Economic Agenda," March 9, 1998]. While the credit for this shift can't be attributed specifically to Soros, his outfits have been active on the issue recently; OSI made a grant several months ago to the libertarian Cato Institute for a conference on forfeiture, and the Lindesmith Center hosted a seminar on the topic. Meanwhile, both the National Academy of Sciences and the National Institutes of Health have issued statements expressing their support for needle exchange, methadone treatment and medical marijuana. Polls nationwide show increased public skepticism toward the war on drugs and, in most cases, favorable opinion for efforts like medical marijuana. (Last year Congress refused to count the vote of a Washington, DC, medical-marijuana initiative; exit polls suggested that it had passed by 69 percent.) In addition, there's growing sympathy among judges, legislators and ordinary citizens for doing away with harsh mandatory-minimum sentences for nonviolent drug offenders.

Lindesmith has been fighting an uphill battle to expand treatment for intravenous drug users, but this past summer the prospects finally became brighter. In July, the Clinton Administration proposed significant changes in methadone treatment policy, including national accreditation for methadone centers and a system for accrediting hospitals and doctors so that they can prescribe the drug. (The final regulations are expected to be issued early next year.) Yet the gap between available treatment slots and drug abusers who want them remains huge.

Even less promising is the status of needle exchange. Despite Soros's $1 million matching grant to fund clean needles—and his support of many foundations working in this area—there has been little change in public policy toward such programs. In April of last year, Secretary of Health and Human Services Donna Shalala was set to give a press conference announcing the government's reversal of its position on needle-exchange funding, but the Clinton Administration reneged at the last minute.

Surveying these wins and losses, Soros himself says he has no intention of remaining the sole patron of the movement. "I think we want to move toward more publicly funded activity rather than being bankrolled by fat cats," he says. He's also pushing for smaller contributions from a larger base. Making good on his promise to allow the whole enterprise to sink or swim, as he has recently done with some of his Central and Eastern European nonprofits, Soros has cut back his donations to the DPF, eliminating funds for the group's operations while continuing to fund its community-treatment grant program. DPF's Tyler Green says that several heavily endowed old-line foundations have already offered to step into the breach (he asked that their names not be used). As for the marijuana initiatives, other funders plan to stay committed. "We're in this for the long haul," says University of Phoenix's Sperling. "We're on a roll." Among other things, they plan to retry initiatives in Maine, Nevada and Colorado, where technicalities prevented them from getting on the ballot last time.

"The first five years have focused on a critique of the current approach," says Gara LaMarche, OSI's director of US programs. "The question is, What now? If the medical-marijuana initiatives showed that the conventional thinking on the war on drugs can be overcome, what's the long-term agenda? We need to focus more on the intersection of drugs and the criminal justice system—to address the disabilities that affect great numbers of people, including drug testing, prosecution of minor offenses and mandatory minimums." Lindesmith, LaMarche says, will probably be spun out as a freestanding organization.

"I think if there is any real challenge the Lindesmith Center and the drug-policy reform movement are facing, it is how to take a political viewpoint and ideology and turn it into a movement," says Lindesmith's Small. "It isn't now.

There's a group of people who share a common perspective, but it hasn't been turned into a plan of action. To be a movement, you have got to be able to communicate goals and aspirations to other communities, especially the minority communities. Those communities are not only not represented in the movement, they're not even aware that a movement exists."

After five years of verbal brickbats from drug warriors, Soros says he doesn't mind being a target: "Other people express more respect for me because I am ready to say something that they would like to say if they could afford it." Even staunch opponents of his views admire Soros's unwavering commitment. "He doesn't care how many articles are written against him," says New York Times columnist and drug warrior A.M. Rosenthal, a heavy critic of Soros who nevertheless notes, "Social responsibility is what is important to him."

Many Americans—especially strong supporters of a tough-on-drugs policy—still imagine drug users as people distinctly different from themselves. As Nadelmann likes to point out, Americans' attitude toward drug users today is reminiscent of our attitude toward homosexuals thirty years ago. "You know one, you just don't know you know one," he says. We also don't know whether enlightened policy models that work in small, relatively low-crime, relatively homogeneous and unfractured European societies will necessarily work here. There are just too many variables. To critics, Soros, Nadelmann and company are proposing a dangerous new course whose consequences are uncertain at best and potentially disastrous. "Lindesmith Center's line is deliberately vague," says UCLA public policy professor Mark Kleiman, a drug-reform moderate. "It's like it used to be with the Old Leftists when you'd ask them, 'What's life going to be like after the revolution?' 'Oh, well, we'll decide that after the revolution.'" Still, few would dispute that Soros is fostering a bracing debate on whether being at war with ourselves is really the best—or only—way to win the "war" against drugs.

WHAT DO WE DO WHEN THE DRUG WAR STOPS?

Rowena Young

This article is based on the pamphlet '*From War to Work: drug treatment, social inclusion and enterprise*' written for the Foreign Policy Center

No one now believes in the war on drugs. The government are quietly dropping their khaki slogans and downgrading the battle against cannabis. Even the right-wing press denounce policies that waste millions and, more importantly, could land their university-educated children with criminal records. But there is no agreement on how the government should withdraw from the battlefield, or what the principles of a new approach would be.

The liberal mantras are more treatment, more education, and more health-care. But the hard truth is that the liberal remedies of choice have been scarcely more effective. Nine-tenths of all treatment fails: most addicts go through the revolving door of treatment and relapse for decades.

The central failure is to treat drug addiction as a "disease." The biomedical approach to drug treatment focuses on weaning addicts off drugs, using opiate substitutes such as methodone and buprenorphine to satisfy their cravings. But dispatching an addict to the most comfortable of rehab clinics far from home only temporarily reduces their physical dependency on drugs. As soon as they return to their home environment, mix with drug using friends, and face the listless boredom of homelessness or unemployment, they easily relapse.

Drug use is a social rather than a medical problem. An ever-expanding army of therapists has failed to acknowledge that social ills are not caused by the substances themselves but by the unstable lives of those using them. Seventy per cent of American frontline servicemen used heroin during the Vietnam War yet only three percent continued using back home. Returning to quiet, civilian lives in Middle America, most had no desire to continue using. Surveys throughout the eighties and nineties in Britain proved that drug use only becomes problematic when it occurs in combination with social isolation or deprivation.

Most teenagers who take ecstasy in clubs on Saturday nights are not at risk of getting an entrenched drug problem because they have emotional and social support that the homeless, long-term unemployed and very poor lack. Cocaine users in the City often check their habits when their performance in the office suffers. Very few have the kind of 'addictive personality' which enslaves the user after a few hits.

Even drugs education, the one policy that wins plaudits all round, isn't the powerful deterrent that its advocates claim. Campaigns which give the impression that one drag on a joint leads to ruin are seen as laughable by a generation of teenagers far savvier than their teachers. The "Heroin Screws You Up" posters of the 1980s were withdrawn after evidence that they had become a darkly glamorous fashion accessory. A recent study by the Drugs Prevention Advisory Service of 14-16-year-olds who had been through a Drugs Education course found that, one year on, the lessons had no impact on their drug-taking.

It should be no surprise that the evidence shows that the most effective way of reducing drug misuse is, unsurprisingly, to encourage self-disciplined and purposeful lives. Many Western health-care professionals would write this philosophy off as "unrealistic" and "bullying." Asked to explain the poor record of drug treatment programmes, they will attribute this to a morally conservative climate and inadequate resourcing. No doubt these do provide barriers to success. But those involved in drugs rehabilitation in India and Pakistan face these problems in spades, and would see western conditions as utopian: yet they achieve much greater success rates with innovative projects.

In Delhi the Sharan project has helped slum-dwellers that have become addicted to the glut of heroin on the streets—where it is cheaper than cannabis or home-brewed alcohol. 90 percent of Delhi's drug users were homeless; many were imprisoned, persecuted, contracted AIDS or were disowned by families ashamed of their behaviour. Prejudice against drug users is deep-felt: the official position ten years ago was that drug users should be left to die. Against a background of fatalism and inertia, the project has combined needle and syringe exchanges and substitute prescribing with training and work. 80 percent of permanent staff—doctors, managers and general drug workers—are now drawn from ex-users.

Unlike most training centres in this country, these schemes do not expect addicts to have overcome their habit before they begin training or work. Instead, they help them through the difficult transition phase, from days dominated by the need to find money to pay for the next hit, to lives filled with training, work shadowing and eventually full time employment. Many of the projects are run by ex-addicts and pay their bills by operating as small businesses—undertaking work as varied as reconditioning jeeps and building houses.

The pioneering Kaleidoscope project in London has implemented some of the lessons of these Asian success stories—creating treatment that combines education, training and treatment in one small organisation. The government could also apply this philosophy to benefit the system. However, most addicts will fall through even schemes targeted at the socially excluded—by failing to commit to training or keep regular appointments. The government should ensure it does everything it can to get them into work—providing transport if necessary to deliver them to work direct. Though this seems expensive, the absolute priority must be to get users back into the structure provided by work. Of course, employers won't want to deal with the messy social problems that addicts bring with them. Private recruitment agencies should be paid by the government to run programmes that combine recruitment, training, management, social support and transport.

There must be recognition by the government that every society in history has had its drug of choice. Instead of promising to halve the use of Class A drugs among young people by 2008, there should be a pledge to reduce the harm associated with drugs misuse. Though legalisation would not be a cure-all, changes in the law could limit the problems associated with drugs. Licensed venues should be established for the safe consumption of drugs and greater penalties should be given to those involved in supplying children.

While British policy remains frozen, other parts of the world are developing drugs policies that are showing de facto signs of success. It will be a major blot on a progressive government's record if it lags behind countries in which the political climate is far more conservative, maintaining drugs policies whose cost—in resources and lives—has already been far too high.

BYO HEROIN

Maurice Frank

From *Mother Jones*, May 5, 2000

FRANKFURT, Germany—"Bleib immer locker" (Always stay mellow) says the sign in the door, an oddly glib piece of advice for the junkies entering a government-funded center to shoot up drugs.

A cross between a youth hostel and a run-down hospital clinic, the place has an antiseptic stench. German hip-hop is playing on a small boom box in the corner. In the waiting area, a dozen men and women are passed out in chairs or on the floor or else twitching nervously, awaiting their turn to inject. Once their names are called, each receives a steel tray containing a new syringe, cotton pads, a sterilized spoon, and a packet of distilled water—everything needed to prepare and inject heroin or cocaine. This they do in the next room, sitting in plastic chairs where others are stripping off their pants in search of a spare vein, or just leaning back and letting the high set in.

The room is one of Frankfurt's four controversial "Druckraum" or injection rooms, where 1,000 times a day, some 600 "clients" inject their own street-bought heroin or cocaine in a safe and clean environment. The rooms are a pragmatically German attempt to create social order, a kind of domestic realpolitik.

"The goal is to get people off the streets. They would be doing this in train station toilets otherwise. Here the risks are minimized," says Wolfgang Barth, the director of one of the injection rooms.

Operating under semi-legal status since 1994, the city-funded rooms were finally legitimized by the German parliament in February. That move has appalled German conservatives and prompted an outcry from the United Nations, which contends that the policy behind the rooms clashes with international treaties on combating the drug trade.

While such centers have existed in the liberal Netherlands for several years, they are more surprising in straight-laced Germany. The appearance of the rooms across the European Union's largest country—several other cities have by now copied Frankfurt's example—has attracted considerable international attention. Spain and Australia are now setting up their own trial injection rooms. Switzerland has even gone a step further with an experimental program in which addicts are administered pharmaceutically produced heroin which they inject under medical supervision. Frankfurt is reportedly also considering such a program, which would cut off injection rooms from the black market supply chain, eliminating the need for addicts to commit crimes to pay for their drugs.

There's little doubt Frankfurt's drug policy—of which injection rooms are merely a part—saves human lives. Juergen Weimer, a laid-back city drugs official, says drug deaths have dropped from 147 in 1992 to 26 last year. In contrast, drug deaths went up 8 percent last year in Germany as a whole. Cheap, impure Afghani heroin flooding the market has led to a rise in addiction in most of Europe—but not in Frankfurt.

Weimer also says that the average age of addicts is getting higher, with virtually no Frankfurt youth getting hooked on heroin. He attributes the success to the city's all-around approach, which includes not only injection rooms, methadone treatment and "rest centers" for addicts, but also a comprehensive youth education and prevention program.

This approach to the drug problem, however, doesn't go down well with the UN. "Treaties require that drug abuse be prevented," says Akira Fujino, deputy secretary of the UN-affiliated International Narcotics Control Board in Vienna. Injection rooms, he says, facilitate the overall traffic in drugs. Conceding that the rooms do save lives, Fujino maintains they could have negative consequences internationally. "Just imagine if other countries started to do the same and the impact (that would have) on international trafficking," he says.

Not that there is a consensus in Germany on injection rooms, either. In other cities where the conservative Christian Democrats are in power, such as Berlin, the authorities staunchly oppose injection rooms."It cannot be the state's job to get people high," said Stefan Paris, Berlin's spokesman on social issues. "Our political stance is to encourage a drug-free, abstinence-oriented life."

In the waiting area of a Frankfurt injection room at 49 Niddastrasse, S. Von Diezelski, 35, is doing her nails, killing time. She's waiting for an appointment with her nearby doctor, to receive her methadone treatment. At any moment she could get up, sign a piece of paper at the reception desk, and shoot up.

Von Diezelski injects heroin here about every four or five days, even though she's on methadone, which means technically she's not allowed to use the injection room. A former prostitute, she comes here to pursue her habit safely.

"The advantage of this place is that you get a clean needle," she says. "Since junk is getting cheaper, and dirtier, and more dangerous, it's good they have medically trained people who can call an ambulance."

There's no registration procedure for junkies here, just an ID check and a few questions to make sure they are over eighteen and not first-time users. Dealing or sharing drugs is banned. "Even if a couple comes in they are not allowed to share," says Josch Steinmetz, head of the Niddastrasse center. Dealing is forbidden inside, but Von Diezelski says it's easy to score just outside the door.

Two hundred yards around the corner, on Elbestrasse, amidst sex-shops, brothels, and kebab stands, is the "Drogennotdienst"—the "drugs emergency service," offering another injection room, a needle exchange station, medical check-ups, methadone clinic, and a cafe with free food. The atmosphere is rowdier here—men are rolling joints and smoking crack pipes on the sidewalk. Relatively new to Germany, crack has made the local drug culture more violent, says Weimer, and it is strictly forbidden inside the centers.

Despite the ruckus out front, Weimer says the number of people shooting up in public spaces in the city has been reduced to nearly zero. He remembers ten years ago, when up to 1,000 addicts would hang out everyday in the park opposite the Deutsche Bank headquarters, littering the area with needles and trash, dealing heroin, selling their bodies for money.

"AIDS changed everything," says Weimer. Soaring HIV rates, caused largely by shared needles, forced the city in the early nineties to begin radically overhauling its drug policy. According to Weimer, social workers sat down with police and had "a non-ideological, pragmatic discussion on what we could immediately do to help users survive." Injection rooms were introduced in 1994 under a liberal mayor; surprisingly, they were continued under the following administration headed by a conservative Christian Democrat, against the will of her own party, which still vehemently opposes injection rooms.

The Frankfurt police have supported injection rooms from the beginning. Junkies still buy their drugs on the street, but no longer have to do them there; and because they are offered treatment programs and advice at the injection rooms, the rooms will likely contribute to a drop in heroin use overall, and a consequent drop in drug-related crimes, says police spokesman Peter Borchardt. Thanks to the rooms, says Borchardt, "Things have improved considerably on the streets here."

WORLD LEADERS ON DOPE: Right Joins Left in Call for an End to the Drug War

Russ Kick

From the *Village Voice*, May 30-June 5, 2001

The American drug war may yet grind on, but one by one, the troops are hiking out. Right-wingers like Jesse Ventura, Gary Johnson, Dan Quayle, William F. Buckley, and George Schultz have all voiced support for either ending the costly campaign of interdiction and imprisonment, or at least decriminalizing pot.

Through the years, in statements little-noted or splashed onto front pages, they've aligned themselves with leaders around the world, all standing in unlikely opposition to the frat-boy chief commander in the White House. President Bush shows no sign of yielding, instead choosing to harden his stance. In May, announcing the appointment of a drug czar who makes John Ashcroft look like a hippie, Bush thundered, "John Walters and I believe the only humane and compassionate response to drug use is a moral refusal to accept it. We emphatically disagree with those who favor drug legalization."

These days, that means disagreeing with a lengthening list of international heavyweights—former presidents of the United States, current presidents of Latin American countries, legislators, governors, high-ranking judges, and law enforcement officials. Not that all of them favor outright legalization—most don't—but each has broached the possibility of relaxing the laws.

Two weeks ago, as the U.S. Supreme Court shot down medical marijuana like Christian missionaries over Peru, the Canadian Parliament was questioning whether soft drugs should be decriminalized. "It's time to be bold," lawmaker Derek Lee told the *Ottawa Citizen.* "Everything has to be on the table."

Bush finds himself hemmed in by opinion south of the border as well, where some of his strongest allies in free trade break radically with his policies on drugs. President Vicente Fox of Mexico, for one, assures the Bush administration he will be an obedient, merciless drug warrior, while he tells his own country's newspapers that someday humanity will recognize universal drug legalization as the best course.

A parade of brutal statistics has long made clear the merit of Fox's legalize-it zeal. According to the National Organization for the Reform of Marijuana Laws, police in 1998 arrested 682,885 Americans for marijuana offenses, more than the number for all violent crimes combined. After eight years of Bill Clinton, a supposed progressive who could have provided relief, some 450,000 drug offenders sat behind bars—a total almost equal to the entire U.S. prison population in 1980. The president who later told *Rolling Stone* he believed small amounts of pot should be decriminalized spent his terms fueling a multibillion-dollar escalation of the drug war, in which people were killed in raids of the wrong homes and constitutional rights were shredded. On average, the Lindesmith Center reports, a federal offender in the Clinton era drew twice as much time for drugs as for manslaughter.

The Drug Policy Foundation calculates that in 1999, the feds spent $1.7 billion to guard America's borders and coasts—$17,700 per mile—only to have 70 percent of the coke and 90 percent of the heroin make it through. Drug use continues to climb, with some 72 million Americans believed to have tried pot.

While the U.S. continues its self-destructive orgy of arrests and wasted money, other parts of the world move forward. The Swiss government has endorsed a plan to legalize pot and hash consumption and allow some shops to sell cannabis. Belgium allows people to grow pot for personal use. The Netherlands allows coffee houses to sell marijuana. Portugal, Spain, and Italy punish the use of any drug (including heroin and coke) with only an administrative sanction, such as a fine.

Britain has loosened its laws a tiny bit, allowing low-level marijuana offenses to be immediately expunged from arrest records. In an effort to control the damage from opiate addiction, Australia has opened the world's largest heroin-injecting room in Sydney.

But it's in the regions most wracked by narco-violence that the cry for legalization rings most clear. Having been shot in the neck by a police officer thought to be acting under orders from drug lords, Patricio Martínez García, governor of the Mexican state of Chihuahua, told *El Universal* in March that he believed a proposal for legalization must be considered. "[B]ecause if the war is going to continue being lost, with the deterioration of the life of communities and even the nation, and with the deterioration of the quality of life for the citizens of the country, well, then, where are we heading?" said García, whose state borders Texas and New Mexico. "There has to be a remaking of the law."

VICENTE FOX - Mexican President

"My opinion is that in Mexico it is not a crime to have a small dose of drugs in one's pocket. . . . But the day that the alternative of freeing the consumption of drugs from punishment comes, it will have to be done in the entire world because we are not going to win anything if Mexico does it, but the production and traffic of the drugs . . . to the United States continues. Thus, humanity will one day view it [legalization] as the best in this sense." (source: *Unomasuno*, March 17, 2001)

JORGE CASTAÑEDA - Mexican Foreign Minister

"In the end, legalization of certain substances may be the only way to bring prices down, and doing so may be the only remedy to some of the worst aspects of the drug plague: violence, corruption, and the collapse of the rule of law." (source: *Newsweek*, September 6, 1999)

JORGE BATLLE - President of Uruguay

"Why don't we just legalize drugs? . . . The day that it is legalized in the United States, it will lose value. And if it loses value, there will be no profit. But as long as the U.S. citizenry doesn't rise up to do something, they will pass this life fighting and fighting." (source: *El Observador*, December 1, 2000)

BILL CLINTON - Former U.S. President

"I think that most small amounts of marijuana have been decriminalized in some places, and should be." (source: *Rolling Stone*, October 6, 2000)

JOE CLARK - Head of Tory Party, member of Canadian Parliament, former Prime Minister

"I believe the least controversial approach is decriminalization [of marijuana], because it's unjust to see someone, because of one decision one night in their youth, carry the stigma—to be barred from studying medicine, law, architecture or other fields where a criminal record could present an obstacle." (source: *Globe and Mail* [Toronto], May 23, 2001)

JIMMY CARTER - Former U.S. President

"Penalties against a drug should not be more damaging to an individual than the use of the drug itself. Nowhere is this more clear than in the laws against possession of marijuana for personal use. The National Commission on Marijuana . . . concluded years ago that marijuana use should be decriminalized, and I believe it is time to implement those basic recommendations." (source: speech to Congress, August 2, 1977)

DAN QUAYLE - Former U.S. Vice President
"Congress should definitely consider decriminalizing possession of marijuana. . . . We should concentrate on prosecuting the rapists and burglars who are a menace to society." (source: *Smoke and Mirrors: The War on Drugs and the Politics of Failure* by Dan Baum, quoting Quayle from 1977)

GEORGE SCHULTZ - Reagan's Secretary of State
"We need at least to consider and examine forms of controlled legalization of drugs." (source: Associated Press, November 6, 1989)

ABIGAIL VAN BUREN - Advice Columnist
"I agree that marijuana laws are overdue for an overhaul. I also favor the medical use of marijuana—if it's prescribed by a physician. I cannot understand why the federal government should interfere with the doctor-patient relationship, nor why it would ignore the will of a majority of voters who have legally approved such legislation." (source: "Dear Abby," March 1, 1999)

WILLIAM F. BUCKLEY - Conservative Author
"Now it's one thing to say (I say it) that people shouldn't consume psychoactive drugs. It is entirely something else to condone marijuana laws the application of which resulted, in 1995, in the arrest of 588,963 Americans. Why are we so afraid to inform ourselves on the question?" (source: syndicated column, October 21, 1997)

GARY JOHNSON - Governor of New Mexico
"Make drugs a controlled substance like alcohol. Legalize it, control it, regulate it, tax it. If you legalize it, we might actually have a healthier society." (source: *The Boston Globe*, October 13, 1999)

BEN CAYETANO - Governor of Hawaii
"I just think it's a matter of time that Congress finally gets around to understanding that the states should be allowed to provide this kind of relief [medical marijuana] to the people. Congress is way, way behind in their thinking." (source: Associated Press, May 15, 2001)

JESSE VENTURA - Governor of Minnesota
"The prohibition of drugs causes crime. You don't have to legalize, just

decriminalize it. Regulate it. Create places where the addict can go get it."
(source: *Playboy*, November 1999)

KURT SCHMOKE - Former Mayor of Baltimore
"Decriminalization would take the profit out of drugs and greatly reduce, if
not eliminate, the drug-related violence that is currently plaguing our streets."
(source: *The Washington Post*, May 15, 1988)

FRANK JORDAN - Former mayor of San Francisco
"I have no problem whatsoever with the use of marijuana for medical purposes. I am sensitive and compassionate to people who have legitimate needs.
We should bend the law and do what's right." (source: *Los Angeles Times*, February 26, 1995)

RON PAUL - U.S. Congressman from Texas
"When we finally decide that drug prohibition has been no more successful
than alcohol prohibition, the drug dealers will disappear." (source: Paul's Web
site, www.house.gov/paul)

JORGE SAMPAIO - President of Portugal
"Policies conceived and enforced to control drug-related problems and
effects have led to disastrous and perverse results. Prohibition is the fundamental
principle of drug policies. If we consider the results achieved, there are profound doubts regarding its effectiveness. Prohibitionist policies have been
unable to control the consumption of narcotics; on the other hand, there has
been an increase of criminality. There is also a high mortality rate related to the
quality of substances and to AIDS or other viral diseases." (source: Madrid's *El
País*, April 7, 1997)

MILTON FRIEDMAN - Nobel Prize winner for economics
"Legalizing drugs would simultaneously reduce the amount of crime and
raise the quality of law enforcement. Can you conceive of any other measure
that would accomplish so much to promote law and order?" (source: *Newsweek*,
May 1, 1972)

MAYOR ROCKY ANDERSON TALKS ABOUT WHAT IT'S LIKE TO . . . DROP THE D.A.R.E. PROGRAM

Alexandra Eyle

From *Reconsider Quarterly*, Winter 2001-2002

[Reconsider Quarterly's] *Editor's Note: Salt Lake City, Utah, Mayor Ross "Rocky" Anderson took office on January 3, 1000, after spending 21 years as an attorney specializing in civil litigation. One of his first acts as mayor was to cut the city's D.A.R.E. programs and to urge the schools to use more effective drug education/prevention programs. He also established other programs for youths, including after-school and arts programs. In this exclusive interview with ReconsiDer Quarterly editor Alexandra Eyle, Anderson talks about what it was like to end D.A.R.E. and the challenges that lie ahead.*

Q: Why did you decide to cut D.A.R.E. from your schools?

A: I had written a column for a local newspaper about this issue, about two years before I was elected. After I became mayor, I updated my research. I studied the literature and found that there were numerous peer-reviewed research articles establishing that D.A.R.E. had no effect on long-term drug use.

Q: As a citizen, and as a mayor, as someone who was investing tax money in D.A.R.E., how did that make you feel?

A: I was—and still am—convinced that the American people had been badly betrayed. D.A.R.E. had created, through its public relations efforts, including t-shirts and bumper stickers and such, the sense, among the public, that we were really doing something by utilizing D.A.R.E. in our public schools to reduce long-term drug use in our public schools. The net result has been lost and ruined lives, many of which could havce been saved through the utilization of effective drug prevention programs. I'm not simply against D.A.R.E.; I'm for effective programs.

Q: Which programs are you thinking of, when you speak of effective programs? As far as I know, none have been objectively peer reviewed by independent researchers, and although the Department of Education recently reviewed 132 programs, reviewers included program developers, and not statisticians.

A: The problem has been that the published research has been by the people who have created the programs. Life Skills Training, for instance, appears to be an outstanding program, but, unfortunately, almost all of the research has been done by Gilbert Botvin, the director of Life Skills. I understand that there are two independent evaluations being conducted now on Life Skills Training and I hope that the outcomes in those research projects will be as positive as Dr. Botvin's have been.

Q: You ended all the D.A.R.E. programs in 2000?

A: Yes.

Q: How did you go about communicating the failures of D.A.R.E. and your vision for the future. Were your constituents resistant at first?

A: Yes. And they are still resistant. It's virtually impossible, no matter how many times you speak out on this issue, regardless of how much the media treats the issue, to overcome the huge public relations campaign conducted by D.A.R.E. I find it really interesting that now that even D.A.R.E. officials themselves admit that the program has not been effective, and when the Surgeon General and the Department of Education have rendered the same sorts of findings, people still proudly drive their cars around with D.A.R.E. bumper stickers on them.

We have a big Pioneer Days parade here every July 24th, and the first year I was in that parade there were pockets of people along the parade route wearing D.A.R.E. t-shirts and the mothers were chanting, "We want D.A.R.E." I'd also go to community meetings and, when challenged about canceling D.A.R.E., I would lay out the research and show them the unequivocal findings that showed the ineffectiveness of the program. There were times when people would look at me in astonishment and shake their heads and say, "I don't believe it!"

Q: The old, "Don't confuse me with the facts!" response!

A: Exactly. And my response was, "This isn't religion. This happens to be science. Unless you can show something that demonstrates D.A.R.E.'s effective, how can you say that we're really pursuing drug prevention when we're actually filling up these time slots and using our resources on something that's proven to be ineffective?" But there's a huge emotional component to this, and D.A.R.E. knows it. That's why they have all their t-shirts and their feel-good approach.

You know, when you talk about how ineffective D.A.R.E. is as a drug program, D.A.R.E. advocates fall back on the argument, "Well, isn't it great to have the police build up a relationship with the students?" I agree with that. I think having officers in the schools is a very good thing. But that begs the question: "What about drug prevention?" That's why D.A.R.E. was there in the first place.

Q: As mayor, you don't control the schools, so it's up to the elected school board to put new programs into place. What program or programs is it installing in the schools?

A: They have put in the ATLAS program, for male high school athletes. And there's an experimental program called Athena for female high school athletes. Besides these programs, they have a sort of homegrown program, called Prevention Dimension, but it hasn't been evaluated. I've been urging the school board and the superintendent to put in place a comprehensive grade 5 through 12 drug prevention program that's research-based and effective.

Q: Do you have one in particular in mind?

A: The two that I've recommended are the STAR and Life Skills programs.

Q: And do you think they'd adopt them?

A: I don't know. It's astounding to me that everybody gets so riled up about drug use, but the school board does not seem all that concerned about putting into place programs that seem to really work.

Q: Why do you think that is?

A: You know, I read a book years ago by Mathea Falco called A *Drug-Free America*, and she pointed out that one of the reasons for D.A.R.E.'s popularity may be the fact that school administrators and faculty can simply wash their hands of the program and turn it over to the police. They don't have to be accountable, and they don't have to do anything to confront the need for drug prevention.

Q: If you were to give advice to a mayor wanting to do what you've done, what advice would you give?

A: First, become familiar with all of the research in the area. Two, learn to communicate very clearly the rationale for terminating the D.A.R.E. program. I did not do this well, but you need to emphasize the positives—that what you want to do is put in place programs that work. You want to get away from the message that it's a termination of D.A.R.E.

D.A.R.E. has built up their infrastructure through a huge fraud on the American people. Now, they've completely lost credibility, but instead of letting them use 37,000 more of our school kids as their guinea pigs as they revamp their program, we ought to be replacing them with programs that have integrity and are effective.

And we need to have a goal of not just keeping kids off drugs entirely but also reducing the harm to those kids who do try drugs. And that's something that just drives a lot of people nuts—to even admit that some kids will do drugs no matter what programs are offered to them. But I think a harm-reduction approach is far more honest and is going to be far more effective in saving lives and in promoting the interests of everybody, including taxpayers.

Q: What has been the response of other mayors to you?

A: I spoke to a group of municipal leaders where one mayor told me that when he raised the issue with his city council as to the advisability of evaluating the effectiveness of D.A.R.E., there was such a public outcry that he had no option but to back down. Some mayors, after the evidence came out as to how ineffective D.A.R.E. has been, still stand by their programs. That's truly cowardly politics. Anybody who takes a look at the literature will understand that by utilizing D.A.R.E. we're depriving kids of effective drug prevention.

Q: At quite a cost.

A: At a huge cost. Both in lives, and monetarily. In Salt Lake City, we were spending $289,000 annually on the officers' salaries, vehicles, and equipment. There have been estimates that over $700 million a year nationwide has been spent on D.A.R.E.

Q: This has been a hot issue for you, and you will no doubt take some bashing in the next election for taking this on. Are you glad you did it anyway?

A: I am always glad to do the right thing.

BREAKING OUT OF THE 12-STEP LOCKSTEP

Maia Szalavitz

From *The Washington Post,* June 9, 2002

In the 1980s and nineties, 12-step programs like Alcoholics Anonymous were the gold standard for addiction treatment. Even among the non-addicted, they had become an accepted part of American culture. In Tim Robbins's 1992 film, *The Player,* the title character attended AA meetings not because he drank too much but because that's where the deals were being made. In 1995, *New York* magazine suggested that single women attend AA to meet men.

But today, the recovery movement—with its emphasis on childhood victimization, lifetime attendance at 12-step groups and complete abstinence from all psychoactive substances—has fallen from pop culture favor. "There was a time when it was almost the 'in' thing to say you were in recovery," says William White, author of *Slaying the Dragon,* a history of addiction treatment. Thankfully, that is no longer the case.

Vogue, Elle and the *New York Times Magazine* have recently run articles critical of the recovery movement. The "addictions" section of the bookstore—once taking up several bookcases in superstores—has shrunk to a few shelves, with a growing proportion of critical books. By the late nineties, the number of inpatient rehab facilities offering treatment centered on the 12-step process was half what it had been earlier in the decade. And AA membership, which grew explosively from the late seventies through the late eighties, has held steady at about 2 million since 1995.

Still, it is difficult to say goodbye to an organization and philosophy that may have helped save my life. Between the ages of seventeen and twenty-three, I was addicted to cocaine and then heroin. For the next twelve years, I was an often enthusiastic participant in 12-step recovery. Eventually, however, it became difficult to imagine defining myself for the rest of my life in relation to behavior that had taken up so few years of it.

During my last five years in the program, I had become increasingly uncomfortable with what it presented as truth: the notion, for example, that addiction is a "chronic, progressive disease" that can only be arrested by 12-stepping. The more research I did, the more I learned that much of what I had been told in rehab was wrong. And yet, I'd indisputably gotten better. Once an unemployed, eighty-pound wreck, I had become a healthy, productive science journalist. That science part, however, became the root of my problem with a model based on anecdote as anodyne.

The 12-step model has always been rife with contradiction. Its adherents recognize, for example, that addiction is a disease, not a sin. But their treatment isn't medical; it's praying, confession, and meeting. And while they claim that the belief in a "God of your understanding" on which the program rests is spiritual, not religious, every court that has ever been asked whether ordering people into such programs violates the separation of church and state has disagreed with the "non-religious" label.

So why have the contradictions come to the fore now? For me, the first step came in 2000 when I wrote about New York's Smithers Addiction Treatment and Research Center and its attempts to modernize treatment. Its director, Alex DeLuca, saw that options needed to be expanded beyond AA. Guided by DeLuca, Smithers began publishing studies funded by the National Institute on Alcoholism and Alcohol Abuse showing that adding treatment options, including support for moderation rather than abstinence, was effective.

However, when a group of people in recovery learned that those options included moderation, they protested, and DeLuca was fired. Imagine cancer or AIDS patients demonstrating against evidence-based treatment offering more options. This deeply distressed me, as did AA's religious aspects. In any other area of medicine, if a physician told you the only cure for your condition was to join a support group that involves "turning your will and your life" over to God (AA's third step), you'd seek a second opinion.

The insistence on the primacy of God in curing addiction also means that treatment can't change in response to empirical evidence. Which leaves us with a rehab system based more on faith than fact. Nowhere is this clearer than in the field's response to medication use. The National Institute on Drug Abuse is pouring big bucks into developing "drugs to fight drugs" but, once approved, they sit on the shelves because many rehab facilities don't believe in medication. Until 1997, for example, the well-known rehab facility Hazelden refused to provide antidepressants to people who had both depression and addiction.

Those who promote just one means of recovery are right to find medication threatening. When I finally tried antidepressants, after years of resisting "drugs" because I'd been told they might lead to relapse, my disillusionment with the recovery movement grew. Years of groups and talking couldn't do what those pills did: allow me not to overreact emotionally, and thus to improve my relationships and worry less. I didn't need to "pray for my character defects to be lifted" (AA's sixth and seventh steps)—I needed to fix my brain chemistry.

This is not to say that I didn't learn anything through recovery groups. The problem is their insistence that their solutions should trump all others. Many recovering people now use medication and groups both—but within the movement there is still an enormous hostility toward this and a sense that people on medications are somehow cheating by avoiding the pain that leads to emotional growth.

Another contradiction in the notion of 12-step programs as a medical treatment shows up in the judicial system. Logically, if addiction were a disease, prison and laws would have no place in its treatment. However, to secure support from the drug-war establishment, many 12-step treatment providers argue that addiction is a disease characterized by "denial"—despite research showing that addicts are no more likely to be in denial than people with other diseases, and that most addicts tell the truth about their drug use when they won't be punished for doing so.

Because of "denial," however, many in-patient treatment providers use methods that would be unheard of for any other condition: restrictions on food and medications, limits on sleep, hours of forced confessions and public humiliation, bans on contact with relatives and, of course, threats of prison for noncompliance.

If these programs wanted what was best for their patients, they would support measures to fund more treatment and divert people from jail. Watching famous 12-steppers such as Martin Sheen fight against California's Proposition 36, which mandates treatment rather than punishment for drug possession, was the final straw for me.

If their argument is that people won't attend treatment without the threat of prison, how do they explain all the alcoholics they treat? How, for that matter, do they explain that 12-step programs were started by volunteers? Their opposition only makes sense in the context of a view of addicts as sinners, not patients.

The view that one can only recover via the moral improvement of the twelve steps is doing more harm than good. It is supporting bad drug policy, preventing people from getting the treatment they need and hampering research.

Yet it is important not to dismiss 12-step programs entirely. They provide a supportive community and should be recommended as an option for people with addictions. Let evidence-based research determine how people are treated medically for drug problems.

DRUG ABUSE TREATMENT
OR DRUG TREATMENT ABUSE

Maia Szalavitz

From *AlterNet*, July 25, 2001

"I experienced five-point restraint, sleep deprivation, denial of privacy, denial of my right to freely practice my religion, no contact with my family, peanut butter and jelly diets, urinating in milk jugs, being locked away in a private prison each night and the ever-dreaded relapse of 'thought.' There was a constant drive to discover the deepest, darkest thoughts in my head and [make me] publicly confess them."

"They served fish and I told them that I was allergic to fish. They said I was lying. I was made to carry the fish around and eventually I was put on the floor in four-point restraint for several hours. They put the food in my mouth and my face became swollen, I started gagging, I could feel my throat closing up. They refused to take me to the hospital. They gave me Benadryl. For a while, I was unable to walk. . . . [Due to another medical condition] my abdomen became swollen. They told me it was intentional and made me wear a diaper when I could not [control my bodily functions. At one point,] someone spat in my face and shoved a soiled diaper in my face."

"They slammed people so hard against a paneled wall, I could see it move from the other side. The guy had bruises all across his shoulders, all over his body. And they kept telling us, 'This is life, this is the boot camp of life.' I heard about a girl who had attempted suicide by drinking Quell shampoo [used for delousing] so I found a bottle. If this is what life was about, I didn't want to be a part of it. I drank half the bottle."

Are these stories from the Gulag? Extracts from accounts of prisoners of war? Tales of torture victims from repressive regimes?

No, they are stories of teenagers who were abused in mainstream American programs for troubled youth. Some of the programs are still in business; others have shut down.

Nancy Reagan's "favorite," Straight Inc., was endorsed by the first Bush administration until state regulators and bad publicity finally closed its last official site in 1993. A founder of Straight Inc., Mel Sembler, has just been nominated by

President Bush II to be ambassador to Italy in spite of the millions of dollars in judgments against his program for the tortures endured by some of its victims.

An affiliated program in New Jersey wasn't shuttered until 1998 and similar programs with many of the same staff are still up and running in Tennessee and Florida. Their methods have spread to the popular "boot camps" and "behavioral modification" programs which now treat thousands of children across the country, despite research showing that they are less effective than other treatments and despite some three dozen deaths in the last decade from things like dehydration, untreated medical problems and improper restraint.

The survivors' stories were told at a ground-breaking conference held in Bethesda, Maryland, this weekend. Titled "Saving Our Children from Drug Treatment Abuse," it was sponsored by the Trebach Institute, a drug policy reform organization. About 50 people attended, mostly victims of abusive programs. It was the first time abusive treatment survivors from different programs and locations had met in person to organize towards protecting others from harm. A second conference is planned for December in Florida.

While the survivors told their stories, there was total silence in the generic hotel conference room. Three of the four speakers on the first panel broke into tears at some point while recalling what had been done to them.

Said Kimberly Fee, who entered a spin-off program of Straight Inc. in 1988, "I still have nightmares. I have friends that left these programs after spending 15 years in them. To know that this still goes on anywhere . . ."

She cried openly, then continued, "I have kids now, I can understand the desire to protect them at any cost. 'She has a booboo, oh my God.' If my kid was doing the things that I was doing, I would do whatever it takes to get help. We need to guide these parents in a better direction. They are just as much victims as we are."

In a second panel, Kamal Manoly, an Egyptian immigrant and father of two, was clearly anguished as he spoke. "I find it absolutely incredible that such programs could exist and thrive today in this twenty-first century, in the land of freedom that I fought to come to thirty-two years ago to escape from the tyranny I was subjected to under a totalitarian regime. . . . How could we be critical of human rights abuses practiced by third world nations, while we still allow organizations such as SAFE [the program his son attended] to destroy the very fabric of our society under the guise of helping our children?"

Manoly's marriage of twenty-seven years broke down just months after his son Chris started treatment at SAFE in 1999. Manoly, Chief of Civil Engineering and

Mechanics for the Nuclear Regulatory Commission, had become skeptical of the program, while his wife wanted to follow its instructions "to the letter." When Chris fled after being denied the "privilege" of being able to write a card saying "I love you" to his father for Christmas, Manoly refused to return him to SAFE.

As a result, Manoly became estranged from his wife and daughter, who refuse to see him. They continue to be involved in the program, which preaches that anyone who does not support the treatment process encourages drug use and is harmful. Many families are torn apart by the program's rigid refusal to accept contradictory viewpoints.

"In some ways, I truly feel sorry for my ex-wife, as I [see] her being torn between her desire to see her beloved son clean from drug use and beginning to lead a normal life, and her desire to see him fail so that she can justify her blind faith in SAFE," said Manoly. Chris is now doing well and preparing to attend college.

The next panel was devoted to possible legal remedies for victims of treatment abuse. The first speaker, New Jersey attorney Philip Elberg, won a $4.5 million medical malpractice judgment in late 1999 against KIDS of North Jersey, a spin-off of Straight run by its former national clinical director.

The woman who brought the suit, Rebecca Ehrlich, had been subjected to complete lack of privacy (participants were monitored even while on the toilet), extreme dietary restrictions, and countless assaults and restraints for six years. During that time, she'd been unable to hold a private conversation, speak to her family privately, listen to music, watch TV, read a book or newspaper, or even the back of a cereal box.

The program claimed to treat behavioral problems, however, Ehrlich was never professionally evaluated or treated for her bipolar disorder.

Elberg was not encouraging about the prospects for similar payoffs in future cases. For most of the survivors at the conference the statute of limitations (which is two to three years after discovery of the injury in most states) has run out. Also, according to Elberg, by the time most of the lawsuits come to trial, the programs have been bankrupted by resultant bad publicity and insurance and tax judgments, so few lawyers are willing to pursue them.

Elberg and the other lawyers suggested that victims determine whether their goal is money, or to ensure that these programs are shut down. If the latter is the objective, negative publicity may be a better weapon than litigation.

However, publicity can be a double-edged sword. The media, in a quest to be fair, plays "success stories" from program supporters against the horror stories of victims.

"Until the Ehrlich case," says Elberg, "the story was framed as whether KIDS was a good or a bad program—'Is Tough Love the Best Way?'—and even when you mentioned assault, people figured maybe the kid deserved it or it was an isolated incident." Elberg stressed that it was crucial to rely on standards of medical practice. Research shows that kind, empathetic, and supportive treatment is both more effective and less likely to cause harm. The abusive approach can potentially create greater long-term damage. Says Elberg, "[These programs] have the potential to be a breeding ground for sociopaths."

Summing up what he believed the conference had achieved, Trebach Institute founder Arnold Trebach, Professor Emeritus at American University, said, "The conference served as a wake-up call, even a firebell in the night, to the entire drug policy reform movement and to the nation that the slogan 'treatment, not jail' is full of anguish. A great deal of work has to be done to define the borders between good and bad treatment. Too often, drug abuse treatment turns out to be drug treatment abuse."

[THE BUSINESS]

RE-ENGINEERING THE DRUG BUSINESS

Matthew Brzezinski

From *The New York Times Magazine*, June 23, 2002

The vial of heroin lands in my lap, and for a few uncomfortable seconds, as an undercover police officer and a very jittery drug dealer both grope my midriff, I worry someone will panic and go for his gun.

The dealer is shouting—for his money, for us to hurry—peppering his exhortations with unprintable expressions. He looks no more than 20, with baggy trousers, high-top sneakers and a Baltimore Orioles baseball cap perched at a rakish angle. His grasping fingers, I can't help noticing, are bejeweled, like those of the rap artists one sees on MTV videos. Lost in the chaotic exchange, and now rolling on the littered floor of the unmarked police pickup truck, is the small vial of heroin. It contains a milligram of opiate in fine powder form and is sealed with a color-coded plastic cap. The top is pink in this instance, but it's also available in an assortment of other hues, each denoting a variation in purity and price, to tap the widest possible customer base. If that sounds incongruously like something out of an M.B.A. textbook, that's because it is: the strategy is called microbranding, and it is the reason so many different varieties of Coca-Cola sit on grocery shelves these days.

The pink-top I have just clumsily purchased has its particular niche, or target market: the "kids from the counties," as middle-class teenagers from the suburbs are known in Maryland. They are the same trendy audience that advertisers slaver over, and Baltimore's inner-city dealers have tailored the pink-top to their finicky needs. The product is just strong enough so that it can be snorted—all the rage nowadays—yet, at $20, cheap enough that it won't make too much of a dent in its average customer's weekly allowance.

Beneath its veneer of violence, narcotics trafficking is a surprisingly sophisticated industry, marketing-driven just like any consumer-products business. Only illegal drugs are a bigger business than most, generating global revenues in excess of $400 billion annually, according to a United Nations study. From source to street, pushing drugs shares many common elements with hawking soda pop or cigarettes. It requires lots of working capital, steady supplies of raw materials, sophisticated manufacturing facilities, reliable shipping contractors and wholesale distributors, the all-important marketing arms and access to retail franchises for maximum market penetration.

Just as in most sectors of the economy, innovation and technology are engines of growth. New uses of old products like heroin, or the introduction of synthetic drugs like methamphetamine and Ecstasy, keep pace with the changing demands of the marketplace, redistributing income from traditional profit centers like marijuana and cocaine. As in the automotive industry, different source nations compete in the global arena, with producers popping up in one country as quickly as they are pushed down in another. Occasionally, aggressive upstarts catch complacent giants unawares, as the Japanese did with Detroit carmakers in the 1980s.

The principal difference between the narcotics trade and legitimate commerce, of course, is that the drug business must operate in the shadow of the law. This throws the entire organizational chart out of whack. Transportation becomes paramount, consolidation and vertical integration—those cherished buzzwords of merger-hungry multinationals—impossible. As a result, the narcotics industry has adapted what might be called the Osama bin Laden approach to management: base your operation in remote safe havens, the more war-torn and chaotic the better; stay small and shifty; use specialized subcontractors or freelancers on a need-to-know basis; vary your routes and routines whenever possible; and most important, always insulate yourself with plenty of expendable intermediaries in case someone gets caught and talks.

September 11 and its new world of heightened border controls has made decentralization doubly important for international smuggling networks, be they Chinese, Colombian, Turkish, or Nigerian. Ever since the big Cali and Medellin cartels were wiped out nearly a decade ago, virtually the entire narcotics trade has radically slimmed down. With the added pressure of 9/11 security measures, drug kingpins have adopted the mantra of their more enlightened corporate cousins, that size does not necessarily create efficiency, and that to survive you have to stay nimble.

Heroin is the perfect drug for the new age of small-batch manufacturing and decentralization, a high-value-added commodity where a little goes a very long way. In fact, it's so well suited to the changing times that many cocaine traffickers are retooling their production lines to include heroin and joining the global trend toward leaner, meaner, terrorist-style operations.

The restructuring is helping the business survive what could otherwise be a difficult period. Despite the military and security measures taken to fight international terrorism and shore up America's borders, Heroin Inc. has had a remarkably good fiscal year. The industry has managed to sustain gains made during the boom of the late 1990s, largely shrug off 9/11 and make further inroads in cocaine markets in the United States. Supplies in America are at an all-time high.

European operations are thriving as well. The Taliban's 2000 ban on poppy cultivation in Afghanistan has had little effect on the bottom line, with existing stockpiles and rerouted deliveries from Southeast Asia more than making up for the temporary shortfall. And the European sector is looking forward to a strong year in 2002. Now that the Taliban has been routed, bumper harvests are projected for Afghanistan. Elsewhere, analysts predict that Colombian distributors will continue their ambitious expansion plans in the Eastern United States. And China's entry into the World Trade Organization is expected to further open a vast new market for both domestic consumption of heroin and its transit to other countries.

The only uncertainty clouding the business's outlook is the long-term effect of September 11. In the post-9/11 era of linking drugs with terror, of beefed-up border security and improved communication between international law-enforcement agencies in both intelligence-gathering and interdiction, the industry is likely to grow even more diffuse. Power will continue shifting from remote producers to highly specialized smuggling subcontractors, and outsourcing in general will become the crucial factor to survival and success. The signs of the industry's new business model can already be seen at the very earliest stages of heroin production, in the distant and troubled lands where poppies grow.

The men with guns and gold watches live down in the valleys below. But it is high in the mist-shrouded mountains along the border between China and Myanmar, as Burma is now known, where the monsoon washes away roads linking lonely villages without electricity or running water, that heroin begins its long journey to America.

By the time it reaches the streets of Baltimore, the world's most powerful narcotic will have traveled through half a dozen countries, soared at least 5,000-fold in price and changed hands a hundred times. The first fingers to touch it, though, belong to a slender thirty-six-year-old mother of seven.

Xiamin Dwan Swan and her husband, Ju—like the other forty families who live in this hilltop hamlet in Myanmar—have been farming opium for generations, ever since the British introduced poppy cultivation to these parts more than a century ago. It's not a lucrative living, judging by the straw huts, mud floors, and barefoot children, but it is the only one that the residents of Chaw Haw have ever known.

The ritual begins every September, when the steep fields are burned and the poppy seeds scattered. They thrive in these altitudes, just about the only crop that does, but it is not only a quirk of climate that allows them to do so. A key competitive advantage of this rugged landscape is that it lies beyond the reach of any law-enforcement agency. As is the case in the world's other opium-producing regions—the guerrilla-controlled jungles of Colombia, the lawless fiefs of Afghanistan—central authorities have no say here. Power is exercised by renegade insurgent groups with prickly notions of territorial sovereignty, not to mention private armies 15,000 to 20,000 strong.

By February, Xiamin Dwan Swan and her husband begin the harvest by scoring each poppy pod with a needle-like knife. A creamy gum oozes from the cuts, and once it turns black it is scraped off with a crescent-shaped tool that has been in her family ever since she can remember. It is painstaking work, and for their labor the Dwan Swans earn $600 annually, barely enough to feed their children, three pigs, and two ornery dogs. Brokers come from the valley in early March to purchase the raw opium gum, which sells for about 1,500 yuan per vis—the equivalent of about $135 a kilogram. (A vis is a unit of measure equal to 1.6 kilos, or about three pounds.)

"I don't know who buys our harvest," Xiamin says, which is the smart answer, but probably not true, given that she and her husband have most likely been dealing with the same broker for the past 20 years. Nor does she claim to know what happens to her harvest once the brokers collect it from Chaw Haw and other villages. This is probably true, since refineries buy their opium gum from the brokers rather than risking exposure by dealing directly with hundreds of separate suppliers.

That is just the first of many layers of insulation that characterize the heroin trade and must be factored into the cost of doing business. For their services, the brokers, usually tribal elders, charge a 20 percent markup, sometimes more if they have lent villagers money in anticipation of their crop. In Helmand Province in Afghanistan, for example, some farmers grew so indebted during Mullah Omar's fatwa banning poppy cultivation that for a time after being liberated by American forces, they were selling raw opium to creditors for as little as $35 per kilogram. (That short-lived ban temporarily toppled Afghanistan from its nearly decade-long dominance among global opium producers, allowing

Myanmar to briefly claim the dubious title, with up to 60 percent of the world total. But once the final tallies are in for this year's harvest, Afghanistan is once again expected to regain the top spot, followed by Myanmar, Colombia, and Mexico.)

Unlike poppy cultivation, refining is a complicated, capital-intensive process, limiting the number of players with the financial wherewithal to participate. This phase of the business is controlled mostly by the Wa, Kokang, and Shan warlords, who run rebel states within Myanmar. "They tax it, or receive money for protection," says Kyaw Thein, a Burmese brigadier general. Indeed, ask a Wa official about opium, and he'll rattle off his town's yields as if he's quoting from the municipal budget. "Four thousand, six hundred vis," says Lu Kyar Shin, a Wa mayor who sports a Rolex and a sidearm. "Down from 10,000 vis a few years ago."

Like the cocaine labs of Colombia, Myanmar's heroin refineries are temporary facilities buried deep in the jungle. They are set up to fill specific orders and can be quickly struck down in case the heat is on. But that only happens occasionally, when central authorities stumble on a refinery that falls within their territorial jurisdiction.

Burmese officials proudly display the precursor chemicals seized in one such recent raid. The materials stand stacked in neat rows of blue and white industrial drums, filling a courtyard lined with papaya trees and barbed wire: 900 gallons of calcium hydroxide needed to cook raw opium into morphine, the first stage of the refining process; liquid ether smuggled into Myanmar by Indian networks; and Chinese-made ammonium chloride, which transforms the morphine into the lower-grade No. 3 heroin, or "brown sugar," as it is popularly known; and finally, out front in a place of honor, 150 gallons of hard-to-come-by acetic anhydride, the key ingredient to producing the 90-percent-pure No. 4 heroin destined for American and European markets, the notorious China White.

Though China White is often packaged by refiners in 700-gram bricks, known as units, the universal measure in the global narcotics business is the 1,000-gram kilo. A kilo that will ultimately fetch in excess of $200,000 (wholesale) in New York City costs as little as $2,500 in Myanmar. That, at least, is what Saikyaw Myat, an unemployed stonemason, was expecting to get for it before being busted by an undercover agent. Ma Lwan Gyi and her two young friends, Ma Kaing Hland and Ma Ban Mong, were nabbed in a similar sting. They had each been promised $20 to deliver a kilo of the famed Double Lion brand into town. All four now sit in leg irons in a stifling corrugated-steel prison, a labyrinth of low wooden cages constructed from thick teak bars, forbidden to move from the lotus position, where they are to contemplate the error of their ways for the next ten years.

The modest price of the China White they carried illustrates how in the overall cost structure of the heroin industry, refining is not a particularly large profit center. That's because the risks of interdiction within Myanmar are too low to factor significantly into the final price. The markup on the finished product is about 20 percent, in line with other forms of contract manufacturing in Asia like semiconductors or cellphones, where the real money goes to designers and distributors.

Once the sourcing and processing stages are complete, isolated countries like Myanmar or Afghanistan lose their competitive advantage. "The Wa or the Kokang don't have the sophistication or international networks to get their product to market," explains Maj. Win Naing, who heads the narcotics task force in the bustling northern Myanmar border town of Muse. "They leave that to foreigners." Much the same holds true with Afghan growers, who despite being the source of 80 percent of the heroin in the $12 billion European market, earned at most only a modest $56 million from opium sales last year, according to a United Nations survey.

The real profits in heroin, to borrow a term from the embattled accounting industry, are all downstream—in transportation and distribution.

To reach global markets, heroin leaves Myanmar through two principal pipelines. With each route, a different set of players, with specific expertise, is involved. The first, and most used, is north through China's Yunnan Province to Hong Kong or the free-trade zones around Guangdong. Chinese smuggling syndicates ply this route, charging as little as $1,000 per kilo to sneak the contraband across the border from Muse to as much as $10,000 per kilo to get it all the way to Hong Kong. One such group operated until recently in Muse, where the border with China is a four-foot-high fence that runs right through the center of town. The syndicate was headed by a thirty-nine-year-old Chinese national by the name of Tan Xiaolin, who set up shop in a large pink-and-green villa a few hundred yards from the frontier. Until his arrest last year through the joint efforts of Chinese and Burmese authorities, he had smuggled more than three tons of pure heroin to Hong Kong, where different trafficking organizations with a more international orientation sent it on to Sydney, Vancouver and the United States. Tan has since been extradited to China and, according to Burmese officials, sentenced to death.

The harsh penalties handed out in Asia for trafficking do not seem to be a great deterrent. That, say American officials, is because you can often buy your way out of jams or simply purchase protection from underpaid local Communist authorities. United States drug-enforcement officials, however, concede that the inner workings of the balkanized China pipeline are somewhat of an intelligence black hole because of spotty relations with Beijing. Much more is known about the second major route out of Myanmar, which travels south and then east, through Thailand.

Much as he tries, Mike Carter finds it hard to blend in with the crowd at his posting in the northern Thai city of Chiang Mai. For one, Carter, a special agent for the Drug Enforcement Administration, is a very large individual; well over six feet tall, a close-cropped former marine who went to college in Texas on a football scholarship and used to maul opponents as a 250-pound linebacker. Then there is the nine-millimeter Glock tucked into the waistband of his jeans. And those dark, wraparound aviator sunglasses.

Even though he has picked up Thai and speaks it more or less grammatically, there's not much chance of passing himself off as a native. So he lurks in the shadows, behind the tinted windows of his silver Toyota, playing a supporting role, waiting for the drugs to come across the border.

Today he has brought some cash to entice traffickers, to expedite matters. It lies temptingly in a green satchel on top of my bag, 5 million baht, just over $116,000 at the current exchange rate. It's what's called "flash money," and it will be shown to a Burmese broker by an undercover Thai policeman posing as a customer.

The deal is set to go down in Chiang Saen, at the confluence of the Mekong and Ruak Rivers, where Myanmar, Thailand, and Laos meet: the heart of the Golden Triangle.

"This all used to be poppy country, and 10 years ago there were refineries everywhere on the Thai side," Carter explains as we drive on broad, freshly paved roads. With all the tour buses and golf resorts around, it's difficult to imagine Thailand as a major heroin producer. But it once was a world leader, until the economy picked up and pressure from the international community forced traffickers to relocate across the border in Myanmar. Much the same happened in Pakistan, Turkey, Bolivia, and Peru in the 1980s, as successful eradication efforts and increased standards of living forced production to shift to the more lawless and impoverished corners of Afghanistan and Colombia. That fluidity is another key feature of the rapid-reaction narcotics business: push it down in one place, and it simply pops up somewhere else. In that sense, heroin is truly a global commodity.

Carter's cellphone rings. It's Col. Dussadee Arajavuth, the head of the Narcotics Suppression Bureau, or N.S.B., in northern Thailand. The Burmese broker, he informs Carter, has taken the bait. Now it's only a matter of time and patience. While we wait, Colonel Arajavuth arranges for me to meet with one of his prized sources, a foot soldier in one of the warlord armies that smuggle heroin across the Thai border. We meet in a hotel room in Chiang Rai, not too far from where the N.S.B. keeps a safe house.

"The heroin leaves the refineries in caravans," the informant begins. "There are usually 50 to 100 people in each caravan. Half are porters carrying up to 500 units of heroin, the other half are soldiers." The soldiers, he continues, are heavily armed with rocket-propelled grenade launchers and are provided—for a fee—by either the United Wa State Army or the Shan State Army, insurgent groups that operate close to the Thai frontier. The final destination is either Thailand proper or Tachileik, a rough Burmese border town that apparently inspires such dread that the superstitious residents of Mae Sai, on the Thai side, have erected a black steel scorpion the size of a tank to ward away their neighbors' evil spirits.

In Tachileik, brokers like the one Agent Carter is currently trying to set up take delivery of the heroin, which, because of high transportation costs, rises in price to $4,500 per kilo. There are approximately twenty such brokers representing the Wa and the Shan in Tachileik, says the informer. "Everyone knows who they are."

Delivering heroin directly into Thailand is a bit trickier, and the added risk is reflected in the slight price hike to $5,500. The drug caravans move over the dense mountain frontier, under cover of night, when Thai border patrols are in their barracks. To see how porous the frontier can be, Carter drives me to the Ban Phai border post atop Mount Doi Tung. We barely make it up the steep road, since Carter's Toyota is loaded down with M-4 assault rifles discreetly tucked into golf bags in the trunk. The firepower is a precaution.

Tensions at the Ban Phai outpost—a collection of bamboo huts reinforced with black sandbags, trenches and M-60 heavy-caliber machine guns—are running high. Just a few days before, two advance scouts from a Wa caravan were caught by a nearby border-patrol unit. The Wa took exception to the arrest and unleashed a mortar barrage. The Thais responded with 105-millimeter Howitzers. Miraculously, only one person was injured.

Once the shipment has arrived in Thailand or Tachileik, a whole new set of players enters the fray. These are Thais from Bangkok, who converge on the border area to pick up heroin. They, too, have their specific niche: moving the product to buyers in Bangkok. One such transportation subcontractor, who had thirty-seven kilos of China White in his black Land Rover, was recently wounded by Burmese border guards in Tachileik. The bust clearly showed just how decentralization keeps the narcotics trade in business. The load was a mix of the Double Lion brand favored by Wa refineries and the 999 brand popular with labs in the Shan region. Under interrogation, the driver could not name his sources and could only provide police with a disconnected contact number to a broker in Tachileik. The chain to the producers was already broken. The transport subcontractors themselves add another layer of protection for both the brokers in the border area and outside buyers, because no one here will do business with a farang, as foreigners are known. They are "too conspicuous," says Colonel Arajavuth. "We'd pick them up right away."

In fact, most of the foreign buyers are West Africans—Nigerians, to be precise—who tend to stick out in the Thai provinces even more than Agent Carter does. They prefer the more cosmopolitan anonymity of Bangkok and are prepared to pay for the added security. In the Thai capital, the local middlemen charge between $7,500 and $9,500 to deliver each kilo of heroin, depending on the quantity ordered. West Africans are not the only foreign customers; there are smugglers from Taiwan and Europe. But the Nigerians are by far the most organized and entrenched group. Their job in heroin's ever-lengthening supply chain is also among the riskiest: to get the heroin into the United States.

Few C.E.O.s of major American corporations lie awake nights agonizing over logistics. That's what companies like DHL or U.P.S. are for. The drug trade, too, has its courier services, outfits such as "Nigeria Express" or Mexico's notorious A.F.O.

The drug runners breach every United States frontier, but one of their main targets is San Ysidro, California, America's busiest border crossing, the fragile demarcation line that separates San Diego from the smuggler's paradise of Tijuana. Between a quarter and a third of the heroin, cocaine, and marijuana entering the country passes through here and four smaller checkpoints in Southern California, and on a good day the Customs Service can hope to make at least a dozen decent-size seizures.

Up to now, it has been relatively easy going for China White traffickers. Nigerians, having taken delivery of the heroin in Bangkok, have either shipped it via couriers to transit countries like Mexico or Canada or, more commonly, have sent it home to Lagos. Given Nigeria's perennial position near the top of the global-corruption rankings, forwarding through Lagos international airport does not pose much of a barrier. In Nigeria, the drugs are repacked into smaller parcels, often into condoms that couriers swallow and transit through nonsource countries like Britain or France to throw Customs officials off the trail. If the heroin is sent directly from Thailand to the United States, Caucasian couriers are usually employed to foil racial profiling. They are often female, in their twenties and thirties.

It is also at this stage that another complication arises for Southeast Asian heroin. As it approaches its target market, it brushes up against the competition, including Mexican-produced Black Tar, known derisively as Mexican Mud because of its poor quality; the superior Mexican Brown in powder form; and especially high-grade Colombian White, its biggest rival. (Afghan heroin is conspicuously absent at San Ysidro and only occasionally shows up in the United States, in places like Detroit. Its principal market is Europe, where it arrives from Turkey, Russia, and the Balkans.)

Colombia is a relative upstart in the international heroin trade, with cocaine traffickers there deciding to get into the business only around 1990. It was a decision based purely on demographics. The cocaine craze of the eighties was waning as the drug fell out of fashion with urban professionals. Moreover, dealers were discovering that unlike heroin addicts, many habitual coke users tended to burn out after five years. Faced with a dwindling customer base in America, cocaine traffickers tried to expand into Europe. But they had only limited success, in places like Spain, England, and, most recently, the Netherlands. The hard drug of choice in the European Union was heroin, and Pakistani and Turkish groups had the market sewn up there. So Colombian cocaine traffickers decided to diversify and launched a poppy-cultivation drive, importing seeds, equipment, and expertise from Southwest Asia.

"It took them three or four years to get it right," recalls Felix J. Jimenez, the D.E.A.'s New York bureau chief, "to procure the proper refining know-how and precursor chemicals like acetic anhydride."

But by the mid-nineties, he says, the Colombians were producing heroin with purity levels exceeding 90 percent. Suddenly Colombian smugglers had a product that was equal to, if not better than, China White. All they had to do was get the new product to the market, past points of entry like San Ysidro.

One sure sign of the high regard in which traffickers hold San Ysidro's defenses is the risk premium attached to making it across. If getting heroin into China or Thailand bears a markup of $1,000 per kilo, here it's a different story altogether. After it makes the 100-yard journey across the border, a kilo of Black Tar will soar in value to $54,000 once safely on the San Diego side. Colombian heroin will rise by as much as twenty times once it gets to Los Angeles. And China White will command well into the six figures once it reaches American soil.

With the stakes so high, smuggling syndicates go to great lengths to keep tabs on what is going on at San Ysidro; when, for instance, shifts are ending, how many rovers are deployed on a given day, which canine units are on patrol. But mostly they just play the numbers game, the law of averages. More than 40 million people enter the United States through San Ysidro annually, and Customs can't check them all.

"We get up to 60,000 cars a day, and you have to keep in mind that 99 percent of the passengers are honest travelers," says Robert Hood, a supervisory Customs inspector. "So the bad guys come straight at us. And if we intercept a few loads, that's just a tax they factor into the cost of doing business."

Most of the China White passing through San Ysidro is spirited through the pedestrian crossing, a long concrete corridor lined with metal detectors, airport-style X-ray scanners and D.E.A. posters offering $2 million for information leading to the arrest of Benjamin Arellano Felix and his brother, Ramon.

The Arellano Felix Organization, A.F.O. for short, is a testament to just how important transportation subcontractors have become in the drug industry. The Tijuana-based outfit started out humbly, smuggling duty-free cigarettes and alcohol in the late seventies. Over time, they moved up to marijuana and were well placed to reap a bonanza from the cocaine craze of the eighties. By the nineties, they were moving tens of billions of dollars in contraband, controlled an estimated three-quarters of everything that passed through San Ysidro and even built complex tunnels into Texas.

"They took over," says Jayson Ahern, director of field operations for United States Customs in Southern California. "They effectively supplanted their old bosses in Colombia and became a cartel of their own." The A.F.O.'s competitive edge was location: right on the Mexican-American border. However, the critical error that would lead to their downfall, as with the Colombian cartels before them, was getting too big and flouting the laws of decentralization.

Colombia's Medellin and Cali cartels were the first drug-trafficking organizations to vertically integrate. Like the big oil companies with gasoline, the cartels tried to hang on to their product through its entire chain of manufacturing, distribution, and sale to consumers. For a while it worked, but the downside of any vertically integrated structure is that one broken link can bring down the whole organization. By using freelance subcontractors who don't know one another or even the identity of their employers, traffickers of China White assiduously avoid this peril.

The Nigerian buyers in Bangkok, for instance, don't even move the heroin themselves. Instead they hire American, European, or Canadian couriers that they send on circuitous journeys to finally enter the United States in places where they hope Customs will have its guard down.

Inspector Hood is familiar with this type of ruse. "I had this one lady pull up to the pedestrian crossing in a cab," he recalls. "I took a look at her passport and it had an exit stamp from Thailand dated three days before. She said her vacation had been cut short because her goddaughter got sick and she had to get back to Baltimore quickly. I didn't buy it. There are definitely more direct routes to Maryland than driving through Mexico."

It turns out that the woman had nearly three kilos of heroin in her luggage and was a courier for Nigerian traffickers. They had hoped that a white waitress would not fit the profile of the Latin American smugglers usually seen at San Ysidro. "They probe for weaknesses," adds Hood, "figuring we are not looking for Southeast Asian heroin here, the way they do on flights arriving from Bangkok to J.F.K."

Many couriers—mules, or body-packers, as they are known in the trade—are swallowers who ingest honey-coated condoms filled with heroin. This makes them perilously hard to detect. Usually, it's only when something goes badly wrong that they get caught. One of Hood's colleagues, for instance, recently stumbled on a jittery gentleman claiming to be a pharmacist from Colombia.

"The guy was too jumpy," recalls the colleague, Chief Inspector Mark Wilkerson. "And he didn't look like a professional type." In other words, he fit the mule profile. Wilkerson asked him to remove his tie and put it back on. "He couldn't do it, couldn't tie a knot," Wilkerson laughs. The faux pharmacist was a mule who had been promised several thousand dollars to make the delivery.

To the uninitiated, all this may seem like a great deal of trouble to go through to move a mere kilo. China White is unusual that way. Of all the branches of the narcotics trafficking trade, it is by far the least efficient on a cost-per-kilo basis. According to a study by an economist, Peter Reuter, Latin American-produced cocaine is as much as ten times cheaper to transport because it is usually shipped in bigger batches, 250 kilos and up. This allows traffickers economies of scale to spread out the, say, $500,000 fee pilots of small aircraft or go-fast boats often charge.

The discrepancy has its roots in the heritage of Colombian cocaine traffickers, many of whom came to the trade from the marijuana rackets, where bigger payloads were always the norm. But it also reflects the nature of heroin and demonstrates why it is increasingly the drug of choice for the savviest smugglers. With its high market value, heroin is ideally suited to traveling tens of thousands of miles, crossing countless borders. It requires far smaller networks to smuggle than the big organizations needed for cocaine or marijuana. And spreading loads over dozens of individual couriers minimizes risk.

"If I had to make any analogies," says Mike Chapman, a senior special agent with the D.E.A. in Washington, "it would be to Al Qaeda."

Heroin traffickers tend to operate more like highly compartmentalized terrorist cells than multinational corporations or the sprawling Colombian cartels of the Pablo Escobar era. But that's also the case, increasingly, across the entire narcotics industry. "This type of activity does not allow concentration of power like legitimate commerce," says Ethan Nadelmann, an economist and drug-policy expert. "If smugglers get too big, they develop security and personnel problems and get targeted by law enforcement."

Indeed, Pablo Escobar—El Patron, as he was known in his heyday—would be living proof of this, had he not been killed in 1993 after one of the most intense international manhunts in history. It's the same story with the high-flying Tan Xiaolin from Muse, who is currently on death row in China along with eighteen of his associates. Even those D.E.A. posters of the Arellano Felix Organization, the closest thing to a cartel since the leaders of the Cali and Medellin gangs were locked up almost a decade ago, are already dated. Ramon is dead, shot in February by Mexican authorities, and his brother Benjamin was arrested in March.

Drug traffickers are also vulnerable to shifting international winds. Smugglers have had a rough time since Sept. 11 changed the way most nations view border security. In late 2001, heroin seizures rose sixteenfold along the California-Mexico border, largely at San Ysidro, which, like every port of entry in America, has been on Level 1 alert since the attacks on the twin towers.

"For the first few weeks," recalls Hood, "we didn't see any drugs whatsoever. It was eerily quiet, as if the traffickers were hanging back, waiting to see what we would do."

But smugglers, like anyone else, have bills to pay and can't afford to sit on inventory for too long. "Eventually they have to move," says Vincent E. Bond, a public affairs officer with United States Customs in San Diego. "And this isn't a very good time to be trying to fly in a Cessna under radar," he adds. "You're liable to have an F-16 up your tail."

So syndicates are shifting away from air routes and big ports of entry, trying to hide their tracks better, bury their loads deeper and use more marine cargo and speedboat deliveries. (The Coast Guard reports making seizures at a pace more than twice last year's.) And, for once, the law of averages is now tilting toward interdiction efforts. "Regular passenger traffic has been way down since 9/11," says Bond. "That gives us more time to scrutinize each entrant."

Once in the territorial United States, heroin typically makes its way to three major collection centers. On the West Coast it travels up Interstate 5 to Los Angeles. There, the wholesale price of a kilo of high-quality heroin jumps to between $86,000 and $100,000, from the $40,000-to-$54,000 range in San Diego.

Along the way, importers jack up the bottom line by cutting the product— "stepping on" it, in street parlance. This is usually the first of many adulterations to follow, all intended to increase profits by decreasing purity, and a variety of agents are used for this purpose: quinine, talcum, even lactose.

In America, as in Europe, immigrants are the major importers and distributors of heroin. This is simply because the smuggling networks prefer to deal with their own and don't trust outsiders. Nigerians will sell to fellow West Africans, Chinese to immigrants from back home and so on.

The American market for heroin, worth about $10 billion annually, is thus roughly divided into ethnic spheres of influence. Los Angeles-based Mexican groups control wholesale markets west of the Mississippi. Nigerians operating out of Chicago have the northern parts of the Midwest. And New York-based Dominican syndicates fronting for Colombians dominate the East Coast. Smaller Chinese gangs operate on the fringes, moving mostly in areas like San Francisco or New York that have large Asian communities.

The divisions, notes Jimenez, the D.E.A.'s top man in New York City and a leading expert on heroin in America, are fluid. Mexican groups, for instance, regularly impinge on the West Africans in Chicago, who, in turn, intrude on Dominican turf in places like Baltimore. The competition can be fierce and at times violent, but more often than not it tends to be fought along straight marketing lines.

One such battle changed the face of the heroin trade on the Eastern

Seaboard. It occurred in New York in the mid-1990s. Up to then, Jimenez explains, the wholesale heroin business on the East Coast belonged to Chinese triads. (They themselves had supplanted Italian crime families the decade before.) But with the entry of the Colombians, the established Chinese rings found themselves with a serious fight on their hands. Astonishingly, what broke out was almost entirely a price war.

China White, which was often smuggled a kilo at a time in people's stomachs, sold for between $160,000 and $180,000 per 700-gram unit, explains Jimenez. But the Colombians would include heroin in their large cocaine shipments, benefiting from drastically lower transportation costs. "They could charge $80,000 a kilo and undercut the Chinese by half."

The Colombians, of course, enjoyed the geographic advantage of closer proximity to the United States. But they had another, equally important, competitive advantage: established distribution centers. "They would force their Dominican cells to take, say, two kilos of heroin for every 100 kilos of coke they ordered and give out free samples to their customers."

The move turned out to be a marketing coup, creating an entirely new clientele for heroin, much the same way that the introduction of crack cocaine in the previous decade had exposed a yuppie drug to the mass market. Because the Colombians insisted that their distributors keep the heroin at high purities, upscale coke users could now snort or smoke it, ridding the product of the stigma of dirty needles and H.I.V. "I put a hidden camera on a street corner where I knew they sold heroin," Jimenez says. "You wouldn't believe the customers we got on film: lawyers, doctors, teachers."

The net result of the innovative strategies, says Jimenez, is that by the new millennium, Colombian heroin dominated markets in New York and throughout the Eastern Seaboard.

From collection centers like New York City, heroin travels down the I-95 corridor to secondary markets like Philadelphia, Baltimore, and Washington, D.C. Dealers from those satellite towns will usually make the trip to New York once every few weeks, picking up anywhere from one to five kilos at a time, explains Detective Lieutenant Michael Tabor of the Baltimore Police Department.

While New York can boast of hundreds of "cells," as Jimenez labels major distribution rings, a city the size of Baltimore will have no more than two dozen dealers capable of buying in kilo quantities. "We know who they are," Tabor says, rattling off names. "We've got phone taps on all of them," he adds. "But they're damn slick."

As you go progressively down the food chain, though, things get a little easier from a law-enforcement perspective. I find myself setting out once again to cruise the streets of Baltimore with narcotics officers.

Special Operations Unit One meets daily at 11:00 a.m. in a newly renovated conference room that appears industriously messy, like the marketing department in a successful midsize company. But no one in Sgt. Mark Janicki's eight-man unit looks remotely corporate: beards, braids, ponytails, and skull-and-bones ear studs form part of the dress code, which leans heavily toward leather and jeans.

Sergeant Janicki goes over the game plan. I am to accompany one under-cover officer on a heroin buy, while the rest of the unit is divided into surveil-lance and enforcement squads. The officer I'm accompanying, a thirty-four-year-old Long Island native who uses the street name Mike, goes off to change into his disguise. We're posing as construction workers—strung-out construction workers by the look of it when Mike returns wearing filthy, tar-splattered jeans, heroin-chic dark eyeliner and a backward baseball cap that pins down his stringy, shoulder-length hair. I'm suddenly glad that I didn't shave this morning.

Janicki gives us a lift to a nearby parking garage, where the department keeps a white Dodge pickup with scaffolding sections scattered in its flatbed for added effect. Kentucky Fried Chicken wrappers and crumpled 7-Eleven coffee cups litter the floor of the cab, more props.

As we head southeast to one of Baltimore's rougher neighborhoods, Mike explains how the lower rungs of the distribution chain are organized. Baltimore's dozen or so big dealers reparcel the newly purchased kilos into more affordable ounce-size lots. Shops or midsize dealers then break down ounces into grams that are resold to crews in "packages" of 100 vials or gelcaps, each containing one milligram. Gelcaps, as opposed to the pink-, blue- or green-tops, cater to the low end of the market, the addicts who inject heroin.

"That's when they're really stepping on the product," says Mike. "The rule is generally six to one," Jimenez elaborates, meaning that from the one kilo pur-chased from wholesalers, up to seven kilos will be produced by adding sundry adulterants by the time it hits the street. "This is where the biggest markups occur," he adds. "From wholesale to retail, because that's where you face the biggest risks. You have to protect yourself not only from the police but from rivals and people in your own organization who know you are carrying large amounts of cash."

As we drive deeper into the drug zone, the violence and poverty that accompany the lowest echelons of the heroin trade become more visible. Mike spots a street corner that is not too busy. He doesn't want to risk leaving me alone with a crowd. He radios Sergeant Janicki to coordinate surveillance. "Corner of East Monument and Belnord," he says, stowing the walkie-talkie. "All right, put away your notebook," he says. "And whatever happens, don't get out of the truck."

We slow down and pull up to the curb. "Yo, man, dope's out?" he calls. Dope is street slang for heroin, which is also sometimes called boy. "I got shirleys," responds the dealer, a tough-looking youth in shiny white sneakers with a stick of red licorice clenched between a solid row of gold teeth. Shirley means crack cocaine, which is also called girl. "He waitin' on a fresh pack," says the youth, nodding across the street to a man with no teeth. A pack is 100 heroin gelcaps, each filled with heavily adulterated heroin—"scramble" in the local dialect—which means he is expecting a delivery from his crew boss.

Mike doesn't like it. To make the buy, he has to get out of the truck and leave me alone. He hesitates for a moment. "Be cool," he finally tells me, and much as I try, I find it hard to follow his instruction, what with the licorice guy eye-balling me menacingly. Mike returns a few nerve-racking minutes later and hands me a clear capsule that looks like cold medicine. It is filled with a chunky white substance. "Scramble," he says, putting the pickup in gear.

Mike paid $10 for the milligram, the purity of which usually ranges from 4 to 7 percent, but recently has been testing as high as 12 percent—a sure sign that heroin is in plentiful supply in Baltimore. "What's that come out to per kilo?" I ask.

"Math was never my strong suit," Mike says. "But a lot." I crunch a few numbers while we drive away, giving Sergeant Janicki and his enforcement unit time to swoop in on the unsuspecting mark. Moments later Janicki radios in to inform us that he has picked up the dealer, a thirty-one-year-old black male with twenty-one prior arrests for heroin and cocaine distribution. "Guy's a junkie," Mike says sadly, shaking his head. "Probably gets fifty bucks and a free fix to sit out there all day."

There are thousands of others like him in Baltimore—and throughout inner cities across the United States—working, much like the stranded peasants of Myanmar, for next to nothing, for a lack perhaps of economic alternatives. And as for the heroin that unites them in their poverty, a lone kilo, which began its economic life cycle so humbly at the hands of a Burmese mother of seven, will have generated sales just shy of a million dollars by the time it ends its deadly journey and enters the American bloodstream.

WORKADAY WORLD, CRACK ECONOMY:
Breaking Rocks in El Barrio

Philippe Bourgois

From *The Nation*, December 4, 1995

I was forced into crack against my will. When I first moved to East Harlem—"El Barrio"—as a newlywed in the spring of 1985,1 was looking for an inexpensive New York City apartment from which I could write about the experience of poverty and ethnic segregation in the heart of one of the most expensive cities in the world. I was interested in the political economy of inner-city street culture I wanted to probe the Achilles's heel of the richest industrialized nation in the world by documenting how it imposes racial segregation and economic marginalization on so many of its Latino/a and African-American citizens.

My original subject was the entire underground (untaxed) economy, from curbside car repairing and baby-sitting to unlicensed off-track betting and drug dealing. I had never even heard of crack when I first arrived in the neighborhood—no one knew about this particular substance yet, because this brittle compound of cocaine and baking soda processed into efficiently smokable pellets was not yet available as a mass-marketed product. By the end of the year, however, most of my friends, neighbors, and acquaintances had been swept into the multibillion-dollar crack cyclone: selling it, smoking it, fretting over it. I followed them, and I watched the murder rate in the projects opposite my crumbling tenement apartment spiral into one of the highest in Manhattan.

But this essay is not about crack, or drugs, per se. Substance abuse in the inner city is merely a symptom—and a vivid symbol—of deeper dynamics of social marginalization and alienation. Of course, on an immediately visible personal level, addiction and substance abuse are among the most immediate, brutal facts shaping daily life on the street. Most important, however, the two dozen street dealers and their families that I befriended were not interested in talking primarily about drugs. On the contrary, they wanted me to learn all about their daily struggles for subsistence and dignity at the poverty line.

Through the 1980s and 1990s, slightly more than one in three familes in El Barrio have received public assistance. Female heads of these impoverished households have to supplement their meager checks in order to keep their children alive. Many are mothers who make extra money by babysitting their neighbors' children, or by housekeeping for a paying boarder. Others may bartend at one of the half-dozen social clubs and after-hours dancing spots scattered throughout the neighborhood. Some work "off the books" in their living rooms as seamstresses for garment contractors. Finally, many also find themselves obliged to establish amorous relationships with men who are willing to make cash contributions to their household expenses.

Male income-generating strategies m the underground economy are more publicly visible. Some men repair cars on the curb; others wait on stoops for unlicensed construction subcontractors to pick them up for fly-by-night demolition jobs or window renovation projects. Many sell "numbers"—the street's version of off-track betting. The most visible cohorts hawk "nickels and dimes" of one illegal drug or another. They are part of the most robust, multibilllon-dollar sector of the booming underground economy. Cocaine and crack, in particular during the mid-1980s and through the early 1990s, followed by heroin in the mid-1990s, have become the fastest-growing—if not the only—equal-opportunity employers of men in Harlem. Retail drug sales easily outcompete other income-generating opportunities, whether legal or illegal.

Why should these young men and women take the subway to work minimum-wage jobs—or even double-minimum-wage jobs—in downtown offices when they can usually earn more, at least m the short run, by selling drugs on the street corner in front of their apartment or schoolyard?? In fact, I am always surprised that so many inner-city men and women remain in the legal economy and work nine-to-five plus overtime, barely making ends meet. According to the 1990 Census of East Harlem, 48 percent of all males and 35 percent of females over 16 were employed in officially reported jobs, compared with a citywide average of 64 percent for men and 49 percent for women. In the census tracts surrounding my apartment, 53 percent of all men over 16 years of age (1,923 out of 3,647) and 28 percent of all women over 16 (1,307 out of 4,626) were working legally in officially censused jobs. An additional 17 percent of the civilian labor force was unemployed but actively looking for work, compared with 16 percent for El Barrio as a whole, and 9 percent for all of New York City.

'IF I WAS WORKING LEGAL . . . '

Street dealers tend to brag to outsiders and to themselves about how much money they make each night. In fact, their income is almost never as consistently high as they report it to be. Most street sellers, like my friend Primo (who, along with other friends and coworkers, allowed me to tape hundreds of hours of conversation with him over five years), are paid on a piece-rate commission basis. When converted into an hourly wage, this is often a relatively paltry sum. According to my calculations, the workers in the Game Room crackhouse, for example, averaged slightly less than double the legal minimum wage—between seven and eight dollars an hour. There were plenty of exceptional nights, however, when they made up to ten times minimum wage—and these are the nights they remember when they reminisce. They forget about all the other shifts when they were unable to work because of police raids,, and they certainly do not count as forfeited working hours the nights they spent in jail.

This was brought home to me symbolically one night as Primo and has co-worker Caesar were shutting down the Game Room. Caesar unscrewed the fuses in the electrical box to disconnect the video games. Primo had finished stashing the leftover bundles of crack vials inside a hollowed-out live electrical socket and was counting the night's thick wad of receipts. I was struck by how thin the handful of bills was that he separated out and folded neatly into his personal billfold. Primo and Caesar then eagerly lowered the iron riot gates over the Game Room's windows and snapped shut the heavy Yale padlocks. They were moving with the smooth, hurried gestures of workers preparing to go home after an honest day's hard labor. Marveling at the universality in the body language of workers rushing at closing time, I felt an urge to compare the wages paid by this alternative economy. I grabbed Primo's wallet out of his back pocket, carefully giving a wide berth to the fatter wad in his front pocket that represented Ray's share of the night's income—and that could cost Primo his life if it were waylaid. Unexpectedly, I pulled out fifteen dollars' worth of food stamps along with two $20 bills. After an embarrassed giggle, Primo stammered that his mother had added him to her food-stamp allotment.

PRIMO: I gave my girl, Maria, half of it. I said, "Here, take it, use it if you need it for whatever." And then the other half I still got it in my wallet for emergencies.

Like that, we always got a couple of dollars here and there, to survive with Because tonight, straight cash, I only got garbage. Forty dollars! Do you believe that?

At the same time that wages can be relatively low in the crack economy, working conditions are often inferior to those in the legal economy. Aside from the obvious dangers of being shot, or of going to prison, the physical work space of most crackhouses is usually unpleasant. The infrastructure of the Game Room, for example, was much worse than that of any legal retail outfit in East Harlem: There was no bathroom, no running water, no telephone, no heat in the winter and no air conditioning in the summer. Primo occasionally complained:

> Everything that you see here [sweeping his arm at the scratched and dented video games, the walls with peeling paint, the floor slippery with litter, the filthy windows pasted over with ripped movie posters] is fucked up. It sucks, man [pointing at the red 40-watt bare bulb hanging from an exposed fixture in the middle of the room and exuding a sickly twilight.]

Indeed, the only furnishings besides the video games were a few grimy milk crates and bent aluminum stools. Worse yet, a smell of urine and vomit usually permeated the locale. For a few months Primo was able to maintain a rudimentary sound system, but it was eventually beaten to a pulp during one of Caesar's drunken rages. Of course, the deficient infrastructure was only one part of the depressing working conditions.

> PRIMO: Plus I don't like to see people fucked up [handing over three vials to a nervously pacing customer! This is fucked-up shit. I don't like this crack dealing. Word up.
> [Gunshots in the distance] Hear that?

In private, especially in the last few years of my residence, Primo admitted that he wanted to go back to the legal economy.

> PRIMO: I just fuck up the money here. I rather be legal.
> PHILIPPE: But you wouldn't be the head man on the block with so many girlfriends.
> PRIMO: I might have women on my dick night now but I would be much cooler If I was working legal I wouldn't be drinking and the coke wouldn't be there every night.
> Plus if I was working legally I would have women on my dick too, because I would have money.
> PHILIPPE: But you make more money here than you could ever make working legit.

PRIMO: O.K. So you want the money but you really don't want to do the job.

I really hate It man. Hate it! I hate the people! I hate the environnent! I hate the whole shit man! But it's like you get caught up with it. You do it and you say "Ay, fuck it today!" Another day another dollar. [pointing at an emaciated customer who was just entering] But I don't really, really think that I would have hoped that I can say I'm gonna be richer one day. I can't say that. I think about it, but I'm just living day to day.

If I was working legal I wouldn't be hanging out so much. I wouldn't be treating you. [pointing to the 16-ounce can of Colt 45 in my hand] In a job, you know, my environment would change . . . totally. 'Cause I'd have different friends. Right after work I'd go out with a co-worker for lunch, for dinner. After work I may go home: I'm too tired for hanging out—I know I gotta work tomorrow.

After working a legal job I'm pretty sure I'd be good.

BURNED IN THE FIRE ECONOMY

The problem is that Primo's good intentions do not lead anywhere when the only legal jobs he can compete for fail to provide him with a livable wage None of the crack dealers were explicitly conscious of the links between their limited options in the legal economy, their addiction to drugs, and their dependence on the crack economy for economic survival and personal dignity. Nevertheless, all of Primo's colleagues and employees told stories of rejecting what they considered to be intolerable working conditions at entry-level jobs.

Most entered the legal labor market at exceptionally young ages. By the time they were twelve they were bagging and delivering groceries at the supermarket for tips stocking beer off the books in local bodegas or running errands. Before reaching twenty-one, however, virtually none had fulfilled their early childhood dreams of finding stable well-paid legal work.

The problem is structural: From the 1950s through the 1980s second-generation inner-city Puerto Ricans were trapped in the most vulnerable niche of a factory-based economy that was rapidly being replaced by service industries. Between 1950 and 1990 the proportion of factory jobs in New York City decreased approximately threefold at the same tune that service-sector jobs doubled. The Department of City Planning calculates that more than 800,000 industrial jobs were lost from the 1960s through the early 1990s while the total number of jobs of all categories remained more or less constant at 3.5 million.

Few scholars have noted the cultural dislocations of the new service economy These cultural clashes have been most pronounced in the office-work service jobs that have multiplied because of the dramatic expansion of the finance real estate, and insurance (FIRE) sector in New York City. Service work in professional offices is the most dynamic place for ambitious inner-city youths to find entry-level jobs if they aspire to upward mobility. Employment as mailroom clerks, photocopiers, and messengers in the high-rise office corridors of the financial district propels many into a wrenching cultural confrontation with the upper-middle-class white world. Obedience to the norms of high-rise office-corridor culture is in direct contradiction to street culture's definitions of personal dignity—especially for males who are socialized not to accept public subordination.

Most of the dealers have not completely withdrawn from the legal economy. On the contrary—they are precariously perched on its edge. Their poverty remains their only constant as they alternate between street-level crack dealing and just-above-minimum-wage legal employment. The working-class jobs they manage to find are objectively recognized to be among the least desirable m U.S. society; hence the following list of just a few of the jobs held by some of the Game Room regulars during the years I knew them: unlicensed asbestos remover, home attendant, street-corner flier distributor, deep-fat fry cook and night-shift security guard on the violent ward at the municipal hospital for the criminally insane.

The stable factory-worker incomes that might have allowed Caesar and Primo to support families have largely disappeared from the inner city. Perhaps if their social network had not been confined to the weakest sector of manufacturing in a period of rapid job loss their teenage working-class dreams might have stabilized them for long enough to enable them to adapt to the restructuring of the local economy. Instead they find themselves propelled headlong into an explosive confrontation between their sense of cultural dignity versus the humiliating interpersonal subordination of service work.

Workers like Caesar and Primo appear inarticulate to their professional supervisors when they try to imitate the language of power in the workplace; they stumble pathetically over the enunciation of unfamiliar words. They cannot decipher the hastily scribbled instructions—rife with mysterious abbreviations—that are left for them by harried office managers on diminutive Post-its. The "common sense" of white-collar work is foreign to them; they do not, for example, understand the logic in filing triplicate copies of memos or for post-dating invoices. When they attempt to improvise or show initiative, they fail miserably and instead appear inefficient—or even hostile—for failing to follow "clearly specified" instructions.

In the high-rise office buildings of midtown Manhattan or Wall Street, newly employed inner-city high school dropouts suddenly realize they look like idiotic buffoons to the men and women for whom they work. But people like Primo and Caesar have not passively accepted their structural victimization. On the contrary, by embroiling themselves in the underground economy and proudly embracing street culture, they are seeking an alternative to their social marginalizatlon. In the process, on a daily level, they become the actual agents administering their own destruction and their community's suffering.

Both Primo and Caesar experienced deep humiliation and insecurity in their attempts to penetrate the foreign-hostile world of high-rise office corridors. Primo had bitter memories of being the mailroom clerk and errand boy at a now-defunct professional trade magazine. The only time he explicitly admitted to having experienced racism was when he described how he was treated at that particular work setting.

PRIMO: I had a prejudiced boss. . . . When she was talking to people she would say. "He's illiterate," as if I was really that stupid that I couldn't understand what she was talking about.

So what I did one day—you see they had this big dictionary right there on the desk, a big heavy motherfucker—so what I just did was open up the dictionary, and I just looked up the word, "illiterate." And that's when I saw what she was calling me.

So she's saying that I'm stupid or something. I'm stupid! [pointing to himself with both thumbs and making a hulking face] "He doesn't know shit."

In contrast in the underground economy Primo never had to risk this kind of threat to his self-worth.

PRIMO: Ray would never disrespect me that way, he wouldn't tell me that because he's illiterate too, plus I've got more education than him. I almost got a G.E.D

The contemporary street sensitivity to being dissed immediately emerges in these memories of office humiliation. The machismo of street culture exacerbates the sense of insult experienced by men because the majority of office supervisors at the entry level are women. In the lowest recesses of New York City's FIRE sector tens of thousands of messengers, photocopy machine operators, and security guards serving the Fortune 500 companies are brusquely ordered about by young white executives—often female—who sometimes make bimonthly salaries superior to their underlings' yearly wages. The extraordinary wealth of Manhattan's financial district exacerbates the sense of sexist-racist insult associated with performing just-above-minimum-wage labor.

'I DON'T EVEN GET A DRESS SHIRT'

Several months earlier, I had watched Primo drop out of a "motivational training" employment program in the basement of his mother's housing project, run by former heroin addicts who had just received a multimillion-dollar private sector grant for their innovative approach to training the "unemployable." Primo felt profoundly disrespected by the program, and he focuses his discontent on the humiliation he faced because of his inappropriate wardrobe. The fundamental philosophy of such motivational job-training programs is that "these people have an attitude problem. They take a boot-camp approach to their unemployed clients, ripping their self-esteem apart during the first week in order to build them back up with an epiphanic realization that they want to find jobs as security guards, messengers, and data-input clerks in just-above-minimum-wage service sector positions The program's highest success rate had been with middle-aged African-American women who wanted to terminate their relationship to welfare once their children leave home.

I originally had a "bad attitude" toward the premise of psychologically motivating and manipulating people to accept boring, poorly paid jobs. At the same time, however, the violence and self-destruction I was witnessing at the Game Room was convincing me that it is better to be exploited at work than to be outside the legal labor market. In any case, I persuaded Primo and a half-dozen of his Game Room associates to sign up for the program. Even Caesar was tempted to join.

None of the crack dealers lasted for more than three sessions. Primo was the first to drop out, after the first day. For several weeks he avoided talking about the experience. I repeatedly pressed him to explain why he "just didn't show up" at the sessions. Only after repeated badgenng on my part did he finally express the deep sense of shame and vulnerability he experienced whenever he attempted to venture into the legal labor market.

PHILIPPE: Yo Primo, listen to me. I worry that there's something taking place that you're not aware of, in terms of yourself. Like the coke that you be sniffing all the time; it's like every night.

PRIMO: What do you mean?

PHILIPPE: Like not showing up at the job training. You say it's just procrastination, but I'm scared that it's something deeper that you're not dealing with. . . .

PRIMO: The truth though—listen Felipe—my biggest worry was the dress code, 'cause my gear is limited. I don't even got a dress shirt, I only got one pair of shoes, and you can't wear sneakers at that program. They wear ties too—don't they? Well I ain't even got ties—I only got the one you lent me.

I would've been there three weeks m the same gear: *T-shirt* and *Jeans*. *Estoy jodido como un bón!* [I'm all fucked up like a bum!]

PHILIPPE: What the fuck kinda bullshit excuse are you talking about? Don't tell me you were thinking that shit. No one notices how people are dressed.

PRIMO: Yo, Felipe, this is for real! Listen to me! I was thinking about that shit hard. Hell yeah!

Hell, yes, they would notice if somebody's wearing a fucked-up tie and shirt.

I don't want to be in a program all *abochornado* [bumlike]. I probably won't even concentrate, getting dished like . . . and being looked at like a sucker. Dirty jeans . . . or like old jeans, because I would have to wear jeans 'cause I only got one slack. Word though! I only got two dress shirts and one of them is missing buttons.

I didn't want to tell you about that because it's like a poor excuse, but that was the only shit I was really thinking about. At the time I just said "Well, I just don't show up."

And Felipe, I'm a stupid [very] skinny nigga'. So I have to be careful how I dress, otherwise people will think I be on the stem [a crack addict who smokes out of a glass-stem pipe].

PHILIPPE: [nervously] Oh shit. I'm even skinnier than you. People must think I'm a total drug addict.

PRIMO: Don't worry. You're white.

[FOREIGN AFFAIRS]

AMERICA'S LONELY DRUG WAR

Adam J. Smith

From *Mother Jones*, December 14, 2001

Last December 5 marked the sixty-eighth anniversary of the effective end of Prohibition, drawing to a close this nation's "noble experiment" with criminalizing alcohol. So it seems ironic that it was also the day on which the United States Senate confirmed John P. Walters as the new director of the Office of National Drug Policy—the nation's drug czar.

Walters, who spent much of the nineties working in various positions at the Federal office he will now lead, has a track record of opposing measures like syringe exchanges while supporting large-scale incarceration for drug users and military action to stop drug production in places like Colombia and Peru. His appointment is the clearest sign yet that the Bush administration is committed to a punishment-based approach to the problems caused by illegal drugs, undeterred by a growing consensus both at home and abroad that the War on Drugs is as ill-conceived as the war on alcohol nearly seven decades ago.

Over the past five years, Americans have voted in favor of nearly every significant state initiative to reform drug policies, from legalizing medical marijuana in Arizona, to banning the seizure of assets of accused but unconvicted drug dealers in Oregon, to last year's Proposition 36 in California which mandates treatment instead of incarceration for drug users. In most cases, that public support came despite strong opposition from the Federal government.

Our allies in Europe have gone much further. The US has had no firmer friend in Europe than the United Kingdom. But even as the UK has enlisted wholeheartedly in the war on terror, it has taken steps toward declaring peace in the War on Drugs.

In late October, Home Secretary David Blunkett announced that the British government will soon abandon the policy of arresting people for marijuana possession. Blunkett also indicated that the New Labour government is ready to discuss expanding the medically supervised distribution of heroin to addicts, while some Labour members in Parliament have called for reducing the penalties for the manufacture, sale, and possession of Ecstasy.

"The drug war, in Western Europe at least, is essentially over," says Paul Flynn, a Labour member of Parliament since 1987 . "Our course is irreversibly moving toward legalized, regulated markets in so-called soft drugs, availability of drugs like opiates for those who are addicted through various health systems, and a more pragmatic approach to substance abuse generally throughout Europe."

Far from being trendsetters in this regard, Britain trails every European Union nation other than Sweden in moving away from criminally enforced prohibition, according to a survey by the European Non-Governmental Organizations Council on Drugs and Development, an umbrella group of advocacy organizations. Holland led the shift starting back in the 1970s, when it "normalized" the cannabis trade—meaning that over the counter sales were tolerated, though not exactly legal. Dutch policymakers hoped that, by separating out the market for "soft" drugs like marijuana from that of "hard" drugs like cocaine and heroin, marijuana users would be less likely to come into contact with more addictive and dangerous substances. That approach seems to have yielded results.

In its latest annual report on drug use, released last month, the European Union's European Monitoring Centre for Drugs and Drug Addiction found that Britain and Ireland rank highest among EU nations in per capita use of cannabis, amphetamines, and cocaine. Per capita usage in the Netherlands, the report indicates, is significantly lower. The incidence of intravenous and long-term regular use of opiates, cocaine, or amphetamines is also two to three times higher in the UK than in the Netherlands, the report indicates.

Due in part to the success of the Dutch model, most Western European countries have over the past five years begun to soften their approach to personal use of most drugs. Spain and Germany no longer arrest people for possession of "soft" drugs such as marijuana, and this year, Portugal essentially decriminalized drug possession altogether.

More controversially, some EU countries are experimenting with programs under which registered addicts can receive legal, measured doses of heroin, along with other health and social services. Switzerland has established such programs as part of its overall health policy, and the Netherlands, Spain, Germany, and Denmark are launching pilot programs.

Several European countries are also testing the benefits of safe injection rooms, places where IV drug users can shoot up under some level of medical supervision. Although the data is still inconclusive, several studies suggest that these facilitites can help reduce the incidence of fatal overdoses and syringe sharing. In Frankfurt, for instance, where injection rooms have been open since 1994, city officials report that overdose fatalities declined from 147 in 1992 to 26 in 1999. There are now injection rooms operating in Germany, the Netherlands, Spain, and Switzerland. City officials in Vancouver, Canada, are also considering opening an injection room.

In the US, of course, things are different—as Walters's nomination makes clear.

"In Europe, the drug problem is viewed as a collection of consequences— AIDS, crime, addiction—which must be dealt with. Not so here, where we tend to look at drug use and intoxication as a moral issue," says Eric Sterling, president of the Washington, D.C.-based Criminal Justice Policy Foundation "We justify the most destructive and least effective of our drug policies as somehow sending an important message to our children."

Indeed, the man set to become America's newest drug czar objects to treatment-based approaches for moral reasons. In 1996, Walters indicated that he opposed syringe exchange on moral grounds; but data from major national and international health organizations—including the National Academy of Sciences, the American Medical Association, and the Joint United Nations Programme on AIDS—indicate that exchange programs reduce the spread of deadly diseases like HIV/AIDS and hepatitis, without increasing drug use.

Walters has also told Congress that he believes foreign drug interdiction programs are "cheap and effective," even though a 1994 federal Government Accounting Office study found that "the supply of illegal drugs reaching the United States via Central America continues virtually uninterrupted, despite years of US drug interdiction efforts." A study the same year by the RAND Corporation, a private research institute, showed that monies spent on treatment are twenty-three times more effective at lowering drug use than those spent on interdiction.

In 1996 Walters, then the president of a private think tank, urged Congress to increase support for a Peruvian policy of shooting suspected drug planes out of the sky, rejecting experts' concerns that the practice would put innocent travellers at risk. Last April, US support for that program was withdrawn after the Peruvian military shot down a plane carrying an American missionary and her daughter—but no drugs.

Walters has also defended the practice of jailing drug offenders, rejecting arguments that too many Americans are imprisoned for simple drug possession and that drug sentences are too long as "among the great urban myths of our time." Walters clings to his beliefs despite the fact that the US has the highest incarceration rate of any country on earth. Thanks largely to the kinds of policies Walters would continue, the US holds more prisoners for drug crimes than are imprisoned in Western Europe for all crimes combined, according to the British Home Office and the US Bureau of Justice Statistics.

By 1933, fourteen years after its inception, it was clear that alcohol prohibition was a disaster. Crime and homicide rates had increased. Machine gun-toting gangsters had become counterculture icons. Impure black market alcohol was causing blindness, disease, and death. Governmental and police corruption was rampant. Children easily obtained alcohol, drinking out of hip flasks, the status symbol of the time.

Nevertheless, to its champions, Prohibition was seen as indistinguishable from society's "message" that excessive drink was a bad and a dangerous thing. How could we stand firm against the sins of drunkenness, spousal and child abuse, violence, and wasted promise, if our laws permitted the legal sale of such deadly stuff? What we needed, according to Prohibitionists, was to redouble our efforts. Those who sought to overturn Prohibition, the hardliners argued, were giving up on our nation, on our quest for an alcohol-free society, on our children.

"We represent here today not only organizations of women, but, as a whole, we represent the home, the school, the church, and we stand firmly for no amendment to the eighteenth amendment . . . but rather a strengthening," Mrs. Henry Peabody, President of the Women's National Committee for Law Enforcement, told the Senate Judiciary Committee on Prohibition in 1926. "We stand for strict law enforcement. . . . It is never the policy of a good mother or teacher to say the children are disobedient—therefore let us give in to them and let them do as they like."

How little things change. Last month, William Bennett, Walters's former boss at ONDCP, penned an op-ed in the *Wall Street Journal* urging Walters's speedy confirmation and accusing the Clinton administration—which oversaw a doubling of the drug war budget and record levels of arrests and incarceration—of "all but giving up" on our children. It is time, said Bennett, not to "go soft" but to "push back."

Today, around the world, in England, in Switzerland, in Germany, in Canada, a new consensus is emerging. It is one which sees substance abuse as a health issue, rather than a criminal justice issue. It seeks pragmatic solutions to the problems of addiction, crime, and AIDS. Here at home, voters are making a statement at the ballot box that moral absolutism might be a fine opinion, but it makes lousy law. Walters and the Bush administration, however, have yet to get the message.

AMERICA'S DiRTY WAR ON DRUGS

Christopher Hitchens

From *The Guardian* (London), July 11, 2001

Good to see that sanity can sometimes be as infectious as insanity. All it takes, apparently, is one lucid moment on the part of one public figure, and a whole realm of illusion can be dissipated. The Peter Lilley moment on soft drugs, closely followed by the David Blunkett one, gives some reason to hope that the American nightmare is not in our future.

Here is what happened in my hometown of Washington, D.C. during the Congressional elections of 1998. A local initiative was attached to the ballot, proposing the "decriminalisation" of marijuana for medical purposes. After the votes had been counted, it was abruptly announced that the result would not be disclosed. The United States Congress, which has ultimate jurisdiction over municipal government in the capital of the free world, ruled that, though it could not prevent a vote being taken, it could prevent the outcome from being made public.

Right away, I knew what I had already guessed—that the citizens had voted overwhelmingly to allow the use of cannabis for the treatment of cancer and glaucoma. But it took a protracted lawsuit to get the ballots counted and the voters decision made known, only to be negated by Congress once again.

In every other state where this simple question has been mooted at election times, it has carried the day by unanswerable majorities. In each instance, Congress or the federal government has intervened to have the decision set aside. The word for this, in commonplace vernacular, is "denial."

The domestic war against the enemy within, which was begun as Richard Nixon's last desperate gamble for panicky popularity, is now in the same shape as the rest of his legacy. It reeks of corruption, police brutality, and overweening bureaucracy. It also involves a demented overseas entanglement, with off-the-record US military aircraft running shady missions over Colombia and Peru, and high-level collaboration with ruthless and unaccountable "Special Forces."

I simply cannot remember the last time, in public or private, that I spoke with a single person who believes this makes the least particle of sense. The opinion pages can occasionally drum up a lone, dull voice, but it's almost invariably that of a paid spokesman for a "war" machine that enjoys funding in inverse proportion to its victories. Again, I know very few habitual drug users, but I also don't know anyone who would be more than two degrees of separation from a reliable supplier, whether that turned out to be a gangsta or a cop.

A striking fact is the predominance of honest and intelligent conservatives on the sane side of the argument. The first editor with any "profile" to call for legalisation was William F. Buckley, the old lion of the right-wing *National Review*. He has been joined by George Schultz, formerly Reagan's secretary of state, and by Gary Johnson, the Republican governor of New Mexico, among many others. The "libertarian" journals have been ahead of the "liberal" ones for the most part. In an eerie way, this matches the recent shift of opinion on capital punishment, where conservatives have again been taking the most moral and political risks. (In both cases, the common factor may be Bill Clinton, the Nixon of the liberals, who expanded the drug war just as he increased the scope of the death penalty.)

Three decades of this grotesque, state-sponsored racketeering have led to unbelievable levels of official corruption and to an unheard-of assault on civil and political liberties. Colombia doesn't look any more like the US as a result, but the US does look a lot more like Colombia. The actual resources expended would have more than paid for national health care: the potential revenue from legal, and therefore clean, narcotics would rebuild the cities from the ground up.

WHY DUTCH DRUG POLICY THREATENS THE U.S.

Craig Reinarman

An earlier version of this article appeared in Het Parool, *July30, 1998*

In 1972, after an exhaustive study by a team of top experts, President Richard Nixon's hand-picked National Commission on Marijuana and Drug Abuse recommended decriminalization of marijuana. Five years later, President Jimmy Carter and many of his top cabinet officials made the same recommendation to Congress. Both the Commission and the Carter administration felt that the "cure" of imprisonment was worse than the "disease" of marijuana use. U.S. drug control officials argued strenuously that Congress should ignore such recommendations, which it did.

At about the same time, however, the Dutch government's own national commission completed its study of the risks of marijuana. The Dutch Commission also concluded that it made no sense to send people to prison for personal possession and use, so Dutch officials designed a policy that first tolerated and later regulated sales of small amounts of marijuana.

DENOUNCING THE DUTCH

Since then, U.S. drug control officials have denounced Dutch drug policy as if it were the devil himself. One former U.S. Drug Czar claimed that all the Dutch youth in Amsterdam's Vondel Park were "stoned zombies." Another said "you can't walk down the street in Amsterdam without tripping over junkies." In the summer of 1998, however, one such denouncement turned into a small scandal. The first part of this chapter examines this incident as a window on the politics of drug policy. The second part offers a more general analysis of why U.S. drug control officials seem to be so threatened by the Dutch example.

In early July, the U.S. Drug Czar, General Barry McCaffrey, announced that he would soon go on a "fact finding tour" of the Netherlands to learn first hand about its drug policy. He quickly made it clear, however, that he would be bringing his own facts. Before he ever left home, McCaffrey denounced the Dutch approach to drugs as "an unmitigated disaster" (CNN, July 9, 1998). If he had let it go at that, the General might have avoided international embarrassment for himself and the Clinton administration. But he proceeded to make claims about drugs and crime in the Netherlands that were incorrect and insulting. Dutch officials and journalists immediately caught him with his evidentiary pants down and publicly rebutted his false charges.

FALSE CLAIMS

McCaffrey asserted that drug abuse problems in The Netherlands are "enormous" (Associated Press, July 13, 1998). In fact, the Dutch have no more drug problems than most neighboring countries which do not have "liberal" drug policies. Further, by virtually all measures the Dutch have less drug use and abuse than the U.S. — from a lower rate of marijuana use among teens to a lower rate of heroin addiction among adults.

McCaffrey also claimed, to a room full of journalists, that "The murder rate in Holland is double that in the United States . . . That's drugs." He cited these figures: 17.58 murders per 100,000 population in the Netherlands, he asserted, vs. 8.22 per 100,000 in the U.S. (Reuters, July 13, 1998). For decades the U.S. has had significantly higher crime rates than other industrialized democracies. This has been reported at least annually by most newspapers and news magazines in the U.S.

Whatever the reason this fact eluded General McCaffrey and his staff, it did not elude the journalists to whom he spoke. In less than 24 hours, the world's media caught and corrected McCaffrey's mistake. They showed that he had arrived at his Dutch figure by lumping homicides together with the much higher number of *attempted* homicides, and that he had *not* done the same for the U.S. figures. Thus, the Drug Czar had compared the U.S. homicide rate with the *combined* rates of homicide and attempted homicide in the Netherlands. The correct Dutch homicide rate, the international press reported, is 1.8 per 100,000, *less than one fourth the U.S. rate* (Centraal Bureau voor de Statistiek, July 13, 1998; Reuters, July 14, 1998). Even this error might have been forgotten if McCaffrey had not gone on to attribute this newfound murderous streak in the Dutch national soul to their drug policy: "That's drugs" he said, apparently unaware that there has never been any evidence that marijuana — the only drug the Dutch ever decriminalized — is a cause of murder.

Then McCaffrey's staff at the Office of National Drug Control Policy dug his agency into a deeper hole. When Dutch Embassy officials confronted Deputy Drug Czar Jim McDonough about the misleading figures, he replied: "Let's say [that's] right. What you're left with is that they [the Dutch] are a much more violent society and more inept [at murder], and that's not much to brag about" (*Washington Times*, July 15, 1998, p. A4). Here, in a stunning blend of ignorance and arrogance, Mr. McDonough compounds his failure to understand the earlier error with an ethnic slur upon the Dutch.

THE DUTCH REACTION

Dutch officials reacted swiftly to all of this. Joris Vos, Dutch Ambassador to the U.S., publicly released a letter he sent to McCaffrey at the White House:

"I am confounded and dismayed by your description of Dutch drug policy as an unmitigated disaster and by your suggestion that the purpose of that policy is to make it easier for young people... Your remarks ... have no basis in the facts and figures which your office has at its disposal and which certainly do not originate only from Dutch sources... Apart from the substance, which I cannot agree with, I must say that I find the timing of your remarks - six days before your planned visit to the Netherlands with a view to gaining first-hand knowledge about Dutch drugs policy and its results, rather astonishing . . . " (Reuters, July 14, 1998; *Washington Times*, July 15, 1998, p. A4).

The Foreign Ministry, Justice Ministry, and Health Ministry issued a joint diplomatic press release which can only be called wry understatement:

The impression had been gained that Mr. McCaffrey was coming to the Netherlands to familiarise himself on the spot with Dutch drugs policy. The Netherlands would not exclude the possibility that if Mr. McCaffrey familiarises himself with the results of Dutch drugs policy, he will bring his views more closely into line with the facts" (*Financial Times* [London], July 16, 1998, p. 2).

The reaction in the Dutch press ranged from a kind of ho-hum, 'what else is new' to genuine outrage. I reviewed coverage of the controversy in five Dutch daily newspapers and on two Amsterdam TV news shows. All agreed on the basic facts. All reported that McCaffrey's claims were simply wrong. The only question seemed to be whether he had intended to be insulting. The liberal press seemed to lean a bit more toward the latter interpretation and responded with ridicule. Amsterdam's TV 5, for example, aired a pair of comedians doing brief satirical sketches mimicking a reporter interviewing the U.S. Drug Czar:

Q: "How have you liked your trip so far, General McCaffrey?"
A: "OK, but the weather has been bad; it's been rainy almost everyday."
Q: "Why do you suppose that's so, General?"
A: "Drugs."
Q: "What are your impressions of the Netherlands so far, General?"
A: "Very interesting. I look forward to going on to Holland."
Q: "But sir, Holland is the same thing as the Netherlands."
A: "What?! The same country with two names? That's drugs for you."

Even the more conservative newspapers, which are sometimes critical of one or another aspect of Dutch drug policy, took McCaffrey to task. *De Volkskrant*, for example, editorialized that the U.S. Drug Czar "had already lost his war," that his false allegations showed the "bankruptcy of prohibitionism," and that the "American crusade against drugs" had "derailed" (July 15, 1998, p. 1). The Christian Democratic paper, *Trouw*, put the story as their top headline, and quoted a police intelligence source who called the Czar's claims "abuse of statistics" (July 15, 1998, p. 1).

WHY DUTCH POLICY POSES A THREAT

The little scandal surrounding McCaffrey's mistakes lasted only a few days in the Dutch press, for they have come to expect this sort of thing from U.S. drug control officials. Dutch citizens of the right and the left, fans and critics of their drug policy, know such claims are false. So do the millions of American tourists who have traveled to The Netherlands. If, as is often said, truth is the first casualty of war, perhaps we should simply expect the same of drug wars.

But such bizarre behavior begs a broader question: Why is a liberal reform in the domestic drug policy of one of the smallest, least powerful nations on earth so threatening to one of the largest and most powerful? U.S. officials are threatened by Dutch drug policy because it cuts directly against the moral ideology underlying U.S. drug policy. And that ideology runs deep in American culture and politics. The U.S. has a history of hysteria about intoxicating substances dating back to the 19th-century Temperance crusade. For over a hundred years, Americans believed that Satan's "demon drink" was the direct cause of poverty, ill health, crime, insanity, and the demise of civilization. This fundamentalist crusade culminated with national alcohol prohibition in 1919.

Alcohol Prohibition agents immediately took over the job of creating U.S. drug policy. Without debate, they chose criminalization. A series of drug scares since then has led to the criminalization of more drugs and the imprisonment of more drug users for longer terms. What animated each of these scares, from the crusade against alcohol on, was less public health than the politics of fear - fear of change, fear of foreigners, fear of communists, of the working class, of non-whites, of rebellious college students, and perhaps most centrally, fear of the loss of self control through drinking and drug use.

CREEPING TOTALITARIANISM

Having scapegoated drugs for so long, U.S. politicians cannot tolerate a tolerant system like the Dutch. They compete for votes on the basis of whose rhetoric is "tougher" on drugs. The Right-wing Republicans who currently control Congress call President Clinton "soft on drugs," even though more drug users have been imprisoned during his administration than under Reagan and Bush. Clinton appointed McCaffrey Drug Czar not because the General had any training or expertise on drug problems, but because he was a military man who would symbolize "toughness."

U.S. drug policy has indeed been getting "tougher." The Czar's budget has increased from $1 billion in 1980 to $17 billion in 1998. The number of drug offenders imprisoned in the U.S. has increased 800 percent since 1980, mostly poor people of color. This has helped the U.S. achieve the highest imprisonment rate in the industrialized world—550 per 100,000 population, compared to the Netherlands' 79 per 100,000. Under the banner of the war on drugs, a kind of creeping totalitarianism tramples more human rights and civil liberties each year. Tens of millions of citizens—most of whom have never used drugs and all of whom are supposed to be presumed innocent—are subjected to supervised urine tests to get jobs and then to keep jobs. Hundreds of thousands more are searched in their homes or, on the basis of racist "trafficker profiles," on freeways and at airports. Houses, cars, and businesses are seized by the state on the slimmest of suspicions alone. And U.S. school children have been bombarded with more antidrug propaganda than any generation in history.

A FAILED WAR

The actual results of all this suggest why U.S. officials lash out defensively against the Dutch. After more than a decade of deepening drug war, U.S. surveys show that illicit drug use by American youth has increased almost every year since 1991. The U.S. Drug Enforcement Administration admits that hard drugs are just as available, less expensive, and more pure than ever. Hard drug abuse and addiction among the urban poor remain widespread. HIV/AIDS continues to spread most rapidly via injection drug users; meanwhile, the needle exchanges that help stem its spread in every other modern nation remain criminalized in the U.S. A growing number of judges—including several high-level federal judges appointed by Republicans—have gone so far as to refuse to apply drug laws that have grown so Draconian they breach all bounds of fairness.

Opinion polls now show a majority of Americans do not believe the war on drugs can be won. More and more are voicing their opposition and seeking alternatives to punitive prohibition. The drug policy reform movement in the U.S. has grown larger and more diverse, attracting support from the American Medical Association, the American Bar Association, the American Public Health Association, the American Society of Criminology, and other professional groups. Not all of these groups support decriminalizing marijuana, but all of them support a shift away from drug war toward the harm-reducing public health approaches pioneered in the Netherlands.

And when such pesky heretics argue that there are alternatives to punitive prohibition, one of their key examples is Dutch drug policy. U.S. drug warriors wish the Netherlands example did not exist, but since they cannot make even small countries disappear, they are reduced to making up their own "facts" about it.

NO DISASTER

Dutch drug policy is also a threat to drug warriors precisely because it has not led to what Czar McCaffrey so confidently called an "unmitigated disaster." Dutch society has its drug problems, of course, but no more and often less than most other modern democracies which have harsher drug laws. Indeed, a higher proportion of people have tried marijuana in the U.S. where millions have been arrested for it than in the Netherlands where citizens may buy it lawfully.

U.S. drug control ideology holds that there is no such thing as use of an illicit drug, only abuse. But drug use patterns in the Netherlands show that for the overwhelming majority of users, marijuana is just one more type of *genotsmiddelen* (foods, spices, and intoxicants which give pleasure to the senses) that the Dutch have been importing and culturally domesticating for centuries.

U.S. drug warriors tend to lump all illicit drugs together, as if all were equally dangerous and addictive. Dutch drug policy makes pragmatic distinctions based on relative risks. When U.S. officials are confronted by scientific evidence showing marijuana to be among the least risky drugs, they fall back on the claim that it is a "stepping stone" to hard drugs. But here, too, the evidence from Dutch surveys is heresy: despite lawful availability, the majority of Dutch people never try marijuana, and most who do try it don't continue to use even marijuana very often, much less harder drugs.

In short, the Dutch facts destroy the Drug Czar's core claims. Those who have built their careers in the U.S. drug control complex fear Dutch drug policy like the Catholic Church feared Gallileo: they must believe the Dutch model is a disaster, for if it is not their whole cosmology shatters.

Leaders more secure about the effectiveness and fairness of their own drug policies would feel less need to slander the Dutch approach. Dutch officials do not proselytize, urging other nations to adopt their approach to drug policy, and the U.S. is obviously not obliged to adopt any part of the Dutch model. By the same logic, the U.S. government should realize that other societies do not share its phobias and do not appreciate its tendency toward drug policy imperialism, particularly with U.S. drug abuse rates being what they are.

A SENSELESS APPROACH

We inhabit an increasingly multicultural world. A multicultural world is also a multi-lifestyle and multi-morality world. Drug policy, therefore, cannot be as simple as stretch socks—"one size fits all." Neither European integration nor globalized markets erase differences in language, culture, behavior, or politics. Thus, a cookie cutter approach to the world's drug problems, in which each nation's drug policy is identical—whether punitive prohibition or any other model—makes no sense.

The Dutch have a long history of tolerance. Many of the Pilgrims who fled religious persecution in England were sheltered in the Netherlands before they came to America in the early 1600s. The Dutch were brutally conquered by the Nazis in World War II, so they know only too well what absolutist states can do to "deviants" and to individual freedom. Down through the centuries the Dutch have developed a deeply democratic culture which has nurtured non-absolutist approaches to many public problems. In the drug policy arena, they have bravely broadened the range of possibilities to examine, which is as useful for those who want to learn something as it is fearful for those who do not.

[CRIMINAL JUSTICE]

THE DRUG WARS: Voices from the Street

Tim Wells and William Triplett

From *Playboy*, March 1992

We think of the drug wars as battles fought among clearly defined antagonists—good versus bad, well-heeled versus impoverished, us versus them. But the conflict is more complicated, more personal, than that. The central figures of this grinding, inconclusive struggle are dealers, addicts, cops, children, parents, doctors, and nurses. All are individuals, all have stories to tell, and all become casualties, whether or not they survive the conflict.

Tim Wells and William Triplett, journalists who work the drug cross fire, became frustrated with the media's narrow coverage of the problem. "We watched the so-called experts on 'Nightline,'" remembers Wells, "and we realized that the most significant people in the drug wars were on the front lines. They were also the most silent."

Wells and Triplett traveled the streets of America's inner cities listening to those previously silent voices. This is what they heard.

THE DOCTORS

"We got a call over the radio informing us that there had been a shooting. We went racing out there with the siren blaring. When we arrived at the scene, the victim was still in his car. He was a teenage kid and he was in the front seat sitting behind the steering wheel. He had been shot right between the eyes at point-blank range.

"This was an obvious drug assassination. This kid had been driving a brand-new sports car and he was wearing all kinds of gold. He had a beeper on his belt, and when the ambulance technicians lifted him, a wad of about three thousand dollars in cash fell from his coat pocket. One look at that bullet hole and I knew he wasn't going to make it. But he was still alive and could still talk.

"After we got him into the ambulance, I leaned real close to him and said, 'This is serious. You've been shot and I don't think you're going to survive. Do you understand what I'm telling you?' He nodded yes.

"'Before you die,' I said, 'do you want to tell me who shot you?'

"He looked me square in the face and, in a voice husky with blood, he said, 'No.'"

"The weekends are unbelievable. The hospital's hallways are always packed with patients. It starts on Friday and doesn't let up until Monday. It's not uncommon to have three, four, or five gunshot victims come in within a span of an hour or two. Then, on top of that, the police are bringing in overdose cases and people who've gone psychotic from using PCP.

"The police are all part of the mix. They'll be in the halls trying to restrain patients, and plain-clothes detectives will be asking questions. Some guy might be lying there dying and the police will want to know who shot him. It's an incredibly chaotic environment in which to try to practice medicine."

*

"You do recognize your handiwork on some of the repeaters. We had one kid come in, a major trauma case, and I opened his chest—but there was no hope. He had taken a bullet right through the heart and it was virtually blown apart. He died, but I thought I recognized him. We undressed him and I saw a fresh scar on his left thigh. He was a kid I'd treated only a few weeks earlier. After we'd patched him up, the drug counselors had worked with him, but then he went right back to selling."

*

"The ones that come in talking are sad because they're in agony and they have that feeling of impending doom. They're pleading with you, and sometimes they'll grab you by the writs and hold on with this death grip. That's a hard thing to deal with. It's like the movies, when you see a hand come out of the grave and grab somebody. It's a lot easier when they come in comatose or unconscious."

IN THE COMBAT ZONE

"This violence wave is butchering the hustling process. It don't make no sense. When I first started dealing heroin back in 1978, it wasn't like that. There wasn't so much unnecessary violence. But these days the young kids out hustling don't understand that. They don't understand the importance of fear. The only things they care about are gold chains and fancy cars. If some dude smokes up some dealer's money, the dealer don't do back with a baseball bat and put fear in the dude. He thinks he's got to save face, so he goes back with his gun and kills the dude straight off the top."

*

"The first time I had to shoot a dude, it was a traumatic experience for me. This guy was a hustler out selling hand to hand. I put a gun on him and said, 'Don't move, man! Just keep real still! Do not move!' But the dude bucked and reached for his vest pocket. I thought, Holy shit! This guy has a weapon! So I shot him. When I fired, it was like the whole world was moving in slow motion. I could see the bullet go into his chest, and the force of the blast lifted the dude off his feet and knocked him to the ground.

"I saw the dude lying on the sidewalk and I ran like hell. It was broad daylight and I was shooting this guy on the street. That scared me. I thought maybe some of his buddies was gonna come after me. When I finally stopped running, my knees were knocking and my hands were shaking. It was very emotional 'cause I'd never had to shoot nobody before. I thought that maybe the dude was dead— that maybe I had killed him.

"The next morning, I read the newspaper real close, looking to see if there was anything in there about a murder. I figure the dude must've lived because I never saw nothin' in the paper about no murder."

*

"Nobody wants to get involved in a drug-murder case. Witnesses are extremely reluctant. They're afraid. They think that if they testify, they're going to get killed. Which is true a lot of times. Witnesses get threatened. They get hurt. They get killed.

"Last night, I went over to where a guy had been shot in the chest. The victim was a drug dealer and he was still conscious when we arrived on the scene. One of our detectives interviewed him, and he told the detective, 'Fuck you. I ain't telling you shit. I'll take care of it myself.'

"Half an hour later, that guy died. So we had a homicide on our hands. We tried to interview his friends and relatives, but they all told us the same thing: 'Fuck you. We'll take care of it ourselves.'

"That's the sort of thing a homicide detective deals with constantly. It never ends. I've had family members who are witnesses to the murder of their uncle or their son, and they won't tell me anything except to tell me to go fuck off.

"You can't help but get disgusted at people. When you're involved in situations where it's dealers shooting dealers, and none of the witnesses will talk, you feel like taking the case and putting it on the shelf and saying, 'To hell with it. Let 'em kill one another.'

"And if you want to know the truth, more and more cases are being handled that way."

THE COPS

"In dope cases, you have to do whatever's necessary to make the case, and that usually means using an informant. Oklahoma has a lot of lakes, resort-type areas, that are well known for gambling and drug activity. I got a girl out of the Alabama penitentiary to be my snitch because I needed someone who wouldn't be known in these areas. I brought her in, got her a false driver's license and sent her up there. She learned that one of the mayors in one of these small resort towns was into buying and distributing dope. She and I sat down and worked out a plan to try to make a case on him.

"She was a cute thing, and she bleached her pubic hair blonde and shaved it into a nice heart shape. On Monday morning, the mayor was in a meeting, so I put her in his office. When he came back, she was there waiting for him. She had on a short skirt, no underpants. He was a middle-aged man, and when she opened her legs, there wasn't a thing he could do. For Christ's sake, he'd been waiting for something like this to walk up to him for forty-five years. She took him right there in the office.

"After he got what he wanted, she told him she wanted some dope, which he was more than happy to supply. She was wired and I was sitting in my car listening to every word. She made the buy from him and that's how we got him. He took one look at that heart and couldn't say no."

*

"Down in Miami, I was sitting with a smuggler in Coconut Grove. He told me, 'One night after we'd gotten several loads in, we brought in all these duffel bags full of money. We started dumping them on the floor, and pretty soon the entire floor in the living room—wall to wall—was covered with money. We were standing knee-deep in twenty-dollar bills.'

"That's why there's so much corruption among law-enforcement people involved in the drug war. Cops will bust a place and one of them will find thousands of dollars stashed away in a back room. He'll grab a handful and stuff it into his pocket. He knows that what he grabs in that handful will be more than his salary for the entire month. He also knows that nobody will be doing any counting until he turns the money in."

*

"There are plenty of abandoned buildings in New York. The drug dealers come in, take over a few apartments and force the good people out. It isn't safe for them to walk in the front door, so they move. After a while, the landlord even stops collecting rent. He leaves a situation like that alone. The place becomes a crack house or a shooting gallery, and it's these buildings where we do most of our work.

"The dealers know we'll be coming after them sooner or later, so they set booby traps for us. They'll kick big holes in the upper floors and cover them with linoleum so that we fall through. Sometimes they'll drive nails into the banisters up a dark flight of stairs. Or they'll weaken the stairs so they collapse when we're about a halfway up, and they'll drive a nail into the banister right where you're most likely to grab when you fall.

"The dealers have started using pit bulls for protection. They'll remove the dogs' vocal cords and train them to go for the groin. You'll go into one of these dark buildings where you can't see a thing, and three or four dogs will come at you. They can't growl, so there's no warning. They just come leaping at your groin.

"I used to be an animal lover, but not anymore. I shoot those dogs without hesitation. This year alone, we've shot hundreds of dogs."

*

"As a cop, you hear about rip-offs all the time. And it's not just stick-up boys knocking off street sellers. There are big-money rip-offs, too.

"My favorite one took place about a year ago. Through an informant, we learned that a transaction was going to take place at a motel, and we had the room wired. On the day of the transaction, a SWAT team was ready to storm the motel.

"When you have an operation like this set up, you never know if it's really going to take place. A lot of informants aren't reliable. They'll feed you all kinds of bullshit and you'll end up spending six hours staking out an empty hole. But on this particular day, the relevant parties showed up right on time. The only thing was, the seller didn't bring any cocaine—he just brought guns because he was planning on ripping off the buyer. But the buyer didn't bring any money because he was going to rip off the seller.

"I was at the command post listening on the wire, laughing my ass off. All I could hear was these two dudes in the motel room shouting at each other, 'You lying motherfucker!'"

CRIMINAL JUSTICE

"Going from the streets to prison is moving from one drug-infested place to another drug-infested place. When a dope fiend wants his dope, he'll take whatever measures are necessary to get it. You'd be amazed at how easy it is to smuggle drugs into this penitentiary. I've been locked up for nine years and I've never had any trouble in getting drugs.

"Probably the most common way is to have a guest bring it in. If you've got a baby, your woman can hide the drugs in the baby's diaper, and when you're holding your little baby, you know where to look. In this prison, we're allowed to have contact visits, so another way is to have your girlfriend stick some drugs up her pussy. When the two of you are alone on the bed, all you got to do is reach between her legs and pull the drugs out. To get past the shakedown when your visit is over, you pack the drugs into a balloon and swallow it or stick it up your anus. It's as easy as that."

*

"There was this one guard here that I used to talk to all the time. I thought he was the squarest dude in the world. Then one day about a month ago, I opened the newspaper and I see this dude's picture. He'd been busted for running a cocaine ring in the prison. Him and another guard would come in with cocaine strapped all up and down their legs. Now, I was talking with this guy for a year, and like I said, I thought he was the squarest guy around. I thought I knew everything that was going on, but I come to find out he was *the man*. I couldn't believe it. I knew that guards were dropping off packages and stuff, but I never would have suspected this guy. He was a sergeant and he was up for promotion. He was going to be a lieutenant. But like everybody else, he got caught up chasing the money."

*

"For every person who goes to jail, eight to ten people pass through the court system. As a judge, I'm permitted an average of four and a half minutes per case. Given these circumstances, we're only able to negotiate pleas. We don't even wield the threat of trying these people. The plea bargain has replaced the indictment in our system. The word on the street is: It doesn't matter what you've done or what you've been arrested for, the courts won't be able to prosecute you.

"The fact that our resources are stretched beyond our ability to cope is evident just by walking through the building. We're using basements for courtrooms. The building's pipes and plumbing are exposed overhead, and every time a toilet flushes in the building, they have to stop the trial because you can't hear over the rushing water. In other basements, the jurors have to wear overcoats because there isn't any heat. There are pretrial examinations being conducted in hallways, and attorney conferences are taking place at Burger King and McDonald's."

*

"On the day that he becomes a policeman, every cop thinks he's going to change the world. He's going to be the cop that puts all the bad guys in jail and makes the streets safe. He's thinking the world is going to be a better place because he has badge and a gun.

"But pretty soon you find out that's not the case. You learn that the system isn't set up to keep people in jail. A lot of the bad guys you arrest, who really do belong in prison, end up copping pleas and don't do any serious time. No matter how many arrests you make, there are still thousands of dealers standing on street corners selling drugs. The murders and robberies and O.D.s keep on coming. The city is like a giant cesspool, and no matter how hard you work, you can't clean it up. The judicial system stinks and that hardens your attitude, makes you a little cynical.

"Pretty soon, you slow down. You don't try so hard. After you've been shot at once or twice, you shy away from potentially dangerous situations. Instead of telling yourself, 'I'm the cop who's going to make the world a better place,' you ask yourself, 'What the fuck am I risking my life for?' "

THE DEALERS

"I first started selling drugs when I was thirteen. By the time I was fifteen, I was doing $10,000 worth of business every day selling cocaine, heroin, bam, and dust. Out of the $10,000, my take would be $2,500. That is a lot of money for a little teenage boy to be bringing in every day.

"I rented my own two bedroom apartment that I used to deal drugs out of and I bought a brand-new Lincoln Town Car. I wasn't old enough to have a driver's license, so my mother cosigned for the car. There I was, driving this big fancy car and buying things that my mother had never been able to buy for me.

"I wasn't a drug user. I was just a dealer, which gave me power over the users. I'd prey on drug users the same way a lion preys on other animals in the jungle. I was strong and they were weak. I never had to do violent things because I could get a drug user to do them for me. It's a mind-boggling thing for a teenager kid to have that power.

"The thing that makes it seem right is, I'd always go home and give money to my mother. She was working, but she wasn't making a whole lot of money. She couldn't afford to buy food and clothes for my brothers and sisters. Life for her was a struggle. A lot of times you'll hear these young kids dealing drugs say, 'Man, my mother needs help.' And that's the truth. To me, that made what I was doing acceptable. My family never had nothing and I was taking care of them. Nobody could say that what I was doing was wrong."

*

"I've only had two real jobs in my entire life. The first was mopping floors and cleaning toilets at the airport, and the second was shining shoes in the men's room at the airport. Do you know what it's like to be working in the shithouse all day, man? People in there be groanin' and fartin'. Some of 'em stink so bad you can smell it coming through the door. It's degrading, man. Degrading.

"After a while, I quit going to work. Why should I be standing in the shithouse when I can make ten times more on the street? Working don't make no sense, man. I ain't got no education. Never even passed the fifth grade. I can't get no good job.

"When I'm on the street, ain't nobody asking how much schoolin' I got. And there ain't nobody telling me to put on clean clothes. All they doing is givin' me rock, sayin', 'Sell 'em, man, sell 'em.'"

*

"I was seven months pregnant when I was arrested. The cop who arrested me kept asking, 'What are you doing selling crack when you're carrying a baby? What do you think that baby is going to be like?'

"I told him I didn't do drugs. I don't smoke crack. I just sell it. Hell, I don't even smoke marijuana. Just cigarettes, that's all. But the policeman kept being mean about the baby. He kept saying, 'What's that baby going to be like?' Tellin' me that I wasn't cut out to be a mother.

"Hell, you can't hurt a baby by *selling* drugs. The baby don't know. It ain't even been born yet."

*

"It ain't hard to spot police. Any educated person like me can do it. Like just a few minutes ago, I saw a guy in a black shirt coming down the street, and it was obvious that the guy was a police officer. He was clean and he had all those big muscles.

"Wanna know how to make a bust? OK, this is how. The police can't be sending in all these big, healthy-looking guys all the time. They got to send in a guy that looks like he's addicted. You got to see it in his eyes. They got to send in a guy who looks like he wants the pipe so bad he'll get down on his knees and suck some dick to get it. If you're a cop and you just want to make a little ten-dollar buy, come in dirty with some stink on you. That's how to make a bust."

*

"The jump-out squad has arrested me three times for selling crack, and that's the worst feeling in the world, man. After sellin' to an undercover, the jump-out squad swarms right down on you. They put you in handcuffs, knee you in the back, rub your nose in the dirt, and leave you lying on the ground. The neighbors all gather round and stand there looking down at you. It makes you feel real stupid. You're thinking, Damn, how could I let this happen?"

*

"A lotta crackheads will tell. They don't want to sit in jail 'cause the only thing they're thinking of is getting more 'caine. So they tell.

"The worst ones are the women. These female crackheads, man, after they flip and start working for the police, they'll have sex with you. They'll screw you real good and be finding out information at the same time. A lot of dudes get busted like that. They'll trust the woman 'cause she's givin' him a piece of pussy. The dude'll think she's all right, but she'll be looking around, seeing where he's hiding all his coke and listening to everything about how his operation runs. Then, as soon as she gets her panties back on, she'll run and tell the police.

"A woman like that gets off two ways, man. She gets a good fuck and she don't have to do no time."

*

"When you're dealing rock, you get a lot of women, man. If I'm on the street and I see a woman that I might want to be with, I find out if she likes rock. If she does, I give her a proposition. I tell her, 'Hey, baby, you give me some head and I'll give you this here rock.' And they do it, man. Really beautiful women, all races, they'll give you head for a little tiny rock.

"A lot of hustlers like to go to bed with crack whores. Not me. I'd never put my penis in their vaginas because I'm thinking 'bout AIDS. A woman pipehead will spread her legs for anybody to get some cocaine.

"Fortunately, I've got a good wife at home. I know there's gonna be times when she wants to make love. That's something I gotta do and I don't want to be bringing no diseases home to my wife. So, I don't go down on no crack whores. I only let 'em give me head."

THE ADDICTS

"I was selling boat [PCP] when crack cocaine first came out, and right away, everybody started putting their money behind crack. So I switched over and was selling crack. I seen how crazy people was acting. I seen dudes getting shot and beat over the head for smoking up product. I seen how women would sell their bodies just to get a little hit. I been in houses where there'd be a little three-, four-month-old baby crying upstairs while the mother was next door selling her body. I'd look in the icebox and there was no food in there. The only thing I'd see in the icebox was some baking soda and some water. I said to myself, 'That ain't right. The baby ain't got no food. No matter what happens, I'll never let myself get this desperate.'

"Then one day my old lady took her mother to the grocery store in my car. While they were gone, I cooked up a rock and said, 'I'm only gonna do it this one time. I'm gonna see what all the fuss is about. And after that—no more.' I cooked up a fifty, put the rock in the pipe, lit it and took a long, deep hit. I held the smoke in my lungs for thirty seconds.

"I felt so free. The feeling was indescribable. I was standing there in front of the window, saying, 'Lord have mercy! This son of a bitch ain't to be fucked with!'"

" That first hit there, that was my downfall. Crack is the worst addiction there is. It's worse than heroin and it's worse than PCP. The craving is so powerful that it makes you lose all your morals and principles. It robs you of your dignity.

"I've seen grown men and grown women sitting down crying, saying, 'I've got to stop living like this. I've got to stop hittin' the pipe. I've got to get some help.'

"But five minutes later, when somebody is knocking on the door with a rock, all the cryin' and shit is history, man. All they thinkin' about is getting' a hit on the pipe."

*

"I remember one time I got jumped for messin' up this dude's money. I was working the street, doing hand to hand, and this dude I was working for come around and gave me some coke. He said, 'Look, man, I'll be back in two hours. If you don't have my money, I'll blow your motherfuckin' brains out.' He was giving me a second chance.

"But as soon as the dude walked way, I run off again. See, when you messin' with crack, you do crazy things.

"I run off to this girl's house. My intention was to screw this girl, 'cause I knew she like to smoke. So me and her started in on these rocks. After we started smoking, I lost interest in sex. I was thinking, You can keep your drawers on, bitch. We'll just smoke. A lotta girls will do that. If you come to trick, they'll try to get you to smoke first because they know you'll just want to keep smoking. You should always make 'em trick first. But that's not what I done this time.

"Me and this girl smoked up all the dude's product. We just smoked and smoked and smoked till it was gone. I didn't have no money to give the dude, so I was ducking and hiding, trying to avoid him. But they found me going into a crack house. Eight dudes run up from behind and jumped me on the street.

"All the people in the neighborhood were looking out of their windows, watching to see what was happening. The dudes carried me back in the alley, and I thought they were gonna kill me because that's what the dude told me he was gonna do. But they just gave me a beating, man. I was lying there on the ground all bloody, and the whole time they was whipping me I was thinking, I wish they'd stop. I wish they'd let me go so I can get a hit of cocaine, man. I *need* a hit.

"And that's exactly what I did. When they finally stopped, I went upstairs to the crack house. People in there took pity on me. This dude said, 'Man, we seen what happened to you.' And he gave me a rock. Another dude gave me some heroin. I wasn't sitting in there two minutes before I had a hypodermic in my arm and the crack pipe in my hand."

*

"After four or five months of heavy crack use, I didn't even look like a human being. I lost a lot of weight and my eyes looked all bloodshot and wired out. I looked like a person off the streets. My boyfriend let me have all the crack I wanted, but he wasn't nice to me anymore. Him and his friends would beat me and rape me. At parties they'd get real rough and throw me around the room. They'd tear off my clothes and screw me, with a bunch of people in the room. I was sixteen years old, getting raped by these men who were thirty and thirty-five years old. But I didn't try to leave. I lived in that environment—let them beat me and rape me—because I wanted crack. Physically, I was still alive, but emotionally, I'd committed suicide."

*

"The first time I walked into a shooting gallery, I couldn't believe my eyes. The gallery was located on the ground floor of a four-story apartment project in a notorious drug area. The entire project was filthy—bare concrete floors with broken glass and needles lying in the halls and stairwells. I'm talking about grinding urban poverty of a sort I didn't know existed in the United States until I saw it with my own eyes.

"In the living room of this gallery three junkies are sitting on a beat-up old sofa and it's obvious they've just finished shooting up. Their eyes are wide and glassy and they're nodding from the high—you know, junkie heaven. I'm standing there trying to talk to one of them when this little three-year-old boy runs up from behind me and starts pulling on my hip pockets, saying, 'Don't touch the needles! Don't touch the needles!' Then he points to all the discarded needles lying on the floor.

"That damn near broke my heart. Instead of learning his A B Cs, the first thing this kid's mother taught him was not to play with the needles because they'd give him AIDS. I'm ashamed to say, the thing I remember most vividly is the way I recoiled from that little boy. Normally, when you see a child in distress, your instinct is to touch him, and I didn't want him touching me. He had open sores on his chest, mossy teeth, and horrible B.O. He'd probably never taken a bath in his life.

"A cop saw me with the kid, and when we got back to the car, the first thing he did was give me a Handi Wipe so I could clean myself off."

THIS IS YOUR BILL OF RIGHTS

Graham Boyd and Jack Hitt

From *Harper's Magazine*, December 1999

The "war on drugs" began as a rhetorical flourish used by Richard Nixon to con-trast his tough stand on crime with LBJ's "war on poverty." But as the Reagan, Bush, and Clinton administrations poured billions of dollars into fighting drugs, the slogan slipped the reins of metaphor to become just a plain old war—with an army (DEA), an enemy (profiled minorities, the poor, the cities), a budget ($17.8 billion), and a shibboleth (the children). As in any war, our political leaders have asked us citizens to make some sacrifices for this higher cause. When George Bush entered office, a Washington Post-ABC News *poll found that 62 percent of Amer-icans "would be willing to give up a few of the freedoms we have" for the war effort. They have gotten their wish. Initially applied only to the buyers and sellers of drugs, exceptions to our fundamental rights have been quickly enlarged to include every one of us. Bill Clinton's legacy is not the drug-free zone he wanted but a moth-eaten Bill of Rights.*

1. Most Americans consider the right to free speech, adopted as the First Amend-ment to our Constitution, to be unassailable. But in less than thirty years the tacticians of the drug war have found ways to erode this bedrock liberty. In 1996 voters in California, by referendum, permitted doctors to recommend mari-juana as part of medical therapy. Alarmed that states were breaking ranks, the federal drug czar, General Barry McCaffrey, threatened to arrest any doctor who merely *mentioned* to a patient that marijuana might alleviate the suffering caused by AIDS, cancer, or other serious illnesses. Still, by last year, voters in seven states had approved the medical use of marijuana. In November 1998 an initiative in the District of Columbia tried to do the same. For almost a year no one knew whether the referendum had passed, because Rep. Bob Barr (R., Gal) impounded the $1.65 it would have cost to tally the vote. Finally, last Sep-tember, the courts overruled Barr. Seven out of ten D.C. voters had decided in favor of legalization. Refusing defeat, Barr pushed a bill through Congress that blocked the spending needed to enact the new law. As fallback, Barr has also proposed a joint resolution of Congress to simply overturn by fiat the will of the people expressed freely and fairly at the ballot box.

2. In 1984, the state of Oregon denied unemployment benefits to two Native American workers fired for using an illegal hallucinogen—peyote—during a religious ceremony that predates the Christian custom of drinking sacramental wine by some 8,000 years. Once upon a time, the decision would have been simple. Freedom of religion. Case closed. But Supreme Court Justice Antonin Scalia, one of the drug war's unacknowledged generals, decided that religious freedom would have to yield to the new drug-war orthodoxy. He declared that any law aimed at the drug menace could restrict religious liberty as long as it wasn't directly couched in bigoted language. But, in short order, the state began plowing directly into the affairs of more traditional religions. In 1993 the bitterest enemies, left and right, banded together to pass the Religious Freedom Restoration Act. Only seven months after the act was passed—by a rare unanimous vote in the House and a nearly unanimous vote in the Senate—a Texas church challenged local zoning laws on religious grounds. The suit eventually appealed its way to the Supreme Court , which, citing the peyote case, declared RFRA unconstitutional. Enraged, Congress has pledged to continue its dangerous constitutional pissing match with the judiciary. All this to prevent two citizens from practicing an ancient rite involving a scarce and rarely abused drug.

3. Assembling peaceably at the voting booth is a waning American tradition these days—in part because the drug war is creating a growing and dangerous population of constitutional outcasts. As more people pass through our prisons, more emerge permanently forbidden from voting. Although most states merely disenfranchise felons in prison or on parole, ten vindictive states—Alabama, Delaware, Florida, Iowa, Kentucky, Mississippi, Nevada, New Mexico, Virginia, and Wyoming—have banished more than one million rehabilitated felons from the voting booth forever. Just who these pariahs are is telling: possession of several grams of crack (a crime for which urban blacks are disproportionately prosecuted) makes you an instant felon, while possession of the same substance as powdered cocaine (a drug predominantly used by whites) results in misdemeanors. According to government statistics, blacks constitute only 14 percent of our drug-using population but 58 percent of those finally convicted. What literacy tests and poll taxes once did in containing black suffrage has found a contemporary replacement. (This is nothing new: in South Carolina at the turn of this century, adultery, arson, and housebreaking were crimes deemed necessary for disenfranchisement;

murder—then thought to be largely a white crime—was not.) In Mississippi there are 145,600 disenfranchised voters, of which 125,000 are ex-felons and 81,700 are black men. Today, one in three black men in both Alabama and Florida is permanently barred from voting.

4. In 1762 the Crown of England sanctioned the use of "writs of assistance"— general warrants that permitted the king's deputies to enter any place at any time in search of contraband, then mainly molasses, tea, and rum. Colonial fury with the writs fueled Americn's rebellion and, later, inspired the prohibition of "unreasonable searches and seizures." Since the early 1980s, the Supreme Court has authorized cascading exceptions to this rule, allowing police helicopters to peer into windows, highway troopers to search the passengers of cars whose drivers seem suspicious, and, most notoriously, state agents to smash down doors without warning and without evidence of a crime. Last August, El Monte, California, police raided the home of sixty-three-year-old grandfather Mario Paz. At least twenty armed officers shot the locks off the back and front doors. They ordered Paz to put his hands on the bed. Although he did, one of the officers believed that Paz was "reaching for something." So the officer shot Paz, who was unarmed in the back two times, killing him. No drugs or any evidence of dealing were found. The man the police had been looking for had lived next door more than fifteen years earlier. These "dynamic entries," as they are called, are on the rise. New York City has had to develop a policy for replacing the doors of homes mistakenly entered. Last year, New York police broke into the home of retired baker Basil Shorter, dragged his retarded, menstruating daughter from the shower and handcuffed her while she bled down her legs. Although no drugs were ever found, investigators insisted that their informant's "information was good." Drug dealers, they explained, can operate out of the homes of innocent people *without their knowledge.*

5. The once sacred protection of property rights is now regularly violated by drug police. Beginning in 1974 the Supreme Court blessed the unholy idea that property could be seized and sold by the government without any arrest, conviction, or due process. Under the strange fiction that property itself can be guilty (e.g., *United States v. One 1974 Cadillac Eldorado Sedan*), the cops take your properly, leaving you to prove that it has no connection to a crime. If you miss the ten-day deadline for challenging the seizure, or can't post

bond, you lose. The rule has been a boon for miserly town councils. In California, when San Jose's police chief asked why he'd been allocated no money for equipment, he was told "just seize it." For years state and local police had little incentive to divert their cruisers from local law enforcement to nabbing drug couriers passing through their jurisdictions. Then the feds pointed out that relaxed search and seizure laws plus easy forfeiture rules equaled windfall profits. Troopers began aggressively trawling their highways, using the new pseudoscience of profiling to determine likely suspects. (Profiling quickly declined into a simple racial litmus test. In 1999 the New Jersey highway patrol admitted that they'd falsified reports to hide their practice of routinely stopping black drivers but finally defended racial profiling because, well, it's just easier.) Law-enforcement agencies became so greedy that some states passed laws diverting the forfeiture treasure to the schools. But the Missouri Highway Patrol has devised a counterscheme tantamount to money laundering. When the locals make a big bust, they call the DEA and let the feds carry out the seizure. On average, the DEA keeps 20 percent of the forfeited property for "processing" costs and kicks back 80 percent to the local police. Since 1993, Missouri law enforcement has earned $41 million in seized assets and handed over less than $12 million to schools.

6. Any grade-school child knows that when you have been accused of a crime, you have a right to confront your accusers. But with drugs it's different. Unlike most felonies that involve a criminal and a victim, drug sales involve two willing participants. So to find out about such transactions, the police rely on inside information, effectively deputizing a posse of faceless informants. Because many snitches are employed more than once, the Supreme Court eliminated the right to face your accuser in a notorious 1983 ruling, *Illinois v. Gates*, which sanctioned the use of anonymous informants. Moreover, any defendant choosing to go to trial risks infuriating the judge by clogging his schedule. Most suspects, innocent or not, plead guilty and then cop a lesser sentence by becoming snitches themselves. Faceless informants are often paid by the police, and many of them continue their drug habits, now subsidized by taxpayers. In effect, the drug war has reduced our justice system to a tournament of snitches.

7. In service to the war on drugs, we have abandoned the traditional requirement that punishment maintain some proportion to the crime committed.

Judges no longer have the discretion to tailor prison sentences to fit individual circumstances. Instead, Congress has dictated "mandatory minimums," reflexively tied to the amount and kind of drug possessed or sold. Sentencing guidelines were born out of the noble intention to reduce inequality in our justice system. Too often judicial discretion meant that blacker, poorer defendants got stiffer sentences than whiter, richer convicts. But the plan has backfired. Poor minorities remain the overwhelming target for harsh sentences, but now the drug war's ever more voracious appetite finds victims within every class and race. Take, for instance, the case of sixty-one-year-old Marvin Harris, the devout Mormon engineer who invented the transistor radio. In 1991, Harris and his wife drove a friend's motor home back from Mexico. When they stopped at the border, a customs agent found 1,500 pounds of cocaine hidden in the vehicle's walls. (The friend has disappeared.) Stunned by the amount of contraband involved, a jury convicted the couple of conspiring to import and distribute cocaine. The judge, tormented that a great injustice was occurring, but now powerless to apply his "judgment," instead wailed from the bench at being forced to sentence them to a mandatory minimum of ten years. Even the prosecutor expressed regret at the outcome. Now in their seventh year of federal incarceration, the Harrises, model inmates, lead fellow prisoners in Bible study. Meanwhile, the machine grinds on.

8. America launched a "war on alcohol" in 1920 and endured many familiar unintended consequences: Rights were eroded. Decent people were redefined as "criminals." And the cops, overwhelmed by an impossible duty, simply collapsed into corruption. When America ended the war in 1933, the public didn't legalize alcohol in every instance. The law forbids minors from drinking, sales are controlled and heavily taxed, and drunkeness does not legally excuse a crime. Alcoholism is now treated in clinics, not in courts. The current drug war could end just as reasonably, except it won't. In September, General McCaffrey announced that the ranks of the enemy had swelled. "The typical drug user is not poor and unemployed," he said, citing a study revealing that seven in ten admitted drug users had full-time jobs. "He or she can be a co-worker, a husband or wife, a parent." Now the enemy is us, creating an eerie sense of historical déjà vu. The necessary "policies"—no-knock entry, property forfeiture, anonymous snitch indictments, frozen elections—would sound quite familiar to Thomas Jefferson, who cited as reasons for rebellion, "swarms of Officers to harass our

People," who "eat out [our] substance" while "depriving us, in many cases, of the benefits of Trial by Jury" and "taking away our Chatters." Not long after the war those words provoked, James Madison warned his young country: "I believe there are more instances of the abridgment of the freedom of the people by gradual and silent encroachments of those in power than by violent and sudden usurpations."

SMASH-UP POLICING: When Law Enforcement Goes Military

Dave Kopel

From *National Review*, May 22, 2000

The seizing of Elian Gonzalez will earn a Pulitzer Prize for photographer Alan Diaz, who caught the federal agent waving a machine gun at the terrified boy. The picture shocked many Americans, but there's something even more shocking that's not in the picture: Similar events — in which people are assaulted in their homes by SWAT teams waving machine guns, spewing foul language, threatening to shoot people, and trashing the house as a tactical distraction — happen every day in the United States, without media attention.

Because of the war on drugs, law enforcement throughout the U.S. has been militarized. The Founding Fathers worked hard to prevent oppression by standing armies, but the militarization of law enforcement is making more and more Americans subject to precisely the kind of violence the founders worried about.

The Los Angeles Police Department started the trend in the 1960s when future police chief Daryl Gates created the first Special Weapons and Tactics (SWAT) team. Gates had originally wanted to call it a "Special Weapons Attack Team," but changed the name for public-relations purposes.

In the 1980s, violent home invasions under the pretext of drug-law enforcement became routine. In 1988, for example, LAPD officers, including members of the department's task force on gangs, broke into and destroyed four apartments on Dalton Avenue; the apartments were suspected to be crack dens, but in fact were not. The officers who participated in the raid were promoted.

The police in Fresno, California, have taken the next step: The Fresno SWAT team now deploys a full-time patrol unit, in complete battle gear. According to criminologist Peter Kraska, the Fresno Police Department considers the SWAT patrol an "unqualified success," and "is encouraging other police agencies to follow suit."

Kraska also notes that "perhaps as many as 20 percent" of police departments in cities with a population over 50,000 have already put their own paramilitary units into street police work. In many cases, money for these deployments comes from "community policing" grants from the federal government.

When law-enforcement agencies create SWAT teams, they often assure the public that the squads will be used for hostage rescue and similar activities. Fortunately, there are not enough actual hostage takings to keep the SWAT teams busy; as a result, the paramilitary units have a tendency to look for other tasks, ones in which there is no need for their special violent skills.

Today, the vast majority of SWAT deployments are to serve search warrants in cases of suspected drug sales or possession. Serving a search warrant by violently breaking into a house (as opposed to knocking first and demanding entry) is justifiable in certain situations—such as when the occupants are known to be armed and dangerous—but not in most. Former New York City Police Commissioner William Bratton has explained: "In those instances where the suspect might be armed, we would call in a special tactics unit. Over time, though, it became common to always use the tactical unit no matter what or who the warrant was for. They used stun grenades each time and looked at it as practice."

The victims of these raids are not just people who break the drug laws. The Rev. Accelynne Williams was a substance-abuse counselor in a poor neighborhood in Boston. One evening in 1994, he was visited in his apartment by a substance abuser who also happened to be an undercover informant in the pay of the Boston police. Later, the informant tried to direct the police to the address of a drug dealer in the apartment above that of Williams—but the police misread the informant's floor plan as directing them to Williams's apartment. Of course, if the police had checked, they would have discovered that the apartment they were actually raiding belonged to a 70-year-old retired Methodist minister, and that there were no signs of drug activity at the apartment. Armed with the search warrant, however, and plenty of firearms, the police broke into Williams's apartment, screamed obscenities at him, chased him into his bedroom, shoved him to the floor, and handcuffed him while pointing guns at his head. He promptly died of a heart attack.

In Denver last September, Ismael Mena was shot dead in his home during an invasion by a SWAT team. The officers were acting on the basis of a search warrant claiming that $20 worth of crack had once been sold in Mena's home. In fact, the "confidential informant" had given the wrong address.

This trend toward excessive use of force has spread well beyond police departments: the *Colorado Daily* has reported that even the campus police at the University of Colorado at Boulder have received SWAT style "sniper training with AR15 rifles, a semiautomatic version of the M-16." (This was deemed necessary for the campus police, even though the Boulder Police Department already had a SWAT unit.)

The desire of smaller law-enforcement agencies to emulate their big brothers is one cause of police militarization; Washington's encouragement is another. A federal statute requires that surplus military equipment (such as M-16 automatic rifles, night-vision scopes, and even combat vehicles) be donated to domestic law enforcement. Another federal law subsidizes local police hiring of ex-military personnel, and it is ex-military who account for almost all SWAT team members. The Navy SEALS, the Army's Delta Force, and other elite military attack forces provide extensive free training to police tactical teams, and this training is funded by congressional drug-war dollars. But military training—which stresses absolute obedience and swift annihilation of the target—is not appropriate for good police behavior, which, after all, requires capturing suspected criminals (not killing them), minimizing the use of force, and acting with a scrupulous regard for the Constitution.

In contrast to ordinary police officers, who usually dress in blue, "tactical officers" are garbed in black to maximize their intimidating effect. Michael Solomon, a Rutgers University professor who studies the psychology of clothing, explains that black uniforms tap "into associations between the color black and authority, invincibility, the power to violate laws with impunity."

The weapon of choice for SWAT teams is the Heckler & Koch MP5 submachine gun—the kind that the INS agent was waving at Elian Gonzalez. Heckler & Koch's advertising to civilian law enforcement conveys the message that by owning the weapon, the civilian officer will be the equivalent of a member of an elite military strike force, such as the Navy SEALS. The ad copy links civilian law enforcement to military combat, with lines like "From the Gulf War to the Drug War."

But the most dangerous aspect of police militarization isn't the machine guns: It's the change in police attitudes. In a constitutional republic, policemen are supposed to be "peace officers." Police militarization promotes maximal use of force as a solution, even when no force at all is required. If the Bureau of Alcohol, Tobacco, and Firearms did not have so many "Special Response Teams," BATF might have reacted differently at Waco—taking up David Koresh's telephone offer to let them come and investigate his guns. What they did instead was "serve" a search warrant through a seventy-six-man helicopter, grenade, and machine-gun attack on a home containing dozens of children.

Janet Reno's initial justification for using a SWAT team (instead of normal immigration agents) to snatch Elian Gonzalez was that somebody in the house or in the crowd outside might have been armed. (She had in mind a security guard who had a handgun-carry permit issued by the state of Florida.) Her theory offers a rationale for SWAT team invasion of any home in the U.S., any time there is a search warrant to be served: About half of all households contain firearms, and the police do not know which ones.

In the 1995 decision in Wilson v. Arkansas, a unanimous Supreme Court rejected the idea that mere invocation of the words "guns" or "drugs" could justify no-knock "dynamic entries." But even after Wilson, no-knock operations carried out by tactical teams are routine in drug cases.

New York University law professor Paul Chevigny points out that in the long run, the police will be the biggest losers from police militarization and its accompanying mentality: "The police think of themselves as an occupying army, and the public comes to think the same. The police lose the connection with the public which is a principal advantage to local policing, and their job becomes progressively more difficult, while they become more unpopular."

An erosion of public confidence in the police has to be a matter of grave concern for anyone who cares about the future of law and order.

CASUALTY IN THE WAR ON DRUGS

Jim Dwyer

From *Playboy*, October 2000

That night after work, they stopped at the Wakamba Cocktail Lounge near Times Square, a working-class side pocket of a joint in the city's glittering wardrobe. No velvet ropes or sneering doormen here: Entry is by buzzer. At a glance, the bartender knew Patrick Dorismond and Kevin Kaiser were OK, recognizing them and a few other guys from their jobs. It was late in the evening of March 15, 2000.

The men worked for the 34th Street Partnership, a semiprivate group that provides neighborhood businesses with services that the government is too tired or too distracted to provide. One such amenity was a private security force of uniformed men resembling police officers, including Kaiser and Dorismond. They passed their days sorting wheat from chaff, directing tourists to Macy's in Harold Square or Pennsylvania Station, or rousting derelicts, dope hustlers, and other unsightly nuisances from the crowded streets.

At home in Flatbush, Dorismond had two kids and a girlfriend. He had grown up in Brooklyn, the son of Haitian immigrants. At the Wakamba, Dorismond and Kaiser stayed for two beers, long enough for Wednesday night to roll into Thursday morning. By 12:30 a.m., they could not face the long, late-night subway ride back out to their homes in Brooklyn.

"Let's get a cab," Dorismond said. Outside the Wakamba, they stopped at the corner of 37th Street and Eighth Avenue, watching for a taxi. Dorismond dialed a number on his cell phone.

"Yo, Yo," a voice called from some shadow. "Yo, homey. Got some weed?" Dorismond turned. The shadow drifted into shape, a street punk, exactly the sort he spent his days running off.

"Get the fuck out of here, man," Dorismond said.

"I just want some weed," the punk whined.

"I don't got none. Don't ask for none. Leave."

Kaiser had turned, noticing that Dorismond was annoyed and that the dirt bag was not alone. A few other shapes lurked nearby.

By now, the punk was making animal noises, snorting like a bull or something, trying to turn Dorismond's anger into a joke. Kaiser locked his eyes on the man and put a hand on Dorismond's shoulder to move him. Dorismond was pissed.

"Chill. Let it be," Kaiser suggested.

The punk barked. Another man stepped from the shadows. "Take your dog around the corner," Dorismond said.

"What are you going to do, rob me?" asked the punk.

Bizarre as the questions seemed, Kaiser and Dorismond did not have long to think about it. The other shadows suddenly took on the form of street skells, swarming around him. Kaiser yelled, "Get the gun."

At that instant, yet another firefight in the war on drugs—the American war that never ends—erupted around them on that street corner.

A black SUV pulled up to the curb, and men in police windbreakers piled out, hollering at them to get on the fucking ground, to put their hands on the wall. Dorismond and one of the shadows shouted and swung at each other, until the fracas finally found its punctuation mark: a single, ringing gun blast.

Dorismond was falling, Kaiser found himself shoved onto the sidewalk, face-down, handcuffs snapped across his wrists.

"Cuff that shot motherfucker, too," ordered one of the officers.

"No, no, that's my friend. Those other guys were bothering us for weed," Kaiser tried to explain.

He was told to shut up. He turned his head. Near him on the sidewalk, Dorismond was trying to roll over. His face an inch above the filthy sidewalk, Dorismond gasped. Blood streamed from his mouth. Kaiser shuddered, then screamed Dorismond's name. "Say another word, I'll put your face on the ground," said a cop.

"It's those other guys, trying to buy weed," Kaiser whispered helplessly. But the cops were going through Dorismond's pockets, speaking urgent, cop talk into radios.

His friend had fallen into a terrible stillness. Dorismond, with a bullet through the chest, was moving fast beyond help. Kaiser was searched, loaded into a police car, and carried it to a precinct station. For the next twelve hours, he answered questions from detectives, trying to rebuild the moment. Much of the time, he was cuffed to a chair. Early on, Kaiser asked about Dorismond, and though the detectives were vague about his condition, they told him that he had been shot by a police officer.

"What about the guys trying to buy the weed?" Kaiser asked. "Did you arrest them?"

Kaiser just didn't get it, so the detectives finally laid it out. The guys trying to buy the weed, they weren't bad guys. They were police officers, too. That strange question—"What are you going to do, rob me?"—was actually a code for help sent over a radio transmitter to a backup team. Hearing it, the other undercovers rushed in. In the struggle with Dorismond, one of these cops fired the shot. It was midmorning before the detectives told Kevin Kaiser that his friend Patrick Dorismond was now on a gurney at the city morgue. He was twenty-six years old.

Today, in the war on drugs, a man ended up dying in the gutter, bleeding to death from a bullet fired by the good guys. Rarely had the malignant stupidity of the anti-drug campaign stood in such stark relief. Dorismond's death was a mistake, but it was also an inevitable expression of official national policy.

In the fall of 1968, a presidential candidate appeared at Disneyland, determinedly climbing out of the early and shallow political grave into which his career had been thrown. If he were elected president, Richard M. Nixon promised America would face down a new enemy. For months, he had crossed the country, nimbly defining law and order as the central issue for a nation heaving with antiwar demonstrations, race riots, and cultural entropy. Speaking at a Republican rally near Disney's Matterhorn ride in September 1968, Nixon sharpened his focus.

"As I look over the problems in this country, I see one that stands out particularly," he said. "The problem of narcotics—the modern curse of the youth, just like the plagues and epidemics of former years. And they are decimating a generation of Americans." No longer would the federal government play a near-invisible role against narcotics trafficking. Nixon campaigned on a plan to end one war, in Vietnam, and the dedication of another—a siege not against a state or people, but on an eclectic list of substances called drugs.

Long after Richard Nixon rose, then fell, and finally passed on, the war against drugs continues. The torch has been passed from Republican to Democrat and back, and no party or politician has been outfervored in fighting drugs. Just in the past ten years, the federal government has spent $150 billion fighting drugs. The federal anti-drug budget this year is $17.8 billion, which is more than 220 times greater than Nixon's 1969 budget of $81 million. Compare that with the $22.2 billion spent per year by the Departments of State, Interior, and Commerce combined.

Thousands of tons of illicit drugs have been seized at borders, ports, and warehouses, from secret compartments in trucks, from hollowed-out holy statues, and from the toilets used by human drug mules detained at airports until they pass the cocaine-packed condoms they swallow. Thousands of people have died on the streets of American cities, in Colombia and in Mexico. By uncounted thousands, law-abiding African Americans and Latinos have been ordered by troopers onto the shoulders of interstate highways, their cars searched, their very races transformed into probable cause for suspicion. Since 1980, the total number of people in prisons on drug offenses has risen from 50,000 to 400,000, most of them confined at an annual cost, per-capita, that would pay for tuition, room, and board at a private college.

A milestone in the war on drugs occurred in 1986 when key members of the House of Representatives, then controlled by the Democrats, saw a chance to take the sting out of Republican charges that Democrats were soft on criminals. The plan was to institute mandatory minimum sentences for drug offenses, a notion that surfaced immediately after the death by cocaine overdose of University of Maryland basketball star Len Bias—in plenty of time for the November midterm elections. The idea was that anyone possessing five grams of crack cocaine would serve five years in prison, with no possibility of parole. Other drugs carried similar mandatory sentences. Normally, such a drastic revision to the federal code, with powerful implications for the entire justice system, would not be undertaken without a detailed consideration of the impact. For this one, though, no hearings were called. The Bureau of Prisons was not consulted. No judges were invited to share their thoughts. Speaker of the House Thomas "Tip" O'Neill, whose Boston constituents were shocked by the death of Bias (who had been drafted by the Celtics), helped the legislation sail through Congress. A new economy was created in the federal courts. The mandatory minimums can be waived only when the Justice Department certifies that one criminal offers incriminating information on another. Incredibly, the sentencing formulas of the supposedly tough legislation permit the convicts to snitch down the criminal food chain, so that drug dealers can cut time off their bits by, say, giving up girlfriends who may have done little more than answer the phones and cook dinner.

As Eric Sterling, former counsel to the House Judiciary Committee, documented for a PBS "Frontline" episode, the doorman in a crack house is now legally responsible for every flake of cocaine in the house or handled by the people who run the house. The new legislation led to an explosion in the number of federal drug offenders in prison, which increased by 300 percent in six years. Only 11 percent of the federal drug-trafficking defendants are classified as major traffickers, and more than half are low-level offenders.

Snitch culture shaped U.S. foreign policy on Manuel Noriega, the hoodlum Panamanian dictator. By occasionally dishing up the shipments or names of cocaine smugglers who used Panama as a trans-shipment point, Noriega earned a batch of hero-grams from U.S. drug enforcement authorities. The feds were happy for the collars; Noriega was content to have the yanquis weed his garden of cohorts or rivals who displeased him. Oliver North provided another coating of Teflon when Noriega promised North help with the Contras.

Inevitably, a narco-industrial complex has risen behind the colossal government expenditures. The Coast Guard deploys high-speed patrol boats, Customs flies early-warning surveillance planes, the DEA uses radar-equipped balloons to watch the Mexican border and local police get grants for narcotics enforcement operations. All these funds stitch the nets that haul in some real drug dealers— and the Patrick Dorismonds of the world.

Earlier this year, President Clinton announced he was sending $1.6 billion in military aid to fight drugs in the jungles of Columbia. The Colombian government will receive sixty new helicopters and enough money to fund two battalions. The aid will help the Colombian government attack just about any opponent or challenger to its authority—and, possibly, pinch off the traffic until it relocates once more.

"As in Vietnam, the policy is designed to fail," says Sylvester Salcedo, a retired naval lieutenant commander who worked for three years in the mid-nineties as intelligence officer on a joint drug task force. "All we're doing is making body counts, although instead of bodies, we're counting seizures—tons of cocaine, kilos of heroin." After learning of the new bolus of money being hurled at Columbia, Salcedo composed a letter of protest to President Clinton and returned the Navy and Marine Corps Achievement Medal he received last year for his work on the task force.

No one involved denies that the seizure scorecard is the body count of the drug war. And no one argues that seizures crimp the supply of drugs on the street.

Today, after three decades of blood and money, neither supply nor demand has flagged. Cheap, potent cocaine, heroin, and marijuana remain abundant.

"It would be hard to think of any area of U.S. social policy that has failed more completely than the war on drugs," writes Michael Massing, author of *The Fix*, an insightful book critical of the drug war.

The futility of the drug war does not make drug abuse any less regrettable. For the poor and working poor, the fallout from addiction runs to child abuse, disintegrating families, inability to hold jobs, and crimes large and small. Of the nation's estimated 4 million hard-core drug users, only about half have access to treatment. While the rich go to Betty Ford, the poor go to jail—particularly African-Americans. Though most drug offenders are white, black men are sent to state prisons at thirteen times the rate of white men.

In the early days of the drug war, criminalization was seen as a dead-end street. After Richard Nixon was elected in 1968, his domestic policy advisers approached America's drug use primarily as a public health issue, not a law-enforcement program. A Nixon aide, Egil "Bud" Krough, designed a model program for the District of Columbia based on drug treatment and addiction alternatives. Only half of Nixon's federal drug budget was spent on law enforcement; the remainder went to treatment. By the late eighties, when drugs replaced communism as the most reliable enemy in U.S. domestic policy debates, the Reagan and Bush administrations repudiated treatment as a policy initiative, and about 80 percent of the money was spent on enforcement. Today, treatment still isn't a priority. Two out of every three dollars are spent on enforcement.

In October 1998, 30 years after Nixon declared the drug war, another Republican politician on the rise flew to North Carolina to make a speech, exasperated by what he saw as a lack of effort by government.

"We get to a drug-free America," Rudolph Giuliani said, "by arresting the people who are selling drugs, putting them in jail for a very, very long time, and recognizing the fact that people who sell those dangerous drugs are very much like murderers because they take people's lives from them."

People simply are not trying hard enough, argued Giuliani. A complicated figure, clownishly belligerent at times, brilliant at others, Giuliani, along with former Senator Alfonse D'Amato, once made a spectacular public relations foray into the Washington Heights section of Manhattan at the height of the crack era, both dressed in their versions of street duds. Giuliani campaigned for mayor in 1993 as a man who would crush New York's drug problem with intensive policing—and also by providing treatment facilities. He kept virtually none of his treatment promises.

By January 2000, Giuliani was being celebrated around the world for the rebirth of New York. He was a candidate in one of the most heavily watched Senate campaigns in modern history: Rudy the crime-buster versus Hillary Rodham Clinton, first lady. But he had a problem. After seven years of decline, the murder rate in New York had crept up in 1999 and was starting to jump again in 2000. In mid-January, Mayor Giuliani and his police commissioner effectively declared a public safety emergency, quietly authorizing virtually unlimited overtime for the police department. Its mission: attack drug dealing, anywhere anytime. The mayor was certain that earlier drug crackdowns—not demographic or other social changes—had led to the drop in crime. And he would do it again, harder.

The new program was called Operation Condor, and it sent a flood of street wretches sloshing down the chutes of precinct houses, holding cells, and criminal courts. "In order to continue working the overtime, you are expected to produce," says Tom Scotto, president of the Detective's Endowment Association.

The official quota, say the undercovers, was five collars per tour for each team. No one sweated about the quality of the arrests. A man selling tamales on the street was busted for not having a permit. Another was grabbed for spitting on the sidewalk. Nearly 80 percent of all the Condor cases were misdemeanors or low-level violations. "We are spending all our time locking up three guys for smoking a joint, and there are no large-scale investigations going on," says one undercover sergeant in the narcotics division. All Patrick Dorismond had to do that fateful evening was surrender a joint, if he had had one, and he would have had a night in jail instead of the morgue.

With crime already low in New York City, the use of undercover officers to arrest people for minor infractions seemed to be a dangerous tactic. "If this is the safest large city in America, where are they finding all these people to arrest?" asked Bill Bratton, the former police commissioner who was given credit for driving down the city's crime rate. "In the early nineties, making arrests was like fishing in a stocked pond. Eventually, you started to have fewer fish. Instead of reducing the number of people fishing in the pond, they actually increased them. So they're reeling out smaller and smaller fish."

Two months into Operation Condor, Police Commissioner Howard Safir declared it a success. The city's murder rate, however, was still climbing. A member of the City Council stated that the name Operation Condor was also the name used for a death squad in Latin America.

"In case you didn't know, a condor is a bird," Safir replied.

Actually, CONDOR stood for Citywide Organized Narcotics Drug Operational Response. "They should call it Operation Band-Aid," remarked the narcotics sergeant.

In the two months since Operation Condor started, police had averaged 350 arrests per day. On the night of Dorismond's death, a Condor team had arrested eight men near the Port Authority Bus Terminal on 42nd Street. With the police van nearly full, the team was just about ready to bring in the night's haul to central booking.

Patrick Dorismond just wanted to catch a taxi. But the drug warriors refused to listen to him. They wanted to make some overtime. The mayor, who got them the overtime money, wanted better crime statistics—and to win another election. And Dorismond ended up dead.

Within hours of Dorismond's death, the mayor and the police commissioner unsealed Dorismond's thirteen-year-old juvenile court record. "I would not want a picture presented of an altar boy, when, in fact, maybe it isn't an altar boy," said the mayor. It turned out Dorismond had been an altar boy—and that he and Giuliani had both been students at Bishop Loughlin High School. Nevertheless, the mayor hurled abuse at the dead Dorismond and at people who did not have respect for the dangerous jobs performed by police officers—flailing at everyone, it seemed, except himself. Even the police officer who shot Dorismond sent regrets and condolences to the victim's mother.

In May, sick with prostate cancer, his poll numbers collapsing after the Dorismond killing, his marriage dissolving, Giuliani pulled out of the Senate race against Hillary Clinton.

One might have thought that the Dorismond shooting would have occasioned soul-searching about the tactics of Operation Condor. But just 11 days after Dorismond died, a team of Condor cops was in the Bedford-Stuyvesant section of Brooklyn, on the prowl for drug offenders. In pursuit of a suspect, cops in an unmarked van swerved into a tree outside a crowded schoolyard, and some of the students thought the noise of the collision was a gunshot. Then the kids, hundreds of them, had more to worry about. The suspect ran through the schoolyard and, eyewitnesses reported, as many as five undercover cops, at least one with a visible drawn gun, followed. One child got cut on the leg and another had an asthma attack in the panic that engulfed the playground. The police got their man, a 19-year-old who, they said, had sold some dope to another young man not far from the school. It was another point tallied on the drug war's endless scoreboard.

"The whole purpose of an action like that," Mayor Giuliani explained, "is to remove drug dealers from the areas around schoolyards and playgrounds because of the great damage that drug dealers do, and the police want to do that without creating disruptions, problems or difficulties for children."

Mission unaccomplished.

THE VIEW FROM THE FORTIETH FLOOR

THERE'S NO JUSTICE IN THE WAR ON DRUGS: Can Our Laws Be Moral if They Have So Racist an Effect?

Milton Friedman

From *The New York Times*, January 11, 1998

Twenty-five years ago, President Richard M. Nixon announced a "War on Drugs." I criticized the action on both moral and expediential grounds in my *Newsweek* column of May 1, 1972, "Prohibition and Drugs": "On ethical grounds, do we have the right to use the machinery of government to prevent an individual from becoming an alcoholic or a drug addict? For children, almost everyone would answer at least a qualified yes. But for responsible adults, I, for one, would answer no. Reason with the potential addict, yes. Tell him the consequences, yes. Pray for and with him, yes. But I believe that we have no right to use force, directly or indirectly, to prevent a fellow man from committing suicide, let alone from drinking alcohol or taking drugs."

That basic ethical flaw has inevitably generated specific evils during the past quarter century, just as it did during our earlier attempt at alcohol prohibition.

1. The use of informers. Informers are not needed in crimes like robbery and murder because the victims of those crimes have a strong incentive to report the crime. In the drug trade, the crime consists of a transaction between a willing buyer and willing seller. Neither has any incentive to report a violation of law. On the contrary, it is in the self-interest of both that the crime not be reported. That is why informers are needed. The use of informers and the immense sums of money at stake inevitably generate corruption — as they did during Prohibition. They also led to violations of the civil rights of innocent people, to the shameful practices of forcible entry, and forfeiture of property without due process.

   As I wrote in 1972: ". . . addicts and pushers are not the only ones corrupted. Immense sums are at stake. It is inevitable that some relatively low-paid police and other government officials — and some high-paid ones as well — will succumb to the temptation to pick up easy money."

2. Filling the prisons. In 1970, 200,000 people were in prison. Today, 1.6 mil-

lion people are. Eight times as many in absolute number, six times as many relative to the increased population. In addition, 2.3 million are on probation and parole. The attempt to prohibit drugs is by far the major source of the horrendous growth in the prison population.

There is no light at the end of that tunnel. How many of our citizens do we want to turn into criminals before we yell "enough"?

3. Disproportionate imprisonment of blacks. Sher Hosonko, at the time Connecticut's director of addiction services, stressed this effect of drug prohibition in a talk given in June 1995:

"Today in this country, we incarcerate 3,109 black men for every 100,000 of them in the population. Just to give you an idea of the drama in this number, our closest competitor for incarcerating black men is South Africa. South Africa—and this is pre-Nelson Mandela and under an overt public policy of apartheid—incarcerated 729 black men for every 100,000. Figure this out: In the land of the Bill of Rights, we jail over four times as many black men as the only country in the world that advertised a political policy of apartheid."

4. Destruction of inner cities. Drug prohibition is one of the most important factors that have combined to reduce our inner cities to their present state. The crowded inner cities have a comparative advantage for selling drugs. Though most customers do not live in the inner cities, most sellers do. Young boys and girls view the swaggering, affluent drug dealers as role models. Compared with the returns from a traditional career of study and hard work, returns from dealing drugs are tempting to young and old alike. And many, especially the young, are not dissuaded by the bullets that fly so freely in disputes between competing drug dealers—bullets that fly only because dealing drugs is illegal. Al Capone epitomizes our earlier attempt at Prohibition; the Crips and Bloods epitomize this one.

5. Compounding the harm to users. Prohibition makes drugs exorbitantly expensive and highly uncertain in quality. A user must associate with criminals to get the drugs, and many are driven to become criminals themselves to finance the habit. Needles, which are hard to get, are often shared, with the predictable effect of spreading disease. Finally, an addict who seeks treatment must confess to being a criminal in order to qualify for a treatment program. Alternatively, professionals who treat addicts must become informers or criminals themselves.

6. Undertreatment of chronic pain. The Federal Department of Health and

Human Services has issued reports showing that two-thirds of all terminal cancer patients do not receive adequate pain medication, and the numbers are surely higher in nonterminally ill patients. Such serious undertreatment of chronic pain is a direct result of the Drug Enforcement Agency's pressures on physicians who prescribe narcotics.

7. Harming foreign countries. Our drug policy has led to thousands of deaths and enormous loss of wealth in countries like Colombia, Peru, and Mexico, and has undermined the stability of their governments. All because we cannot enforce our laws at home. If we did, there would be no market for imported drugs. There would be no Cali cartel. The foreign countries would not have to suffer the loss of sovereignty involved in letting our "advisers" and troops operate on their soil, search their vessels, and encourage local militaries to shoot down their planes. They could run their own affairs, and we, in turn, could avoid the diversion of military forces from their proper function.

Can any policy, however high-minded, be moral if it leads to widespread corruption, imprisons so many, has so racist an effect, destroys our inner cities, wreaks havoc on misguided and vulnerable individuals and brings death and destruction to foreign countries?

COMMONSENSE DRUG POLICY

Ethan A. Nadelmann

From *Foreign Affairs*, January/February 1998

FIRST, REDUCE HARM

In 1988 Congress passed a resolution proclaiming its goal of "a drug-free America by 1995." U.S. drug policy has failed persistently over the decades because it has preferred such rhetoric to reality, and moralism to pragmatism. Politicians confess their youthful indiscretions, then call for tougher drug laws. Drug control officials make assertions with no basis in fact or science. Police officers, generals, politicians, and guardians of public morals qualify as drug czars—but not, to date, a single doctor or public health figure. Independent commissions are appointed to evaluate drug policies, only to see their recommendations ignored as politically risky. And drug policies are designed, implemented, and enforced with virtually no input from the millions of Americans they affect most: drug users. Drug abuse is a serious problem, both for individual citizens and society at large, but the "war on drugs" has made matters worse, not better. Drug warriors often point to the 1980s as a time in which the drug war really worked. Illicit drug use by teenagers peaked around 1980, then fell more than 50 percent over the next twelve years. During the 1996 presidential campaign, Republican challenger Bob Dole made much of the recent rise in teenagers' use of illicit drugs, contrasting it with the sharp drop during the Reagan and Bush administrations. President Clinton's response was tepid, in part because he accepted the notion that teen drug use is the principal measure of drug policy's success or failure; at best, he could point out that the level was still barely half what it had been in 1980.

In 1980, however, no one had ever heard of the cheap, smokable form of cocaine called crack, or drug-related HIV infection or AIDS. By the 1990s, both had reached epidemic proportions in American cities, largely driven by prohibitionist economics and morals indifferent to the human consequences of the drug war. In 1980, the federal budget for drug control was about $16 billion, two-thirds of it for law enforcement agencies, and state and local funding to at least that. On any day in 1980, approximately 50,000 people were behind bars for violating a drug law. By 1997, the number had increased eightfold, to about

400,000. These are the results of a drug policy overreliant on criminal justice "solutions," ideologically wedded to abstinence-only treatment, and insulated from cost-benefit analysis.

Imagine instead a policy that starts by acknowledging that drugs are here to stay, and that we have no choice but to learn how to live with them so that they cause the least possible harm. Imagine a policy that focuses on reducing not illicit drug use per se but the crime and misery caused by both drug abuse and prohibitionist policies. And imagine a drug policy based not on the fear, prejudice, and ignorance that drive America's current approach but rather on common sense, science, public health concerns, and human rights. Such a policy is possible in the United States, especially if Americans are willing to learn from the experiences of other countries where such policies are emerging.

ATTITUDES ABROAD

Americans are not averse to looking abroad for solutions to the nation's drug problems. Unfortunately, they have been looking in the wrong places: Asia and Latin America, where much of the world's heroin and cocaine originates. Decades of U.S. efforts to keep drugs from being produced abroad and exported to American markets have failed. Illicit drug production is bigger business than ever before. The opium poppy, source of morphine and heroin, and *cannabis sativa*, from which marijuana and hashish are prepared, grow readily around the world; the coca plant, from whose leaves cocaine is extracted, can be cultivated far from its native environment in the Andes. Crop substitution programs designed to persuade Third World peasants to grow legal crops cannot compete with the profits that drug prohibition makes inevitable. Crop eradication campaigns occasionally reduce production in one country, but new suppliers pop up elsewhere. International law enforcement efforts can disrupt drug trafficking organizations and routes, but they rarely have much impact on U.S. drug markets.

Even if foreign supplies could be cut off, the drug abuse problem in the United States would scarcely abate. Most of America's drug-related problems are associated with domestically produced alcohol and tobacco. Much if not most of the marijuana, amphetamine, hallucinogens, and illicitly diverted pharmaceutical drugs consumed in the country are made in the U.S.A. The same is true of the glue, gasoline, and other solvents used by kids too young or too poor to obtain other psychoactive substances. No doubt such drugs, as well as new products, would quickly substitute for imported heroin and cocaine if the flow from abroad dried up.

While looking to Latin America and Asia for supply-reduction solutions to America's drug problems is futile, the harm-reduction approaches spreading throughout Europe and Australia and even into corners of North America show promise. These approaches start by acknowledging that supply-reduction initiatives are inherently limited, that criminal justice responses can be costly and counterproductive, and that single-minded pursuit of a "drug-free society" is dangerously quixotic. Demand-reduction efforts to prevent drug abuse among children and adults are important, but so are harm-reduction efforts to lessen the damage to those unable or unwilling to stop using drugs immediately, and to those around them.

Most proponents of harm reduction do not favor legalization. They recognize that prohibition has failed to curtail drug abuse, that it is responsible for much of the crime, corruption, disease, and death associated with drugs, and that its costs mount every year. But they also see legalization as politically unwise and as risking increased drug use. The challenge is thus making drug prohibition work better, but with a focus on reducing the negative consequences of both drug use and prohibitionist policies.

Countries that have turned to harm-reduction strategies for help in alleviating their drug woes are not so different from the United States. Drugs, crime, and race problems, and other socioeconomic problems are inextricably linked. As in America, criminal justice authorities still prosecute and imprison major drug traffickers as well as petty dealers who create public nuisances. Parents worry that their children might get involved with drugs. Politicians remain fond of drug war rhetoric. But by contrast with U.S. drug policy, public health goals have priority, and public health authorities have substantial influence. Doctors have far more latitude in treating addiction and associated problems. Police view the sale and use of illicit drugs as similar to prostitution—vice activities that cannot be stamped out but can be effectively regulated. Moralists focus less on any inherent evils of drugs than on the need to deal with drug use and addiction pragmatically and humanely. And more politicians dare to speak out in favor of alternatives to punitive prohibitionist policies.

Harm-reduction innovations include efforts to stem the spread of HIV by making sterile syringes readily available and collecting used syringes; allowing doctors to prescribe oral methadone for heroin addiction treatment, as well as heroin and other drugs for addicts who would otherwise buy them on the black market; establishing "safe injection rooms" so addicts do not congregate in public places or dangerous "shooting galleries"; employing drug analysis units at the large dance parties called raves to test the quality and potency of MDMA, known as ecstasy, and other drugs that patrons buy and consume there; decriminalizing (but not legalizing) possession and retail sale of cannabis and, in some cases, possession of small amounts of "hard" drugs; and integrating harm-reduction policies and principles into community policing strategies. Some of these measures are under way or under consideration in parts of the United States, but rarely to the extent found in growing numbers of foreign countries.

STOPPING HIV WITH STERILE SYRINGES

The spread of HIV, the virus that causes AIDS, among people who inject drugs illegally was what prompted governments in Europe and Australia to experiment with harm-reduction policies. During the early 1980s public health officials realized that infected users were spreading HIV by sharing needles. Having already experienced a hepatitis epidemic attributed to the same mode of transmission, the Dutch were the first to tell drug users about the risks of needle sharing and to make sterile syringes available and collect dirty needles through pharmacies, needle exchange and methadone programs, and public health services. Governments elsewhere in Europe and in Australia soon followed suit. The few countries in which a prescription was necessary to obtain a syringe dropped the requirement. Local authorities in Germany, Switzerland, and other European countries authorized needle exchange machines to ensure 24-hour access. In some European cities, addicts can exchange used syringes for clean ones at local police stations without fear of prosecution or harassment. Prisons are instituting similar policies to help discourage the spread of HIV among inmates, recognizing that illegal drug injecting cannot be eliminated even behind bars.

These initiatives were not adopted without controversy. Conservative politicians argued that needle exchange programs condoned illicit and immoral behavior and that government policies should focus on punishing drug users or making them drug-free. But by the late 1980s, the consensus in most of Western Europe, Oceania, and Canada was that while drug abuse was a serious problem, AIDS was worse. Slowing the spread of a fatal disease for which no cure exists was the greater moral imperative. There was also a fiscal imperative. Needle exchange programs' costs are minuscule compared with those of treating people who would otherwise become infected with HIV.

Only in the United States has this logic not prevailed, even though AIDS was the leading killer of Americans ages twenty-five to forty-four for most of the

1990s and is now No. 2. The Centers for Disease Control (CDC) estimates that half of new HIV infections in the country stem from injection drug use. Yet both the White House and Congress block allocation of AIDS or drug-abuse prevention funds for needle exchange, and virtually all state governments retain drug paraphernalia laws, pharmacy regulations, and other restrictions on access to sterile syringes. During the 1980s, AIDS activists engaging in civil disobedience set up more syringe exchange programs than state and local governments. There are now more than 100 such programs in twenty-eight states, Washington, D.C., and Puerto Rico, but they reach only an estimated 10 percent of injection drug users.

Governments at all levels in the United States refuse to fund needle exchange for political reasons, even though dozens of scientific studies, domestic and foreign, have found that needle exchange and other distribution programs reduce needle sharing, bring hard-to-reach drug users into contact with health care systems, and inform addicts about treatment programs, yet do not increase illegal drug use. In 1991 the National AIDS Commission appointed by President Bush called the lack of federal support for such programs "bewildering and tragic." In 1993 a CDC-sponsored review of research on needle exchange recommended federal funding, but top officials in the Clinton administration suppressed a favorable evaluation of the report within the Department of Health and Human Services. In July 1996 President Clinton's Advisory Council on HIV/AIDS criticized the administration for its failure to heed the National Academy of Sciences's recommendation that it authorize the use of federal money to support needle exchange programs. An independent panel convened by the National Institute of Health reached the same conclusion in February 1997. Last summer, the American Medical Association, the American Bar Association, and even the politicized U.S. Conference of Mayors endorsed the concept of needle exchange. In the fall, an endorsement followed from the World Bank.

To date, America's failure in this regard is conservatively estimated to have resulted in the infection of up to 10,000 people with HIV. Mounting scientific evidence and the stark reality of the continuing AIDS crisis have convinced the public, if not politicians, that needle exchange saves lives; polls consistently find that a majority of Americans support needle exchange, with approval highest among those most familiar with the notion. Prejudice and political cowardice are poor excuses for allowing more citizens to suffer from and die of AIDS, especially when effective interventions are cheap, safe, and easy.

METHADONE AND OTHER ALTERNATIVES

The United States pioneered the use of the synthetic opiate methadone to treat heroin addiction in the 1960s and 1970s, but now lags behind much of Europe and Australia in making methadone accessible and effective. Methadone is the best available treatment in terms of reducing illicit heroin use and associated crime, disease, and death. In the early 1990s the National Academy of Sciences's Institute of Medicine stated that of all forms of drug treatment, "methadone maintenance has been the most rigorously studied modality and has yielded the most incontrovertibly positive results . . . Consumption of all illicit drugs, especially heroin, declines. Crime is reduced, fewer individuals become HIV positive, and individual functioning is improved." However, the institute went on to declare, "Current policy . . . puts too much emphasis on protecting society from methadone, and not enough on protecting society from the epidemics of addiction, violence, and infectious diseases that methadone can help reduce."

Methadone is to street heroin what nicotine skin patches and chewing gum are to cigarettes—with the added benefit of legality. Taken orally, methadone has little of injected heroin's effect on mood or cognition. It can be consumed for decades with few if any negative health consequences, and its purity and concentration, unlike street heroin's, are assured. Like other opiates, it can create physical dependence if taken regularly, but the "addiction" is more like a diabetic's "addiction" to insulin than a heroin addict's to product bought on the street. Methadone patients can and do drive safely, hold good jobs, and care for their children. When prescribed adequate doses, they can be indistinguishable from people who have never used heroin or methadone.

Popular misconceptions and prejudice, however, have all but prevented any expansion of methadone treatment in the United States. The 115,000 Americans receiving methadone today represent only a small increase over the number twenty years ago. For every ten heroin addicts, there are only one or two methadone treatment slots. Methadone is the most tightly controlled drug in the pharmacopoeia, subject to unique federal and state restrictions. Doctors cannot prescribe it for addiction treatment outside designated programs. Regulations dictate not only security, documentation, and staffing requirements but maximum doses, admission criteria, time spent in the program, and a host of other specifics, none of which has much to do with quality of treatment. Moreover, the regulations do not prevent poor treatment; many clinics provide insufficient doses, prematurely detoxify clients, expel clients for offensive behavior, and engage in other practices that would be regarded as unethical in any other field of medicine. Attempts to open new clinics tend to be blocked by residents who don't want addicts in their neighborhood.

In much of Europe and Australia, methadone treatment was at first even more controversial than in the United States; some countries, including Germany, France, and Greece, prohibited it well into the 1980s and 1990s. But where methadone has been accepted, doctors have substantial latitude in deciding how and when to prescribe it so as to maximize its efficacy. There are methadone treatment programs for addicts looking for rehabilitation and programs for those simply trying to reduce their heroin consumption. Doctors in regular medical practice can prescribe the drug, and patients fill their prescriptions at local pharmacies. Thousands of general practitioners throughout Europe, Australia, New Zealand, and Canada (notably in Ontario and British Columbia) are now involved in methadone maintenance. In Belgium, Germany, and Australia this is the principal means of distribution. Integrating methadone with mainstream medicine makes treatment more accessible, improves its quality, and allocates ancillary services more efficiently. It also helps reduce the stigma of methadone programs and community resistance to them.

Many factors prevent American doctors from experimenting with the more flexible treatment programs of their European counterparts. The Drug Enforcement Administration contends that looser regulations would fuel the illicit market in diverted methadone. But the black market, in which virtually all buyers are heroin addicts who cannot or will not enroll in methadone programs, is primarily a product of the inadequate legal availability of methadone. Some conventional providers do not want to cede their near-monopoly over methadone treatment and are reluctant to take on addicts who can't or won't commit to quitting heroin. And all efforts to make methadone more available in the United States run up against the many Americans who dismiss methadone treatment as substituting one addictive drug for another and are wary of any treatment that does not leave the patient "drug free."

Oral methadone works best for hundreds of thousands of heroin addicts, but some fare better with other opiate substitutes. In England, doctors prescribe injectable methadone for about 10 percent of recovering patients, who may like the modest "rush" upon injection or the ritual of injecting. Doctors in Austria, Switzerland, and Australia are experimenting with prescribing oral morphine to determine whether it works better than oral methadone for some users. Several treatment programs in the Netherlands have conducted trials with oral morphine and palfium. In Germany, where methadone treatment was initially shunned, thousands of addicts have been maintained on codeine, which many doctors and patients still prefer to methadone. The same is true of buprenorphine in France.

In England, doctors have broad discretion to prescribe whatever drugs help addicted patients manage their lives and stay away from illegal drugs and their dealers. Beginning in the 1920s, thousands of English addicts were maintained on legal prescriptions of heroin, morphine, amphetamine, cocaine, and other pharmaceutical drugs. This tradition flourished until the 1960s, and has reemerged in response to AIDS and to growing disappointment with the Americanization of British prescribing practices during the 1970s and 1980s, when illicit heroin use in Britain increased almost tenfold. Doctors in other European countries and Australia are also trying heroin prescription.

The Swiss government began a nationwide trial in 1994 to determine whether prescribing heroin, morphine, or injectable methadone could reduce crime, disease, and other drug-related ills. Some 1,000 volunteers—only heroin addicts with at least two unsuccessful experiences in methadone or other conventional treatment programs were considered—took part in the experiment. The trial quickly determined that virtually all participants preferred heroin, and doctors subsequently prescribed it for them. Last July the government reported the results so far: Criminal offenses and the number of criminal offenders dropped 60 percent, the percentage of income from illegal and semilegal activities fell from 69 to 10 percent, illegal heroin *and* cocaine use declined dramatically (although use of alcohol, cannabis, and tranquilizers like Valium remained fairly constant), stable employment increased from 14 to 32 percent, physical health improved enormously, and most participants greatly reduced their contact with the drug scene. There were no deaths from overdoses, and no prescribed drugs were diverted to the black market. More than half those who dropped out of the study switched to another form of drug treatment, including eighty-three who began abstinence therapy. A cost-benefit analysis of the program found a net economic benefit of $30 per patient per day, mostly because of reduced criminal justice and health care costs.

The Swiss study has undermined several myths about heroin and its habitual users. The results to date demonstrate that, given relatively unlimited availability, heroin users will voluntarily stabilize or reduce their dosage and some will even choose abstinence; that long-addicted users can lead relatively normal, stable lives if provided legal access to their drug of choice; and that ordinary citizens will support such initiatives. In recent referendums in Zurich, Basel, and Zug, substantial majorities voted to continue funding local arms of the experiment. And last September, a nationwide referendum to end the government's heroin maintenance and other harm-reduction initiatives was rejected by 71 percent of Swiss voters, including majorities in all twenty-six cantons.

The Netherlands plans its own heroin prescription study in 1998, and similar trials are under consideration elsewhere in Europe, including Luxembourg and Spain, as well as Canada. In Germany, the federal government has opposed heroin prescription trials and other harm-reduction innovations, but the League of Cities has petitioned it for permission to undertake them; a survey early last year found that police chiefs in ten of the country's twelve largest cities favored letting states implement controlled heroin distribution programs. In Australia last summer, a majority of state health ministers approved a heroin prescription trial, but Prime Minister John Howard blocked it. And in Denmark, a September 1996 poll found that 66 percent of voters supported an experiment that would provide registered addicts with free heroin to be consumed in centers set up for the purpose.

Switzerland, attempting to reduce overdoses, dangerous injecting practices, and shooting up in public places, has also taken the lead in establishing "safe injection rooms" where users can inject their drugs under secure, sanitary conditions. There are now about a dozen such rooms in the country, and initial evaluations are positive. In Germany, Frankfurt has set up three, and there are also officially sanctioned facilities in Hamburg and Saarbrucken. Cities elsewhere in Europe and in Australia are expected to open safe injection rooms soon.

REEFER SANITY

Cannabis, in the form of marijuana and hashish, is by far the most popular illicit drug in the United States. More than a quarter of Americans admit to having tried it. Marijuana's popularity peaked in 1980, dropped steadily until the early 1990s, and is now on the rise again. Although it is not entirely safe, especially when consumed by children, smoked heavily, or used when driving, it is clearly among the least dangerous psychoactive drugs in common use. In 1988 the administrative law judge for the Drug Enforcement Administration, Francis Young, reviewed the evidence and concluded that "marihuana, in its natural form, is one of the safest therapeutically active substances known to man."

As with needle exchange and methadone treatment, American politicians have ignored or spurned the findings of government commissions and scientific organizations concerning marijuana policy. In 1972 the National Commission on Marihuana and Drug Abuse—created by President Nixon and chaired by a former Republican governor, Raymond Shafer—recommended that possession of up to one ounce of marijuana be decriminalized. Nixon rejected the recommendation. In 1982 a panel appointed by the National Academy of Sciences reached the same conclusion as the Shafer Commission.

Between 1973 and 1978, with attitudes changing, eleven states approved decriminalization statutes that reclassified marijuana possession as a misdemeanor, petty offense, or civil violation punishable by no more than a $100 fine. Consumption trends in those states and in states that retained stricter sanctions were indistinguishable. A 1988 scholarly evaluation of the Moscone Act, California's 1976 decriminalization law, estimated that the state had saved half a billion dollars in arrest costs since the law's passage. Nonetheless, public opinion began to shift in 1978. No other states decriminalized marijuana, and some eventually recriminalized it.

Between 1973 and 1989, annual arrests on marijuana charges by state and local police ranged between 360,000 and 460,000. The annual total fell to 283,700 in 1991, but has since more than doubled. In 1996, 641,642 people were arrested for marijuana, 85 percent of them for possession, not sale, of the drug. Prompted by concern over rising marijuana use among adolescents and fears of being labeled soft on drugs, the Clinton administration launched its own anti-marijuana campaign in 1995. But the administration's claims to have identified new risks of marijuana consumption—including a purported link between marijuana and violent behavior—have not withstood scrutiny.[1] Neither Congress nor the White House seems likely to put the issue of marijuana policy before a truly independent advisory commission, given the consistency with which such commissions have reached politically unacceptable conclusions.

In contrast, governments in Australia and Europe, notably in the Netherlands, have reconsidered their cannabis policies. In 1976 the Baan Commission in the Netherlands recommended, and the Dutch government adopted, a policy of separating the "soft" and "hard" drug markets. Criminal penalties for and police efforts against heroin trafficking were increased, while those against cannabis were relaxed. Marijuana and hashish can now be bought in hundreds of "coffee shops" throughout the country. Advertising, open displays, and sales to minors are prohibited. Police quickly close coffee shops caught selling hard drugs. Almost no one is arrested or even fined for cannabis possession, and the government collects taxes on the gray market sales.

In the Netherlands today, cannabis consumption for most age groups is similar to that in the United States. Young Dutch teenagers, however, are less likely to sample marijuana than their American peers; from 1992 to 1994, only 7.2 percent of Dutch youths between the ages of twelve and fifteen reported having tried marijuana, compared to 13.5 percent of Americans in that age bracket. Far fewer Dutch youths, moreover, experiment with cocaine, buttressing officials' claims of success in separating the markets for hard and soft drugs. Most Dutch parents regard the "reefer madness" anti-marijuana campaigns of the United States as silly.

Dutch coffee shops have not been problem-free. Many citizens have complained about the proliferation of coffee shops, as well as nuisances created by foreign youth flocking to party in Dutch border cities. Organized crime involvement in the growing domestic cannabis industry is of increasing concern. The Dutch government's efforts to address the problem by more openly and systematically regulating supplies to coffee shops, along with some of its other drug policy initiatives, have run up against pressure from abroad, notably from Paris, Stockholm, Bonn, and Washington. In late 1995 French President Jacques Chirac began publicly berating The Hague for its drug policies, even threatening to suspend implementation of the Schengen Agreement allowing the free movement of people across borders of European Union (EU) countries. Some of Chirac's political allies called the Netherlands a narco-state. Dutch officials responded with evidence of the relative success of their policies, while pointing out that most cannabis seized in France originates in Morocco (which Chirac has refrained from criticizing because of his government's close relations with King Hassan). The Hague, however, did announce reductions in the number of coffee shops and the amount of cannabis customers can buy there. But it still sanctions the coffee shops, and a few municipalities actually operate them.

Notwithstanding the attacks, in the 1990s the trend toward decriminalization of cannabis has accelerated in Europe. Across much of Western Europe, possession and even minor sales of the drug are effectively decriminalized. Spain decriminalized private use of cannabis in 1983. In Germany, the Federal Constitutional Court effectively sanctioned a cautious liberalization of cannabis policy in a widely publicized 1994 decision. German states vary considerably in their attitude; some, like Bavaria, persist in a highly punitive policy, but most now favor the Dutch approach. So far the Kohl administration has refused to approve state proposals to legalize and regulate cannabis sales, but it appears aware of the rising support in the country for Dutch and Swiss approaches to local drug problems.

In June 1996 Luxembourg's parliament voted to decriminalize cannabis and push for standardization of drug laws in the Benelux countries. The Belgian government is now considering a more modest decriminalization of cannabis combined with tougher measures against organized crime and heroin traffickers. In Australia, cannabis has been decriminalized in South Australia, the Australian Capital Territory (Canberra), and the Northern Territory, and other states are considering the step. Even in France, Chirac's outburst followed recommendations of cannabis decriminalization by three distinguished national commissions. Chirac must now contend with a new prime minister, Lionel Jospin, who declared himself in favor of decriminalization before his Socialist Party won the 1997 parliamentary elections. Public opinion is clearly shifting. A recent poll found that 51 percent of Canadians favor decriminalizing marijuana.

WILL IT WORK?

Both at home and abroad, the U.S. government has attempted to block resolutions supporting harm reduction, suppress scientific studies that reached politically inconvenient conclusions, and silence critics of official drug policy. In May 1994 the State Department forced the last-minute cancellation of a World Bank conference on drug trafficking to which critics of U.S. drug policy had been invited. That December the U.S. delegation to an international meeting of the U.N. Drug Control Program refused to sign any statement incorporating the phrase "harm reduction." In early 1995 the State Department successfully pressured the World Health Organization to scuttle the release of a report it had commissioned from a panel that included many of the world's leading experts on cocaine because it included the scientifically incontrovertible observations that traditional use of coca leaf in the Andes causes little harm to users and that most consumers of cocaine use the drug in moderation with few detrimental effects. Hundreds of congressional hearings have addressed multitudinous aspects of the drug problem, but few have inquired into the European harm-reduction policies described above. When former Secretary of State George Shultz, then-Surgeon General M. Joycelyn Elders, and Baltimore Mayor Kurt Schmoke pointed to the failure of current policies and called for new approaches, they were mocked, fired, and ignored, respectively—and thereafter mischaracterized as advocating the outright legalization of drugs.

In Europe, in contrast, informed, public debate about drug policy is increasingly common in government, even at the EU level. In June 1995 the European Parliament issued a report acknowledging that "there will always be a demand for drugs in our societies . . . the policies followed so far have not been able to prevent the illegal drug trade from flourishing." The EU called for serious consideration of the Frankfurt Resolution, a statement of harm-reduction principles supported by a transnational coalition of thirty-one cities and regions. In October 1996 Emma Bonino, the European commissioner for consumer policy, advocated decriminalizing soft drugs and initiating a broad prescription program for hard drugs. Greece's minister for European affairs, George Papandreou, seconded her. Last February the monarch of Liechtenstein, Prince Hans Adam, spoke out in favor of controlled drug legalization. Even Raymond Kendall, secretary general of Interpol, was quoted in the August 20, 1994, *Guardian* as saying, "The prosecution of thousands of otherwise law-abiding citizens every year is both hypocritical and an affront to individual, civil, and human rights. . . . Drug use should no longer be a criminal offense. I am totally against legalization, but in favor of decriminalization for the user."

One can, of course, exaggerate the differences between attitudes in the United States and those in Europe and Australia. Many European leaders still echo Chirac's U.S.-style antidrug pronouncements. Most capital cities endorse the Stockholm Resolution, a statement backing punitive prohibitionist policies that was drafted in response to the Frankfurt Resolution. And the Dutch have had to struggle against French and other efforts to standardize more punitive drug laws and policies within the EU.

Conversely, support for harm-reduction approaches is growing in the United States, notably and vocally among public health professionals but also, more discreetly, among urban politicians and police officials. Some of the world's most innovative needle exchange and other harm-reduction programs can be found in America. The 1996 victories at the polls for California's Proposition 215, which legalizes the medicinal use of marijuana, and Arizona's Proposition 200, which allows doctors to prescribe any drug they deem appropriate and mandates treatment rather than jail for those arrested for possession, suggest that Americans are more receptive to drug policy reform than politicians acknowledge.

But Europe and Australia are generally ahead of the United States in their willingness to discuss openly and experiment pragmatically with alternative policies that might reduce the harm to both addicts and society. Public health officials in many European cities work closely with police, politicians, private physicians, and others to coordinate efforts. Community policing treats drug dealers and users as elements of the community that need not be expelled but can be made less troublesome. Such efforts, including crackdowns on open drug scenes in Zurich, Bern, and Frankfurt, are devised and implemented in tandem with initiatives to address health and housing problems. In the United States, in contrast, politicians presented with new approaches do not ask, "Will they work?" but only, "Are they tough enough?" Many legislators are reluctant to support drug treatment programs that are not punitive, coercive, and prison-based, and many criminal justice officials still view prison as a quick and easy solution for drug problems.

The lessons from Europe and Australia are compelling. Drug control policies should focus on reducing drug-related crime, disease, and death, not the number of casual drug users. Stopping the spread of HIV by and among drug users by making sterile syringes and methadone readily available must be the first priority. American politicians need to explore, not ignore or automatically condemn, promising policy options such as cannabis decriminalization, heroin prescription, and the integration of harm-reduction principles into community policing strategies. Central governments must back, or at least not hinder, the efforts of municipal officials and citizens to devise pragmatic approaches to local drug problems. Like citizens in Europe, the American public has supported such innovations when they are adequately explained and allowed to prove themselves. As the evidence comes in, what works is increasingly apparent. All that remains is mustering the political courage.

NOTE

1. Lynn Zimmer and John P. Morgan, *Marijuana Myths, Marijuana Facts: A Review of the Scientific Evidence*, New York: Lindesmith Center, 1997.

MY PROBLEM WITH THE WAR ON DRUGS

P. J. O'Rourke;

From *Rolling Stone*, Jan. 20, 2000

I am in favor of legalizing drugs, because I am a staunch libertarian who believes that a human being has the right to exercise individual freedoms, including the freedom to snort mounds of blow, the freedom to get fired, the freedom to be kicked out of his condominium, and the freedom to end up sleeping on my sofa for months, except he doesn't sleep, he sits up all night dribbling snot and drool on the slipcovers and yammering about the great times we had back when we were both majoring in street pharmacology at bong state, blah, blah, blah, until I'm ready to shoot him, and—because I'm a staunch libertarian and thus an opponent of gun control—I will.

But don't tell my wife I'm a libertarian. She thinks I'm an old loadie. In her opinion, this produces less sofa wear and tear than libertarianism: one husband-size butt print facing the TV vs. an entire old college buddy with saliva pools, coke boogers, bullet damage, bloodstains, etc.

However, calling me an old loadie is unfair. I don't do drugs anymore. They interfere with the Prozac, lithium, Viagra, and painkillers. Anyway, if drugs were legal, I wouldn't abuse them. I would take drugs with the same discipline and moderation that I exercise in my consumption of alcohol, unless I've had a hard day, or lunch with a client, or the Washington Redskins have been losing. And I wouldn't even touch the hard stuff. You have to be nuts to fool with tootski. Nuts or really tired. Because sometimes it's nice to have a little bump to get you through the evening. It's like coffee. And if you buy your coffee at Starbucks, cocaine's probably cheaper. It's like coffee that you can't stop drinking even though you're swollen to the width of a wheelchair access toilet stall and you're spurting used java out of every body orifice. Still, you keep chug-a-lugging, the hotter the better—get up on the counter, wiggle on your back, slide your head right onto the Mr. Coffee hot plate. Smell those neck hairs burn. Suck that filter paper. Feel your tongue split and pop like a Ball Park Frank. Who needs tongues? Tongues just get in the way of drinking more coffee, of getting more awake, more alert, more. . . . Speaking of alert, have you noticed that Starbucks aren't built? They just appear. You'll be crossing the street, there's a dry cleaner over there, you look up to check the walk light, look back and there's a Starbucks. I'm calling "X-Files." Ouch, who boiled my gums? And why's this toilet stall ankle-deep in latte? I'd better take some heroin to calm down.

As I was saying, I am against legalizing drugs, because I am a stoner dirtbag who believes that a human being—given half a chance—will get fuck-witted and do stuff that sucks.

Man, you'd think all those drugs were legal already, I'm so confused about drug legalization. And I'm not the only one talking through my hat. There's the president of the United States. He says, in his foreword to the Office of National Drug Control Policy's 1999 report to Congress, "Youth drug use has leveled off and in many instances is on the decline." While on page 4 of that report we read, "During the decade of the nineties, with the exception of the past two years, the rate of substance abuse by children has risen dramatically."

Retired Gen. Barry R. McCaffrey, the director of the Office of National Drug Control Policy, is otherwise known as the drug czar, which is easily the coolest government job title ever—sort of like hip, young Anastasia got Nicholas II and the czarina to ditch Rasputin and go to a Phish concert. It really makes you think how the Russian Revolution could have been mellower. I mean, it does if you've had a couple of tokes. But I digress. The drug czar, in his report to Congress, uses arguments against drugs that could be used against anything. Notice how the following quotes (with slight modifications appearing in brackets) make an effective plea for banning the penis: "[Penis] abuse impairs rational thinking and the potential for a full, productive life." "[Penises] drain the physical, intellectual, spiritual and moral strength of America." "Crime, violence, workplace accidents, family misery, [penis]-exposed children and addiction are only part of the price imposed on society [by penises]." The worst thing about these arguments is that the drug czar is right—about drugs and penises.

On the other hand, the drug czar's report also contains some powerful reasoning in favor of drug legalization, although I don't think it means to, unless Jerry Garcia isn't really dead but has assumed a disguise and gone undercover as a mole in the ONDCP. Funny how you never see all ten of McCaffrey's fingers. The federal drug control budget has gone from an average of $11.25 billion a year during the Bush administration to $17.9 billion in 1999. But the drug czar's report says that half a million more Americans used drugs in 1997 than in 1991. In the same period, the number of marijuana smokers increased by 700,000, which is the population of a medium-size city (a city with record pizza, potato-chip and Mallomar sales). And adolescent dope takers went from 1.4 million to 2.6 million, which explains Eminem, Tommy Hilfiger clothes, and why the kid behind the McDonald's counter gets lost on his way to the french fries. Meanwhile, between 1991 and 1998, the wholesale price of a gram of cocaine declined from $68.08 to $44.30, and the price of a gram of heroin fell by $549.28. These are figures obtained by the Drug Enforcement Administration. God knows how cheap smack is if you don't show your badge when buying it. Jerry is doing a great job at the ONDCP.

The people fighting drugs may be a fifth column. But the people fighting drug prohibition are working for the other side, too. There is, for example, the legalizers' argument that banning drugs is ridiculous when it's the perfectly legal substances, alcohol and tobacco, that cause most of America's health problems. Like, after we're through with the hooch and the coffin nails, let's go stand out in a thunderstorm with car antennas in our hands.

Then there's the argument that if drugs were legal, the free market would somehow keep people from taking them. Steven Duke and Albert Gross, authors of *America's Longest War: Rethinking Our Tragic Crusade against Drugs*, claim that the number of drug bums wouldn't increase, because "the use of heroin and cocaine in a free-market system would adversely affect the quality of the lives of the users." Am I missing something about the current non-free-market system? Is there a special Joy-Popper Visa card that gives me frequent-overdose discounts?

Legalizing drugs will lower their price, the more so if price is measured not only in dollars but also in time spent with dangerous maniacs in dark parking lots, not to mention time spent in jail. If drugs turn out to be a case study showing that price has no connection to demand, every economics textbook will have to be rewritten. This will be an enormous bother—if all the economists are stoned.

Maybe there's some other way to avoid more drug taking. The pro-legalization Netherlands Drug Policy Foundation has a pamphlet containing the following sentence: "Young people who want to experiment with drugs will be stimulated to learn to do so in a controlled way." Our boy Hans is doing so well in history and mathematics, but he's flunking LSD.

A certain weird—not to say high and spacey—optimism can come over people when they discuss opening the floodgates on the Grand Coulee Dam of drug legislation and letting America's river of junk bunnies, blow fiends, hop hounds, pipe hogs, mezz rollers, hypo-smackers and yen-shee babies find their own level. Milton Friedman believes that the crack epidemic was the result of cocaine being against the law. He says crack "was invented because the high cost of illegal drugs made it profitable to provide a cheaper version." Milton Friedman is a brilliant man, a courageous defender of liberty. I respect Milton Friedman. I revere Milton Friedman. But from drugs Milton Friedman doesn't know. Crack is less expensive than powdered cocaine for ten seconds. It was the marketing guys who thought up crack, not the people in accounting.

Ethan Nadelmann has a Ph.D. from Harvard and an M.A. from the London School of Economics. He's the director of the Lindesmith Center, a drug-policy research institute funded by one of the richest men in the world, currency trader George Soros. Nadelmann is no vulgar legalizer but a champion of the medically pragmatic and the politically possible. He is one of the most sophisticated advocates of drug-law reform. And even he can get fuzzy: "Perhaps the most reassuring reason," Nadelmann writes, "for believing that repeal of the drug-prohibition laws will not lead to tremendous increases in drug-abuse levels is the fact that we have learned something from our past experiences with alcohol and tobacco abuse." Ethan, what I have learned from my past experiences with alcohol and tobacco abuse is that I am a pig dog—a pig dog with a bad cough and a liver that looks like Chechnya.

The problem with illicit drugs is that nobody knows anything about them (except for those of us who found out too much, and we have memory problems). There are precedents for this. Tobacco smoking among educated people began in the sixteenth century, and it took those educated people until 1964 to figure out that tobacco killed them. Beer has been around since Neolithic times. That's 10,000 years of experience that wives have had handling husbands who've been ice fishing. And my wife still can't reason with me when I'm blotto. So how is society supposed to cope with ecstasy, which dates back only to the first Reagan administration? We may be talking A.D. 20,000 before anybody knows what to do about a complete stranger who hugs you on the dance floor and says she's in love with the purple aura that's shining out your nose.

Drug research doesn't add much to the debate. Eighty-five percent of the world's research on the health aspects of drug abuse and addiction is funded by the U.S. government's National Institute on Drug Abuse. Scientists studying drugs are getting their money from the politicians who made drugs illegal. Do you think the scientists want to get more money? What kind of conclusions do you think the scientists will reach? Compare and contrast these conclusions with the conclusions reached by scientists funded by the Medellin cartel.

Even assuming that the scientists aren't crooked, imagine the problems involved in studying something that's illegal, secret, shameful, sometimes heavily armed, and always stupid. And imagine doing this when you're pretty stupid yourself, as the Department of Health and Human Services famously is. The HHS National Household Survey on Drug Abuse is cited all over the place whenever drug policy is discussed. The household survey is America's main source of information on everything from sniffing paint (14.2 percent of white non-Hispanics ages eighteen to twenty-five have used inhalants) to dipping snuff (0.1 percent of blacks ages twelve to seventeen are current users of smokeless tobacco). And do you know how the survey takers get the—to use a dated but apposite slang expression—inside dope? They go door-to-door and ask people. They really do.

"Hi, I'm from the government. Do you use illegal drugs?"

To which everyone responds, "Yessiree, Bob. Come on in, we're just cooking up a batch of meth."

Then the survey takers "adjust for non-response through imputation," which is called, in layman's terms, making things up.

It's hard to exaggerate official ignorance about drugs. In the wake of Clinton-Lewinsky et al., America's governing class will confess to most things, but what you can't get a political figure to admit is that he doesn't know what he's talking about. An admirable exception is William von Raab, who was customs commissioner under President Reagan. Commissioner von Raab instituted the "zero tolerance" policy that meant if you sailed into Miami with so much as one soggy roach in the scuppers of your bazillion-dollar yacht, you lost the whole bikini barge. Drug-law reformers did not like von Raab, but I did. Zero tolerance gave me hours of pleasure just thinking about planting blunts on the floating gin palaces of Donald Trump, Ted Turner, and their ilk. Anyway, von Raab came up with zero tolerance because, as he says, "You can be for legalization or against legalization, and no one knows what you mean." The commissioner decided to find out what we mean when we say it's illegal to import drugs into the United States. He found out we didn't mean it. "Zero tolerance," says von Raab with a smile of satisfaction, "was something of a public-relations disaster."

When von Raab was appointed customs commissioner, the secretary of the treasury, Nicholas Brady, asked him a straightforward question: "How does the cocaine business work?" The secretary wanted to know what it cost to grow coca and refine it, who the farmers and middlemen were and what kind of profits they made, how the distribution network was organized, who provided venture capital—all the things a good Republican normally wants to find out about a company he plans to squash like a bug. Commissioner von Raab didn't know. He called a meeting of the various federal law-enforcement agencies. They didn't know. Upper ranks asked middle ranks. Middle ranks asked lower ranks. "Finally," says von Raab, "someone found an article in *High Times.*"

U.S. drug policy was being guided by the incoherent scribblings of some half-starved freelancer who . . . wait a minute. I was a half-starved freelancer back then. That article could be by me. I may have been in control of U.S. drug policy. I wish I'd known. "Cocaine comes from, um, Mars," I would have written, "and enters the United States only on yachts owned by Donald Trump and Ted Turner."

Maybe when we're arguing about drugs, we should stick to what we do know. And we do know a few things. Drugs have bad effects. Even chamomile does— to judge by the morons who drink herb tea. And let's not kid ourselves with the likes of medical-marijuana initiatives. (Good slogan possibility; Medical marijuana makes me sick!) But the bad effects of drugs themselves (as opposed to the bad effects of drug laws, drug gangs, drug money or, for that matter, drug legalization) are bad effects mostly for us drug users. And we're bad already. There are worse things than overdosing that John Belushi could have done. He could have lived to make infomercials. We don't deserve sympathy. And we don't deserve help. What we deserve is to have drugs legalized. No, subsidized. No, given to us free until we're put to bed with a shovel and are out of everybody's way. You may think that Draconian drug laws are hardhearted, that mandatory minimums are horrible. And, indeed, sending federal agents to troll the Lilith Fair parking lot so that nineteen-year-olds can spend ten years in the pen for selling grocery-store 'shrooms is not warm and caring. But legalization is cold, too. Smoking crack is a way for people who couldn't afford college to study the works of Charles Darwin.

Drugs have bad effects; likewise the war against drugs. In the first place, the paradigm stinks. War excuses everything. You can drop an A-bomb on the Japanese. No sacrifice is too great, no expense is too high to win a war. This is why politicians love the war thing. War is steroids and free weights for government. Budgets, bureaucracies, and the whole scope of legal and regulatory authority get pumped and buff. This is why we have the War on Poverty and the War on Cancer. But you don't cure lymphoma by dropping an A-bomb. Rather the reverse. Who do you draft in a war against drugs? Certainly not eighteen-year-old boys. They're the enemy. If poverty surrenders, do we put the poor on trial, like the Nazis at Nuremberg? Some people, including a number of fricasseed residents of Hiroshima, think that "the War on ____" isn't a good idea, even during a war.

Furthermore, it is very expensive to mistake Robert Downey Jr.'s impulse-control problems for an attack on Pearl Harbor. There's the federal government's aforementioned $17.9 billion anti-drug budget, plus an almost equal amount of state and local spending, plus the more than $8.6 billion that it costs to keep War on Drugs POWs incarcerated. That's about $44 billion a year to stop the use of narcotics, mostly wasted, because the drug czar's office itself estimates that Americans are spending $57 billion a year to keep the use of narcotics going. (And those Americans are presumably wasted, too.)

The drug war has also taken a toll on an institution that's even more noble and venerated than our wallet. Drug-control zealotry has led to what constitutional scholar Roger Pilon calls "the drug exception to the Bill of Rights":

I. Freedom of religion—except for religions involving peyote.

II. Right to keep and bear arms—except when you point one at ninja-dressed members of a SWAT team that breaks through the wrong door at 3:00 a.m.

III. Quartering soldiers in our houses—to be fair, I haven't noticed any soldiers actually in the house, but some National Guard helicopters have been hovering over my backyard marijuana patch.

IV. No unreasonable searches and seizures—except mandatory random piss tests.

V. No self-incrimination—except that urine in the bottle.

VI. Right to counsel—except if the government suspects your lawyer is being paid with drug money.

VII. Right to trial by jury—except in the case of RICO property forfeitures.

VIII. No cruel or unusual punishments—except to those caught selling 'shrooms at rock concerts.

IX. The enumeration of certain rights shall not be construed to deny others—except when it looks like you might have drugs in your car.

X. The powers not delegated to the United States by the Constitution are reserved for the DEA.

So let's protest and sing folk songs ("The answer, my friend, is blowin' up your nose") and stuff flowers into . . . mmm. . . . the jaws of drug-sniffing dogs at airports. Peace now!

But how, exactly, shall we make our peace with drugs? All societies regulate the consumption of intoxicants, either by law or by custom, or by waiting until you pass out and rubbing Limburger cheese under your nose and putting a live frog in your BVDs. The most libertarian of governments would have some regulations, at least to protect the frog.

One easy and uncontroversial reform would be to get rid of insane penalties. Even the drug czar favors something called "equitable sentencing policies," which would eliminate one or two federal mandatory minimums for simple possession. I personally think that people caught with drugs should be made to go door-to-door taking the National Household Survey on Drug Abuse.

As for legalization, each drug ought to be considered individually and judged on its own merits. (What fun to be on the jury.) First, take the case of marijuana. Pot has become America's Beer Jr. Weed is not going away, especially since weed is, in fact, a weed and grows like one. Besides, how much can you really say against a drug that makes teenage boys drive slow?

Nonetheless, I'm reluctant to see marijuana legalized. No drug will be permitted by law in the United States without being licensed, regulated, taxed, and hemmed in with legalization like alcohol is. No advocate of legalization is asking for anything else. Ethan Nadelmann says marijuana should be "decriminalized, taxed, and regulated." New Mexico Gov. Gary Johnson favors moving the drug economy "from illegal to legal, where it's taxed and regulated." And Milton Friedman bases his arguments for repeat of drug prohibition on the assumption that drugs would be "handled exactly the same way alcohol is now handled."

So instead of the National Guard hovering over my marijuana patch, I've got the Food and Drug Administration, the Department of Agriculture, ATF&D (Alcohol, Tobacco, Firearms and Doobies), the Internal Revenue Service, and the Environmental Protection Agency. Instead of going to jail for growing pot, I'm going to jail for violation of the federal wetlands-protection act. And marijuana has legal standing, so the next time some fifteen-year-old sucks a goof butt and walks through a glass patio slider, me and every other old hippie selling nickel bags are defendants in a gigantic class-action lawsuit—same as the gun and cigarette companies. Since only the richest corporation in the world can stand the expense and bother of selling marijuana, you'll end up trying to get a virtual high off a digital joint delivered via the Microsoft server.

All that is nothing compared with the cow-having that would be involved in legalizing anything other than marijuana. In fact, it probably won't happen. Americans are remarkably puritanical—when they aren't high as kites. (To understand this aspect of our national character, it helps to have a very bad hangover.) What probably will happen, rather than legalization, is therapy. America will go from the punishment mode to the treatment mode with hard-drug users. We do it already when we catch our own kids using hard drugs — if we have the lawyers, doctors, and money. What was a crime will be a disease. Junkies might even get an Rx for heroin. This, of course, will do nothing to stop murder, theft, corruption, or the black market in drugs. Since when was going to the doctor cheaper than hanging out on the corner? We'll end up building thousands of "treatment facilities" and sending dopers there instead of prison. The countryside will be festooned with Betty Ford Centers, except bigger, with barbed wire around them and with no cute actors, rich kids, or politicians' wives inside. At least in prison you get out when your sentence is up. In treatment you don't get out until you're "cured." Who gets to decide? I hope it's not my wife.

"No legalization without no treatment" is my motto. And maybe no legalization even then. Suppose that we do manage to obtain an unregulated free market for all drugs. And suppose that this somehow doesn't cause a horrendous head-on collision between "pursuit of happiness" and "Where's the party?" Suppose we legalize and it works. It won't work anyway.

Give Americans a legal right and they'll think they've got a federal entitlement. As I said before, we drug users deserve free drugs. Sounds like a vote getter to me. Pretty soon Democrats in Congress will be lambasting Republicans for cutting school-lunch morphine portions. And if you think Social Security is expensive now, wait until Medicare covers granny's freebase.

Nor should we imagine that drug legalization will get us our $44 billion back. General McCaffrey won't get fired or end up sleeping on my sofa. He'll just shift the focus of his efforts from jailing Woody Harrelson and annoying the peasants of Peru to educating America's youth: "It may be lawful, but ain't it awful." Maybe the drug czar will spend the $44 billion on more of those very trippy anti-drug TV ads. Have you seen the one with the cute chick busting up the kitchen? "This is what your family goes through!" she yells as she whacks the dinner china with a skillet. Who hasn't wanted to do that to the relatives?

What's the sensible answer to America's drug-policy conundrum? It's the same as the sensible answer to the National Household Survey of Drug Abuse: Just lie. I don't do drugs anymore. You don't do drugs anymore. End of discussion. New topic. And everyone who's involved in America's drug-policy debate take a powder.

THE WAR ON DRUGS IS LOST

William F. Buckley Jr., Kurt Schmoke, Joseph McNamara, and Robert W. Sweet

From *National Review*, July 1, 1996

[*Editor's Note:* When this article was originally published in the *National Review*, Ethan A Nadelmann, Thomas Szasz and Steven B. Duke were included in the discussion. Due to space restraints we were unable to reproduce their comments.]

National Review has attempted during its tenure as, so to speak, keeper of the conservative tablets, to analyze public problems and to recommend intelligent thought. The magazine has acknowledged a variety of positions by right-minded thinkers and analysts who sometimes reach conflicting conclusions about public policy. As recently as on the question of troops to Bosnia, there was dissent within the family from our corporate conclusion that we'd be best off staying home.

For many years we have published analyses of the drug problem. An important and frequently cited essay by Professor Michael Gazzaniga [Feb. 5, 1990] brought a scientist's discipline into the picture, shedding light on matters vital to an understanding of the drug question. He wrote, for instance, about different rates of addiction, and about ambient pressures that bear on addiction. Elsewhere, Professor James Q. Wilson, now of UCLA, has written eloquently in defense of the drug war. Milton Friedman from the beginning said it would not work, and would do damage.

We have found Dr. Gazzaniga and others who have written on the subject persuasive in arguing that the weight of the evidence is against the current attempt to prohibit drugs. But *National Review* has not, until now, opined formally on the subject. We do so at this point. To put off a declarative judgment would be morally and intellectually weak-kneed.

Things being as they are, and people as they are, there is no way to prevent somebody, somewhere, from concluding that "*National Review* favors drugs." We don't; we deplore their use; we urge the stiffest feasible sentences against anyone convicted of selling a drug to a minor. But that said, it is our judgment that the war on drugs has failed, that it is diverting intelligent energy away from how to deal with the problem of addiction, that it is wasting our resources, and that it is encouraging civil, judicial, and penal procedures associated with police states. We all agree on movement toward legalization, even though we may differ on just how far.

We are joined in our judgment by Ethan A. Nadelmann, a scholar and researcher [*This article is not included in* Busted–M.G.]; Kurt Schmoke, a mayor and former prosecutor; Joseph D. McNamara, a former police chief; Robert W. Sweet, a federal judge and former prosecutor; Thomas Szasz, a psychiatrist [*This article is not included in* Busted–M.G.]; and Steven B. Duke, a law professor [*This article is not included in* Busted–M.G.]. Each has his own emphases, as one might expect. All agree that the celebrated war has failed, and that it is time to go home, and to mobilize fresh thought on the drug problem in the context of a free society. This symposium is our contribution to such thought.

—The Editors

WILLIAM F. BUCKLEY JR.

Last summer WFB was asked by the New York Bar Association to make a statement to the panel of lawyers considering the drug question. He made the following statement:

We are speaking of a plague that consumes an estimated $75 billion per year of public money, exacts an estimated $70 billion a year from consumers, is responsible for nearly 50 percent of the million Americans who are today in jail, occupies an estimated 50 per-cent of the trial time of our judiciary, and takes the time of 400,000 policemen—yet a plague for which no cure is at hand, nor in prospect.

Perhaps you, ladies and gentlemen of the Bar, will understand it if I chronicle my own itinerary on the subject of drugs and public policy. When I ran for mayor of New York, the political race was jocular, but the thought given to municipal problems was entirely serious, and in my paper on drugs and in my post-election book I advocated their continued embargo, but on unusual grounds. I had read—and I think the evidence continues to affirm it—that drug-taking is a gregarious activity. What this means, I said, is that an addict is in pursuit of company and therefore attempts to entice others to share his habit with him. Under the circumstances, I said, it can reasonably be held that drug-taking is a contagious disease and, accordingly, subject to the conventional restrictions employed to shield the innocent from Typhoid Mary. Some sport was made of my position by libertarians, including Professor Milton Friedman, who asked whether the police might legitimately be summoned if it were established that keeping company with me was a contagious activity.

I recall all of this in search of philosophical perspective. Back in 1965 I sought to pay conventional deference to libertarian presumptions against outlawing any activity potentially harmful only to the person who engages in that activity. I cited

John Stuart Mill and, while at it, opined that there was no warrant for requiring motorcyclists to wear a helmet. I was seeking, and I thought I had found, a reason to override the presumption against intercession by the state.

About ten years later, I deferred to a different allegiance, this one not the presumptive opposition to state intervention, but a different order of priorities. A conservative should evaluate the practicality of a legal constriction, as, for instance, in those states whose statute books continue to outlaw sodomy, which interdiction is unenforceable, making the law nothing more than print-on-paper. I came to the conclusion that the so-called war against drugs was not working, that it would not work absent a change in the structure of the civil rights to which we are accustomed and to which we cling as a valuable part of our patrimony. And that therefore if that war against drugs is not working, we should look into what effects the war has, a canvass of the casualties consequent on its failure to work. That consideration encouraged me to weigh utilitarian principles: the Benthamite calculus of pain and pleasure introduced by the illegalization of drugs.

A year or so ago I thought to calculate a ratio, however roughly arrived at, toward the elaboration of which I would need to place a dollar figure on deprivations that do not lend themselves to quantification. Yet the law, lacking any other recourse, every day countenances such quantifications, as when asking a jury to put a dollar figure on the damage done by the loss of a plaintiff's right arm, amputated by defective machinery at the factory. My enterprise became allegorical in character—I couldn't do the arithmetic—but the model, I think, proves useful in sharpening perspectives.

Professor Steven Duke of Yale Law School, in his valuable book, *America's Longest War: Rethinking Our Tragic Crusade against Drugs*, and scholarly essay, "Drug Prohibition: An Unnatural Disaster," reminds us that it isn't the use of illegal drugs that we have any business complaining about, it is the abuse of such drugs. It is acknowledged that tens of millions of Americans (I have seen the figure 85 million) have at one time or another consumed, or exposed themselves to, an illegal drug. But the estimate authorized by the federal agency charged with such explorations is that there are not more than 1 million regular cocaine users, defined as those who have used the drug at least once in the preceding week. There are (again, an informed estimate) 5 million Americans who regularly use marijuana; and again, an estimated 70 million who once upon a time, or even twice upon a time, inhaled marijuana. From the above we reasonably deduce that Americans who abuse a drug, here defined as Americans who become addicted to it or even habituated to it, are a very small percentage of those who have experimented with a drug, or who continue to use a drug without any observable distraction in their lives or careers. About such users one might say that they are the equivalent of those Americans who drink liquor but do not become alcoholics, or those Americans who smoke cigarettes but do not suffer a shortened lifespan as a result.

Curiosity naturally flows to ask, next, How many users of illegal drugs in fact die from the use of them? The answer is complicated in part because marijuana finds itself lumped together with cocaine and heroin, and nobody has ever been found dead from marijuana. The question of deaths from cocaine is complicated by the factor of impurity. It would not be useful to draw any conclusions about alcohol consumption, for instance, by observing that, in 1931, 1,000 Americans died from alcohol consumption if it happened that half of those deaths, or more than half, were the result of drinking alcohol with toxic ingredients extrinsic to the drug as conventionally used. When alcohol was illegal, the consumer could never know whether he had been given relatively harmless alcohol to drink — such alcoholic beverages as we find today in the liquor store — or whether the bootlegger had come up with paralyzing rotgut. By the same token, purchasers of illegal cocaine and heroin cannot know whether they are consuming a drug that would qualify for regulated consumption after clinical analysis.

But we do know this, and I approach the nexus of my inquiry, which is that more people die every year as a result of the war against drugs than die from what we call, generically, overdosing. These fatalities include, perhaps most prominently, drug merchants who compete for commercial territory, but include also people who are robbed and killed by those desperate for money to buy the drug to which they have become addicted.

This is perhaps the moment to note that the pharmaceutical cost of cocaine and heroin is approximately 2 percent of the street price of those drugs. Since a cocaine addict can spend as much as $1,000 per week to sustain his habit, he would need to come up with that $1,000. The approximate fencing cost of stolen goods is 80 percent, so that to come up with $1,000 can require stealing $5,000 worth of jewels, cars, whatever. We can see that at free-market rates, $20 per week would provide the addict with the cocaine which, in this wartime drug situation, requires of him $1,000.

My mind turned, then, to auxiliary expenses — auxiliary pains, if you wish. The crime rate, whatever one made of its modest curtsy last year toward diminution, continues its secular rise. Serious crime is 480 percent higher than in 1965. The correlation is not absolute, but it is suggestive: crime is reduced by the number of available enforcers of law and order, namely policemen. The heralded new crime legislation, passed last year and acclaimed by President Clinton, provides for 100,000 extra policemen, even if only for a limited amount of time. But 400,000 policemen would be freed to pursue criminals engaged in activity other than the sale and distribution of drugs if such sale and distribution, at a price at which there was no profit, were to be done by, say, a federal drugstore.

So then we attempt to put a value on the goods stolen by addicts. The figure arrived at by Professor Duke is $10 billion. But we need to add to this pain of stolen property, surely, the extra-material pain suffered by victims of robbers. If someone breaks into your house at night, perhaps holding you at gunpoint while taking your money and your jewelry and whatever, it is reasonable to assign a higher "cost" to the episode than the commercial value of the stolen money and jewelry. If we were modest, we might reasonably, however arbitrarily, put at $1,000 the "value" of the victim's pain. But then the hurt, the psychological trauma, might be evaluated by a jury at ten times, or one hundred times, that sum.

But we must consider other factors, not readily quantifiable, but no less tangible. Fifty years ago, to walk at night across Central Park was no more adventurous than to walk down Fifth Avenue. But walking across the park is no longer done, save by the kind of people who climb the Matterhorn. Is it fair to put a value on a lost amenity? If the Metropolitan Museum were to close, mightn't we, without fear of distortion, judge that we had been deprived of something valuable? What value might we assign to confidence that, at night, one can sleep without fear of intrusion by criminals seeking money or goods exchangeable for drugs?

Pursuing utilitarian analysis, we ask: What are the relative costs, on the one hand, of medical and psychological treatment for addicts and, on the other, incarceration for drug offenses? It transpires that treatment is seven times more cost-effective. By this is meant that one dollar spent on the treatment of an addict reduces the probability of continued addiction seven times more than one dollar spent on incarceration. Looked at another way: Treatment is not now available for almost half of those who would benefit from it. Yet we are willing to build more and more jails in which to isolate drug users even though at one-seventh the cost of building and maintaining jail space and pursuing, detaining, and prosecuting the drug user, we could subsidize commensurately effective medical care and psychological treatment.

I have spared you, even as I spared myself, an arithmetical consummation of my inquiry, but the data here cited instruct us that the cost of the drug war is many times more painful, in all its manifestations, than would be the licensing of drugs combined with intensive education of non-users and intensive education designed to warn those who experiment with drugs. We have seen a substantial reduction in the use of tobacco over the last thirty years, and this is not because tobacco became illegal but because a sentient community began, in substantial numbers, to apprehend the high cost of tobacco to human health, even as, we can assume, a growing number of Americans desist from practicing unsafe sex and using polluted needles in this age of AIDS. If 80 million Americans can experiment with drugs and resist addiction using information publicly available, we can reasonably hope that approximately the same number would resist the temptation to purchase such drugs even if they were available at a federal drugstore at the mere cost of production.

And added to the above is the point of civil justice. Those who suffer from the abuse of drugs have themselves to blame for it. This does not mean that society is absolved from active concern for their plight. It does mean that their plight is subordinate to the plight of those citizens who do not experiment with drugs but whose life, liberty, and property are substantially affected by the illegalization of the drugs sought after by the minority.

I have not spoken of the cost to our society of the astonishing legal weapons available now to policemen and prosecutors; of the penalty of forfeiture of one's home and property for violation of laws which, though designed to advance the war against drugs, could legally be used—I am told by learned counsel—as penalties for the neglect of one's pets. I leave it at this, that it is outrageous to live in a society whose laws tolerate sending young people to life in prison because they grew, or distributed, a dozen ounces of marijuana. I would hope that the good offices of your vital profession would mobilize at least to protest such excesses of wartime zeal, the legal equivalent of a My Lai massacre. And perhaps proceed to recommend the legalization of the sale of most drugs, except to minors.

KURT SCHMOKE

Mayor Kurt Schmoke of Baltimore may be the only sitting politician who advocates, if not outright legalization, reforms in that direction. But even if he is lonely, he is not hopeless on the question of democratic political enlightenment. Mr. Schmoke was first elected mayor in 1987. He is a graduate of Yale University and a Rhodes Scholar.

Serious problems require serious minds. That may help explain why William F. Buckley Jr. was one of the first public figures to acknowledge that the war on drugs is a failure. I don't know how Mr. Buckley's early apostasy about the war on drugs was greeted by his conservative colleagues—although it's not hard to guess—but I remember the reaction in 1988 to my own call for a national debate on that war. A leading congressional liberal called me the most dangerous man in America. A national magazine referred to me as "a nice young man who had a bright future." Many of my political supporters encouraged me to drop the subject and stick to potholes.

Potholes are important, but, as Mr. Buckley argued to the New York Bar Association, dropping the subject of the war on drugs means dropping any hope of solving some of America's most difficult social problems. The war on drugs isn't a solution in search of a problem. It's a problem in search of a solution.

How big a problem? Very big. As Mr. Buckley points out, "More people die every year as a result of the war on drugs than die from what we call, generically, overdosing." He is similarly correct in noting that blanket prohibition is a major source of crime: it inflates the price of drugs, inviting new criminals to enter the trade; reduces the number of police officers available to investigate violent crime; fosters adulterated, even poisonous, drugs; and contributes significantly to the transmission of HIV. These are not problems that are merely tangential to the war on drugs. These are problems caused, or made substantially worse, by the war on drugs.

That is why I have long advocated that the war on drugs be fought as a public-health war. This is sometimes called medicalization, or regulated distribution. Under this alternative to the war on drugs, the government would set up a regulatory regime to pull addicts into the public-health system. The government, not criminal traffickers, would control the price, distribution, and purity of addictive substances—which it already does with prescription drugs. This would take most of the profit out of drug trafficking, and it is profits that drive the crime. Addicts would be treated—and if necessary maintained—under medical auspices. Children would find it harder, not easier, to get their hands on drugs. And law enforcement would be able to concentrate on the highest echelons of drug-trafficking enterprises.

I do not specifically endorse the idea of a federal drugstore, particularly if that means selling drugs to people who are not already physically or psychologically addicted. On the other hand, I do support a national commission to study *all* possible alternatives (including legalization) to our failed strategy of blanket prohibition. This commission would be similar to the 1929 Wickersham Commission, which President Hoover set up to study how to enforce alcohol prohibition more strictly. Although Hoover tried to conceal the results, the commission concluded that alcohol prohibition was, in the words of Walter Lippmann, a "helpless failure." I believe that an objective and nonpartisan inquiry would come to the same conclusion about the war on drugs.

I also support Mr. Buckley's idea of applying a "utilitarian" calculus to the war on drugs. Congress is quite enthusiastic about weighing the costs and benefits of health care, welfare, community development, and other domestic programs. It should apply a similar analysis to the war on drugs, a war that is now costing the Federal Government $14 billion a year.

In weighing the costs and benefits, Congress would not have to start from scratch. There have been many studies and experiments, including our needle-exchange program in Baltimore. This program costs $160,000 a year. The cost to the state of Maryland of taking care of just one adult AIDS patient infected through the sharing of a syringe is $102,000 to $120,000. In other words, if just two addicts are protected from HIV through the city's needle exchange, the program will have paid for itself.

But a cost-benefit analysis for the war on drugs would do more than offer a guide to the sensible allocation of federal dollars. It would also make advocating changes in the war on drugs less politically risky for elected officials. Unfortunately, that risk has kept most political leaders in lockstep support of the war on drugs.

I understand their reluctance to call for an end to blanket prohibition, especially since individual mayors and governors cannot, by themselves, end the war on drugs or its devastating effects on their communities. However, I also believe that the political risks of debating and criticizing the war on drugs have been overstated. I have been reelected twice since 1988. In my most recent election, last year, my opponent specifically attacked my call for a new strategy in the war on drugs. She advocated "zero tolerance," which is more of a slogan than a policy, and said she would sign the Atlanta resolution, which supports the status quo. In spite of her distortions of my record on drug policy, I won re-election by a 20-point margin, the widest margin in my political career.

Although I strongly believe that changes in national drug policy must be national in scope, I have nevertheless tried to demonstrate that some reforms can be made on the local level. For example, in 1993 I formed a Mayor's Working Group on Drug Policy Reform, and I have since implemented most of its major recommendations. These recommendations included providing for more community policing; encouraging Baltimore's teaching hospitals to make addiction treatment a larger part of their curriculum; and, most important, developing the needle-exchange program mentioned above.

Needle exchange was my top legislative priority in 1994. We could not begin the program without a change in the state's drug-paraphernalia laws. In the previous two years, lawmakers had been reluctant to go along, in part out of fear that they would be accused of condoning drug use. But in 1994, we were able to convince the legislature that needle exchange would not increase drug use but instead would save lives, and perhaps even reduce crime.

The most politically effective argument in selling needle exchange was that it would slow the spread of AIDS. That is because 70 percent of new AIDS cases in Baltimore are related to intravenous drug use, and AIDS is now the number-one killer of both young men and young women in Baltimore. (This crisis is not unique to Baltimore, and the problem is especially horrendous for African-Americans. A recent report entitled "Health Emergency: The Spread of Drug-Related AIDS among African-Americans and Latinos," shows that 73,000 African-Americans have drug-related AIDS or have died from it. Among people who inject drugs, African-Americans are almost five times as likely as whites to be diagnosed with AIDS. And for African-Americans, the risk of getting AIDS is seven times greater than the risk of dying from an overdose.)

I'm proud that Baltimore now has the largest government-run needle exchange program in the country. That program is being thoroughly evaluated by the Johns Hopkins School of Public Health and Hygiene. I expect that evaluation to show that needle exchange is saving lives, a claim that the war on drugs has not been able to make for more than eighty years.

Mario Cuomo once made an observation that both liberals and conservatives should feel comfortable endorsing. He said that policymakers must distinguish between ideas that sound good and good ideas that are sound. The current war on drugs is an idea that sounds good, but it is not a good idea that is sound. After hundreds of billions of dollars spent trying to stop the supply and demand of drugs, after the break-up of thousands of families because of the arrest of a non-violent drug offender, after eight decades of failure, how much longer will the war on drugs continue?

I once told a television reporter that the war on drugs was our domestic Vietnam. Conservatives and liberals disagree about the justice of that war. But we generally agree that the strategy for fighting it didn't work, and as a result the war lasted too long and cost too many lives. The same is true of the war on drugs. It's time to bring this enervating war to an end. It's time for peace.

JOSEPH D. McNAMARA

We turned next to a former police chief—Mr. McNamara was chief of police in Kansas City, Missouri, and San Jose, California—to inquire into the special problems of the war on drugs on the street. Mr. McNamara, who has a doctorate in public administration from Harvard, is the author of four books on policing and is currently a research fellow at the Hoover Institution.

"It's the money, stupid." After 35 years as a police officer in three of the country's largest cities, that is my message to the righteous politicians who obstinately proclaim that a war on drugs will lead to a drug-free America. About $500 worth of heroin or cocaine in a source country will bring in as much as $100,000 on the streets of an American city. All the cops, armies, prisons, and executions in the world cannot impede a market with that kind of tax-free profit margin. It is the illegality that permits the obscene markup, enriching drug traffickers, distributors, dealers, crooked cops, lawyers, judges, politicians, bankers, businessmen.

Naturally, these people are against reform of the drug laws. Drug crooks align themselves with their avowed enemies, such as the Drug Enforcement Administration, in opposing drug reform. They are joined by many others with vested economic interests. President Eisenhower warned of a military-industrial complex that would elevate the defense budget unnecessarily. That military-industrial complex pales in comparison to the host of industries catering to our national puritanical hypocrisy—researchers willing to tell the government what it wants to hear, prison builders, correction and parole officers' associations, drug-testing companies, and dubious purveyors of anti-drug education. Mayor Schmoke is correct about the vested interests in the drug war.

Sadly, the police have been pushed into a war they did not start and cannot win. It was not the police who lobbied in 1914 for passage of the Harrison Act, which first criminalized drugs. It was the Protestant missionary societies in China, the Woman's Christian Temperance Union, and other such organizations that viewed the taking of psychoactive substances as sinful. These groups gradually got their religious tenets enacted into penal statutes under which the "sinners" go to jail. The religious origin is significant for two reasons. If drugs had been outlawed because the police had complained that drug use caused crime and disorder, the policy would have been more acceptable to the public and won more compliance. And the conviction that the use of certain drugs is immoral chills the ability to scrutinize rationally and to debate the effects of the drug war. When Ethan Nadelmann pointed out once that it was illogical for the most hazardous drugs, alcohol, and nicotine to be legal while less dangerous drugs were illegal, he was roundly denounced. A leading conservative supporter of the drug war contended that while alcohol and nicotine addiction was unhealthy and could even cost lives, addiction to illegal drugs could result in the loss of one's soul. No empirical proof was given.

The demonizing of these drugs and their users encourages demagoguery. William Bennett, the nation's first drug czar, would cut off the heads of drug sellers. Bennett's anti-drug rhetoric is echoed by Joseph Califano, the liberal former Secretary of Health, Education, and Welfare, now chairman of the Center on Addic-

tion and Substance Abuse at Columbia University. Last June, the Center hysteri-
cally suggested (with great media coverage) that binge drinking and other substance abuse were taking over the nation's colleges, leading to an increase in rapes,
assaults, and murders and to the spread of AIDS and other sexually transmitted diseases. The validity of the research in Califano's report was persuasively debunked
by Kathy McNamara-Meis, writing in *Forbes Media Critic*. She was equally critical
of the media for accepting the Center's sensational statements.

Conservatives like Bennett normally advocate minimal government. Liberals
like Califano ordinarily recoil from the draconian prison sentences and property
seizures used in the drug war. This illustrates why it is so difficult to get politicians to concede that alternative approaches to drug control need to be studied.
We are familiar with the perception that the first casualty in any war is truth.
Eighty years of drug-war propaganda has so influenced public opinion that most
politicians believe they will lose their jobs if their opponents can claim they are
soft on drugs and crime. Yet, public doubt is growing. Gallup reports that in
1990 only 4 percent of Americans believed that "arresting the people who use
drugs" is the best way for the government to allocate resources.

It was my own experience as a policeman trying to enforce the laws against
drugs that led me to change my attitude about drug-control policy. The analogy
to the Vietnam War is fitting. I was a willing foot soldier at the start of the
modern drug war, pounding a beat in Harlem. During the early 1960s, as heroin
use spread, we made many arrests, but it did not take long before cops realized
that arrests did not lessen drug selling or drug use.

I came to realize just how ineffective we were in deterring drug use one day
when my partner and I arrested an addict for possession of a hypodermic needle
and heroin. Our prisoner had already shot up, but the heroin charge we were
prepared to level at him was based on the tiny residue in the bottle cap used to
heat the fix. It was petty, but then—and now—such arrests are valued because
they can be used to claim success, like the body counts during the Vietnam War.

In this case the addict offered to "give" us a pusher in exchange for letting
him go. He would lure the pusher into a hallway where we could then arrest
him in the act of selling drugs. We trailed the addict along Lenox Avenue. To
our surprise, he spoke to one man after another.

It suddenly struck me as humiliating, the whole scene. Here it was, broad
daylight. We were brilliantly visible, in uniform, in a marked police car: and yet
a few feet away, our quarry was attempting one drug transaction after another.
The first two dealers weren't deterred by our presence—they were simply sold

out, and we could not arrest them without the goods. We finally arrested the third pusher, letting the first addict escape, as we had covenanted. The man we brought in was selling drugs only to support his own habit.

Another inherent difficulty in drug enforcement is that violators are engaging in consensual activity and seek privacy. Every day, millions of drug crimes similar to what took place in front of our police car occur without police knowledge. To enforce drug laws the police have to resort to undercover work, which is dangerous to them and also to innocent bystanders. Drug enforcement often involves questionable ethical behavior by the police, such as what we did in letting a guilty person go free because he enticed someone else into violating the law.

Soldiers in a war need to dehumanize the enemy, and many cops look on drug users as less than human. A former police chief of Los Angeles, Daryl Gates, testified before the United States Senate that casual users should be taken out and shot. He defended the statement to the *Los Angeles Times* by saying, "We're in a war." New York police officers convicted of beating and robbing drug dealers (their boss at the time is now Director of the White House's Office of National Drug Control Policy) rationalized their crimes by saying it was impossible to stop drug dealing and these guys were the enemy. Why should they get to keep all the money?

Police scandals are an untallied cost of the drug war. The FBI, the Drug Enforcement Administration, and even the Coast Guard have had to admit to corruption. The gravity of the police crimes is as disturbing as the volume. In New Orleans, a uniformed cop in league with a drug dealer has been convicted of murdering her partner and shop owners during a robbery committed while she was on patrol. In Washington, D.C., and in Atlanta, cops in drug stings were arrested for stealing and taking bribes. New York State troopers falsified drug evidence that sent people to prison.

And it is not just the rank and file. The former police chief of Detroit went to prison for stealing police drug-buy money. In a small New England town, the chief stole drugs from the evidence locker for his own use. And the DEA agent who arrested Panama's General Noriega is in jail for stealing laundered drug money.

The drug war is as lethal as it is corrupting. And the police and drug criminals are not the only casualties. An innocent 75-year-old African-American minister died of a heart attack struggling with Boston cops who were mistakenly arresting him because an informant had given them the wrong address. A rancher in Ventura County, California, was killed by a police SWAT team serving a search warrant in the mistaken belief that he was growing marijuana. In Los Angeles, a three-year-old girl died of gunshot wounds after her mother took a wrong turn into a street controlled by a drug-dealing gang. They fired on the car because it had invaded their marketplace.

The violence comes from the competition for illegal profits among dealers, not from crazed drug users. Professor Milton Friedman has estimated that as many as 10,000 additional homicides a year are plausibly attributed to the drug war.

Worse still, the drug war has become a race war in which nonwhites are arrested and imprisoned at four to five times the rate whites are, even though most drug crimes are committed by whites. The Sentencing Research Project reports that one-third of black men are in jail or under penal supervision, largely because of drug arrests. The drug war has established thriving criminal enterprises which recruit teenagers into criminal careers.

It was such issues that engaged law-enforcement leaders—most of them police chiefs—from fifty agencies during a two-day conference at the Hoover Institution in May 1995. Among the speakers was our colleague in this symposium, Mayor Kurt Schmoke, who told the group that he had visited a high school and asked the students if the high dropout rate was due to kids being hooked on drugs. He was told that the kids were dropping out because they were hooked on drug money, not drugs. He also told us that when he went to community meetings he would ask the audience three questions. 1) "Have we won the drug war?" People laughed. 2) "Are we winning the drug war?" People shook their heads. 3) "If we keep doing what we are doing will we have won the drug war in ten years?" The answer was a resounding No.

At the end of the conference, the police participants completed an evaluation form. Ninety percent voted no confidence in the war on drugs. They were unanimous in favoring more treatment and education over more arrests and prisons. They were unanimous in recommending a presidential blue-ribbon commission to evaluate the drug war and to explore alternative methods of drug control. In sum, the tough-minded law-enforcement officials took positions directly contrary to those of Congress and the President.

One hopes that politicians will realize that no one can accuse them of being soft on drugs if they vote for changes suggested by many thoughtful people in law enforcement. If the politicians tone down their rhetoric it will permit police leaders to expose the costs of our present drug-control policies. Public opinion will then allow policy changes to decriminalize marijuana and stop the arrest of hundreds of thousands of people every year. The enormous savings can be used for what the public really wants—the prevention of violent crime.

ROBERT W. SWEET

To ponder the legal and judicial problems that arise from the drug war we turned to Robert Sweet, a District Judge in New York City. He has served as an Assistant U.S. Attorney and as Deputy Mayor of New York City under John Lindsay. He is a graduate of Yale and of Yale Law School.

Why does a sitting judge, constitutionally charged with enforcing the laws of the United States, seek the abolition of the criminal penalties attached to drug use and distribution? The answer in my case stems from personal experience, leading to the conviction that our present policy debases the rule of law and that its fundamental premise is flawed.

In college in the forties, while experimenting with the drug of choice—alcohol—I cheerfully sang the lyrics of "Cocaine Bill and Morphine Sue," without any understanding of the reality behind the words. As an Assistant United States Attorney in the fifties, I accepted the enforcement of the drug laws without question. In the sixties, as Deputy Mayor of the City of New York, I supported methadone and various modalities of treatment and rehabilitation. After becoming a federal trial judge in 1978, I presided over drug trials and sought to impose just sentences ranging from probation to twenty years.

Then Congress enacted mandatory minimum sentences, and judicial discretion was radically restricted. The day in the fall of 1988 that I was mandated to sentence Luis Quinones, an eighteen-year-old with no prior record, to ten years of real time because he was a bouncer in an apartment where drugs were being sold, I faced our national drug policy and the need to reexamine it. Assisted by the writings of Professor Ethan Nadelmann I concluded that our present policy of criminal prohibition was a monumental error. A number of other judges have reached the same conclusion. Judge Weinstein has characterized our present policy as "utter futility," and Judge Knapp has likened it to "taking minnows out of the pond."

As Chief McNamara writes, the realities of criminal prohibition are becoming recognized. The first and foremost effect is the creation of a pervasive and unbelievably powerful underground economy.

The *Economist* estimates that the markup on cocaine and heroin is not 5,000 percent, as Messrs. Buckley and Duke suggest, but 20,000 percent. The drug market in the United States is estimated at $150 billion a year. At least one group of distributors in a case before me sold 37,500 kilos of cocaine a month for gross sales of almost $20 million a month, and this group was but one of a number operating here.

While this economic engine drives forward, so have our efforts to punish those who operate it. Today we have the highest incarceration rate for any Western nation, almost 1 million [there are higher estimates.—ED.] in jails or prisons at a cost of $20 billion a year. Federal drug cases have trebled in ten years, up 25 percent in 1993 alone, with marijuana cases up 17 percent. The total federal expenditure on the drug war this year under the proposed budget will exceed $17 billion. Ten years ago the annual expenditure on the drug war was $5 billion for all governments, federal, state, and local.

While our expenditures have increased tenfold, the number of Americans using drugs has remained relatively constant at 40 million. Steady users are estimated to be 6 million, with 1 to 2 million of those seriously disordered. Our present prohibition policy has failed, flatly and without serious question.

Secondly, the rule of law has been debased by the use of criminal sanctions to alter personal conduct. Of course, the same effort was made in the twenties and thirties with respect to alcohol, with the same results. Al Capone and Nicky Barnes are interchangeable. Drive-by shootings, turf wars, mugging, and random violence are all the direct result of criminal prohibition. Courts are clogged with drug cases to such an extent that in some jurisdictions (the Eastern District of New York and the Southern District of Florida, for example) it is difficult to find the resources to try civil cases; yet, the street-corner availability of drugs is known to every citizen.

The rights of the individual have been curtailed in the name of the War on Drugs. We have seen the elimination of an accused's right to pretrial release for most charges under the drug laws; heightened restrictions on post-conviction bail; and invasions into the attorney-client relationship through criminal forfeiture.

The criteria for securing a search warrant have been relaxed. In drug cases, the Supreme Court has permitted the issuance of search warrants based on anonymous tips and tips from informants known to be corrupt and unreliable; permitted warrantless searches of fields, barns, and private property near a residence; and upheld evidence obtained under defective search warrants if the officers executing the warrant acted in "good faith." Taken together, these holdings have been characterized as "the drug exception to the Fourth Amendment."

Police corruption and the unwholesome practice of using confidential informants (one of whom made over $100,000 in a case before me) have been noted by Chief McNamara.

Finally, the fundamental flaw, which will ultimately destroy this prohibition as it did the last one, is that criminal sanctions cannot, and should not attempt to, prohibit personal conduct which does no harm to others. Personal liberty surely must extend to what, when, and how much a citizen can ingest.

The Framers of our Constitution explicitly acknowledged that the individual possesses certain rights not enumerated in the text of the Constitution and not contingent upon the relationship between the individual and the Federal Government. When a right has been narrowly defined as, for example, the right to possess marijuana or cocaine, the courts have refused to recognize it as one that is fundamental in nature. However, when the right to ingest substances is considered in more general terms as the right to self-determination, that right has a constitutional foundation as yet undeclared.

To overturn the present policy will not be easy, given the established bureaucracy, but President Kennedy at the Berlin Wall was correct: "Change is the law of life." We must recognize that drug use is first and foremost a health problem, and that, as Professor Nadelmann has established, mind-altering substances are a part of modern life to be understood and their effects ameliorated, rather than grounds for prosecution.

Alcohol and tobacco have a social cost when abused, and society has properly concluded that abuse of these drugs is a health problem, not a criminal issue. Indeed, our experience with the reduction of 50 percent in the use of tobacco—the most addicting of drugs, which results in 400,000 deaths a year—confirms the wisdom of that policy. To distinguish between these substances and heroin or cocaine is mere tautology.

While the medicalization of the issue is going forward, Congress should accept the recommendations of President Nixon's commission on the drug laws and of the National Academy of Sciences in 1982 and end the criminalization of marijuana, which is now widely acknowledged to be without deleterious effect. That reform alone would take 450,000 arrests out of the system.

The latest crime bill proposed a study of violence and crime encompassing drug policy but failed to fund it. The Surgeon General proposed such a study and got fired. Such a study, if fairly conducted, would compel the abolition of criminal prohibition of drugs by the Federal Government, permitting all drugs to be treated much the same as alcohol: restricted by the individual states as to time and place of sale, barred from minors, subject to truth in advertising, and made the source of tax revenue. As with alcohol, those who harm or pose a threat to others while under the influence of drugs would face criminal sanctions.

The effect of the underworld drug economy, the debasement of the rule of law, and the undermining of fundamental fairness and individual rights under the war on drugs all combine to require that the criminal prohibition against drug use and distribution be ended.

THE POLITICS OF ECSTASY

Charles S. Grob, M.D.

From the *Journal of Psychoactive Drugs*, April-June 2002

Several decades into the monolithic and largely ineffectual War On Drugs, the latest object of media sensationalism and government agency hyperbole has been the phenomenon of ecstasy use. In spite of a vigorous and lavishly funded propaganda campaign designed to portray ecstasy as a vehicle for horrific central nervous system damage, its degree of use by the vulnerable young people and concomitant risk for serious injury has steadily risen. Unfortunately, and not for the first time, a misguided political agenda armed with biased and misleading science has yielded counterproductive results. In order to successfully reduce the risks of harm that young people face in the future, it will be necessary to step back from the zealous and disturbed policies that have brought us to our current distressing state of affairs, and instead create a new foundation based on common sense and honest interpretation of the scientific process.

Mirroring the history of hallucinogen research in the 1950s and 1960s, when highly promising psychiatric investigations were precipitously terminated by an increasingly angry and reactive political establishment, attempts in the 1980s and 1990s to conduct sanctioned research into the value of the MDMA (3,4-methylenedioxymethamphetamine) treatment model were met with a similar fate. Loathe to provide the opportunity to explore such a putative challenge to the multibillion dollar pharmaceutical industry's domination of contemporary psychiatric treatment, government regulatory and funding agencies have resisted the development of research programs designed to explore alternative models. Regrettably, a potentially valuable dialogue on the relative merits of the MDMA treatment model has been stifled, while sensational claims reinforcing the worst fears of a vulnerable populace have been regularly trumpeted in the press. It is an unfortunate fact that keeping apace with the repression of the hallucinogen and MDMA treatment models, the serious degree of dangerous drug and alcohol abuse engaged in by young people in contemporary society has continued unabated.

The centerpiece of the anti-Ecstasy campaign over the last several years has been the National Institute of Drug Abuse (NIDA) Club Drug Initiative, budgeted in excess of 50 million dollars per year. It is telling that while fervently disseminating information on the real and embellished dangers of what NIDA considers to be the prototype club drug, Ecstasy, any discussion of the short and long term dangers of alcohol, arguably the most dangerous and potentially lethal of club drugs, is virtually ignored. Whereas recent U.S. data estimates Ecstasy accounts for approximately thirty to forty deaths per year (all tragic and for the most part preventable), alcohol is annually responsible for 100,000 fatalities. What role the wealthy and politically powerful alcohol industry lobby plays in determining such government drug policy bias is waiting to be elucidated.

Over the last two decades, the long arm of a seriously disturbed drug policy has also insinuated itself into modern cultural trends, with serious adverse consequences. In addition to compounding the risk of drug uses inflicting irreparable harm to themselves, official policy has also regrettably tarnished the actual scientific process. In the mid 1980s, MDMA was declared a Schedule I drug by the Drug Enforcement Administration, overruling a judicial recommendation that its status recognize a potential for medical use in well-controlled settings. While inhibiting legitimate therapeutic research with MDMA, this policy has not deterred the increasingly dangerous recreational use of Ecstasy of young people.

Although at one time equivalent to MDMA, ecstasy in recent years has been the object of increasing degrees of drug substitution. In some surveys of marketed Ecstasy, more than 50% of the samples have been identified as consisting of variety of substituted compounds sold to naïve youth. These range from relatively benign substances like aspirin of caffeine to more dangerous ones such as methamphetamine, phencyclidine (PCP) and dextromethorphan (DXM), to potentially lethal paramethoxyamphetamine (PMA). Efforts to institute harm reduction programs (e.g., pill testing), modeled after Dutch efforts that have significantly reduced mortality at raves, have been obstructed. Ironically, scheduling MDMA as a tightly controlled Schedule I drug has only denied qualified researchers the opportunity to investigate the range of physiological and psychological effects caused by the drug, while young people appear to have little difficulty obtaining their supplies of Ecstasy.

Recent proposed legislation to prosecute rave promoters under the crack house law, actively target available supplies of water and chill-out rooms as evidence of felonious conduct. Harm reduction efforts, often fiercely condemned by mainstream policymakers, emphasize the need to maintain adequate hydration, ventilation and rest as critical to diminishing morbidity and mortality at raves and dance clubs. To a regrettable degree, official drug policy has gone far beyond resisting harm reduction alternatives to a de facto maximization of the potential harm likely to be incurred through recreational Ecstasy use.

Our medical and public health systems rely on accurate and objective knowledge, behavior and policies. We place our trust in the honesty and integrity of the scientific process. In the case of ecstasy and MDMA, among other highly sensationalized stories of injurious outcome, the media has regularly presented reports of irreversible brain damage, often from published articles in our most prestigious medical and scientific journals. Close inspection of some of these studies alleging MDMA neurotoxicity, however, reveals a pattern of flawed research methodologies and deceptive practices of data analysis (for a review see Grob 2000; Grob & Poland 1997). A particularly egregious example is the unreported preselection bias of MDMA experienced subjects for an L-tryptophan challenge study (Price et al. 1989) on the basis of their low levels of CSF 5-hydroxyindole acetic acid (5-HIAA), as measured for a prior study looking into effects on serotonin function. In a companion investigation, some of these same subjects were judged to have neuropsychological deficits (albeit subtle) (Krystal et al. 1992) after having been flown from the West Coast to the East Coast the day before and had been on the receiving end of sedating intravenous L-tryptophan a few hours prior to cognitive testing. The published articles disingenuously misreported the actual procedures and analytic methods used. Other high profile research evaluations of the so-called serotonin neurotoxicity effect in humans have consistently suffered from neglect of the critical roles polydrug abuse, sleep and nutritional deprivation, and underlying psychopathology have on psychobiologic correlates (McCann et al. 1999, 1998; Bolla et al. 1998). Selective concealment of data sets, designed to hide statistical manipulations employed to yield even marginally positive results, raise serious ethical questions.

Almost two decades after the scheduling of MDMA, the use of recreational ecstasy has evolved into an increasingly dangerous activity, while the controlled investigation of a potentially new and valuable treatment model has remained taboo. Given the serious lack of demonstrated effectiveness of our drug policy, it is time to begin a fresh dialogue that will allow for the examination of alternative perspectives designed to reduce the risk of injury. When it comes to official policy that will affect the health and safety of the young, the most sensible and ethical position would be to reduce the potential for harm while raising the standards necessary to ensure genuine scientific credibility. For those who not are able to *Just Say No*, measures must be taken to protect them from preventable injury. Ultimately, young people might surprise us with their capacity to protect themselves if we were to instead *Just Tell the Truth*.

REFERENCES

Bolla, K. I.: McCann, U. D. & Ricaurte, G. A. 1998. Memory impairment in abstinent MDMA ("ecstasy") users. *Neurology* 51: 1532-37.

Grob, C. S. 2000. Deconstructing ecstasy: The politics of MDMA research. *Addiction Research* 8:549-588.

Grob, C. S. & Poland, R. E. 1997. MDMA. In: J. H. Lowinson, P. Ruiz, R. B. Millman & J. G. Langrod (Eds.) *Substance Abuse: A Comprehensive Textbook, Third Edition.* Baltimore, Maryland: Williams and Wilkins.

Krystal, J. H.; Price, L. H.: Opsahl, C.; Ricaurte, G. A. & Heninger, G. R. 1992. Chronic 3,4-methylenedioxymethamphetamine (MDMA) use: Effects on mood and neuropsychological function. *American Journal of Drug and Alcohol Abuse*18:331-41.

McCann, U. D.; Mertl, M.; Eligulashvili, V. & Ricaurte, G. A. 1999. Cognitive performance in 3,4-methylenedioxymethamphetamine (MDMA, "ecstasy") users: A controlled study. *Psychopharmacology* 143: 417-25.

McCann, U. D.; Szubo, Z.: Scheffel, U.: Dannals, R. F. & Rucarte, G. A. 1998. Positron emission tomographic evidence of toxic effects of MDMA ("ecstasy") on brain serotonin neurons in human beings. *Lancet* 352: 1433-37.

Price, L. H.: Ricaurte, G. A.; Krystal, J. H. & Henninger, G. R. 1989. Neuroendocrine and mood responses to intravenous l-tryptophan in 3,4-methylenedioxymethamphetamine (MDMA) users. *Archives of General Psychiatry* 46: 20-2.

A MOTHER'S ADVICE ABOUT DRUGS

Marsha Rosenbaum, Ph.D.

From *The San Francisco Chronicle*, September 7, 1998

Dear Johnny,

This fall you will be entering high school, and like most American teenagers, you'll have to navigate drugs. As most parents, I would prefer that you not use drugs. However, I realize that despite my wishes, you might experiment. I will not use scare tactics to deter you. Instead, having spent the past 25 years researching drug use, abuse, and policy, I will tell you a little about what I have learned, hoping this will let you to make wise choices. My only concern is your health and safety.

When people talk about "drugs," they are generally referring to illegal substances such as marijuana, cocaine, methamphetamine (speed), psychedelic drugs (LSD, ecstasy, "Schrooms") and heroin.

These are not the only drugs that make you high. Alcohol, cigarettes, and many other substances (like glue) cause intoxication of some sort. The fact that one drug or another is illegal does not mean one is better or worse for you. All of them temporarily change the way you perceive things and the way you think.

Some people will tell you that drugs feel good, and that's why they use them. But drugs are not always fun. Cocaine and methamphetamine speed up your heart; LSD can make you feel disoriented; alcohol intoxication impairs driving; cigarette smoking leads to addiction and sometimes lung cancer; and people sometimes die suddenly from taking heroin. Marijuana does not often lead to physical dependence or overdose, but it does alter the way people think, behave, and react.

I have tried to give you a short description of the drugs you might encounter. I choose not to try to scare you by distorting information because I want you to have confidence in what I tell you. Although I won't lie to you about their effects, there are many reasons for a person your age to not use drugs or alcohol.

First, being high on marijuana or any other drug often interferes with normal life. It is difficult to retain information while high, so using it—especially daily—affects your ability to learn.

Second, if you think you might try marijuana, please wait until you are older. Adults with drug problems often started using at a very early age.

Finally, your father and I don't want you to get into trouble. Drug and alcohol use is illegal, and the consequences of being caught are huge. Here in the United States, the number of arrests for possession of marijuana has more than doubled in the past six years. Adults are serious about "zero tolerance." If caught, you could be arrested, expelled from school, barred from playing sports, lose your driver's license, denied a college loan, and/or rejected for college.

Despite my advice to abstain, you may one day choose to experiment. I will say again that this is not a good idea, but if you do, I urge you to learn as much as you can, and use common sense. There are many excellent books and references, including the Internet, that give you credible information about drugs. You can, of course, always talk to me. If I don't know the answers to your questions, I will try to help you find them.

If you are offered drugs, be cautious. Watch how people behave, but understand that everyone responds differently—even to the same substance. If you do decide to experiment, be sure you are surrounded by people you can count upon. Plan your transportation and under no circumstances drive or get into a car with anyone else who has been using alcohol or other drugs. Call us or any of our close friends any time, day or night, and we will pick you up—no questions asked and no consequences.

And please, Johnny, use moderation. It is impossible to know what is contained in illegal drugs because they are not regulated. The majority of fatal overdoses occur because young people do not know the strength of the drugs they consume, or how they combine with other drugs. Please do not participate in drinking contests, which have killed too many young people. Whereas marijuana by itself is not fatal, too much can cause you to become disoriented and sometimes paranoid. And of course, smoking can hurt your lungs, later in life and now.

Johnny, as your father and I have always told you about a range of activities (including sex), think about the consequences of your actions before you act. Drugs are no different. Be skeptical and most of all, be safe.

Love, Mom

THE MYTH OF "HARMLESS" MARIJUANA

John P. Walters

From The *Washington Post*, May 1, 2002

Last December the University of Michigan released its annual survey "Monitoring the Future," which measures drug use among American youth. Very little had changed from the previous year's report; most indicators were flat. The report generated little in the way of public comment.

Yet what it brought to light was deeply disturbing. Drug use among our nation's teens remains stable, but at near-record levels, with some 49 percent of high school seniors experimenting with marijuana at least once prior to graduation—and 22 percent smoking marijuana at least once a month.

After years of giggling at quaintly outdated marijuana scare stories like the 1936 movie *Reefer Madness*, we've become almost conditioned to think that any warnings about the true dangers of marijuana are overblown. But marijuana is far from "harmless"—it is pernicious. Parents are often unaware that today's marijuana is different from that of a generation ago, with potency levels 10 to 20 times stronger than the marijuana with which they were familiar.

Marijuana directly affects the brain. Researchers have learned that it impairs the ability of young people to concentrate and retain information during their peak learning years, and when their brains are still developing. The THC in marijuana attaches itself to receptors in the hippocampal region of the brain, weakening short-term memory and interfering with the mechanisms that form long-term memory. Do our struggling schools really need another obstacle to student achievement?

Marijuana smoking can hurt more than just grades. According to the Department of Health and Human Services, every year more than 2,500 admissions to the District of Columbia's overtaxed emergency rooms—some 300 of them for patients under age 18—are linked to marijuana smoking, and the number of marijuana-related emergencies is growing. Each year, for example, marijuana use is linked to tens of thousands of serious traffic accidents.

Research has now established that marijuana is in fact addictive. Of the 4.3 million Americans who meet the diagnostic criteria for needing drug treatment (criteria developed by the American Psychiatric Association, not police departments or prosecutors) two-thirds are dependent on marijuana, according to

HHS. These are not occasional pot smokers but people with real problems directly traceable to their use of marijuana, including significant health problems, emotional problems, and difficulty in cutting down on use. Sixty percent of teens in drug treatment have a primary marijuana diagnosis.

Despite this and other strong scientific evidence of marijuana's destructive effects, a cynical campaign is underway, in the District and elsewhere, to proclaim the virtues of "medical" marijuana. By now most Americans realize that the push to "normalize" marijuana for medical use is part of the drug legalization agenda. Its chief funders, George Soros, John Sperling, and Peter Lewis, have spent millions to help pay for referendums and ballot initiatives in states from Alaska to Maine. Now it appears that a medical marijuana campaign may be on the horizon for the District.

Why? Is the American health care system—the most sophisticated in the world—really being hobbled by a lack of smoked medicines? The University of California's Center for Medicinal Cannabis Research is currently conducting scientific studies to determine the efficacy of marijuana in treating various ailments. Until that research is concluded, however, most of what the public hears from marijuana activists is little more than a compilation of anecdotes. Many questions remain unanswered, but the science is clear on a few things. Example: Marijuana contains hundreds of carcinogens.

Moreover, anti-smoking efforts aimed at youth have been remarkably effective by building on a campaign to erode the social acceptability of tobacco. Should we undermine those efforts by promoting smoked marijuana as though it were a medicine?

While medical marijuana initiatives are based on pseudo-science, their effects on the criminal justice system are anything but imaginary. By opening up legal loopholes, existing medical marijuana laws have caused police and prosecutors to stay away from marijuana prosecutions.

Giving marijuana dealers a free pass is a terrible idea. In fact, thanks in part to excellent reporting in the *Washington Post*, District residents are increasingly aware that marijuana dealers are dangerous criminals. The recent life-without-parole convictions of leaders of Washington's K Street Crew are only the latest evidence of this.

As reported in the *Washington Post*, the K Street Crew was a vicious group of marijuana dealers whose decade-long reign of terror was brought to an end only this year after a massive prosecution effort by Michael Volkov, chief gang prosecutor for the U.S. attorney's office. The K Street Crew is credited with at least

17 murders, including systematic killings of potential witnesses. (It should not be confused with the L Street Crew, a D.C. marijuana gang that killed eight people in the course of doing business.)

Says prosecutor Volkov: "The experience in D.C. shows that marijuana dealers are no less violent than cocaine and heroin traffickers. They have just as much money to lose, just as much turf to lose, and just as many reasons to kill as any drug trafficker."

Skeptics will charge that this kind of violence is just one more reason to legalize marijuana. A review of the nation's history with drug use suggests otherwise: When marijuana is inexpensive, as it would be if legal, use soars—bad news for the District's schools, streets, and emergency rooms.

THE PROBLEM IS POT PROHIBITION

Keith Stroup & Paul Armentano

An earlier version of this response appeared in the Washington Post, *May 4, 2002*

It's ironic that Drug Czar John Walters cites the movie "Reefer Madness" in his op/ed, "The Myth of 'Harmless' Marijuana." Indeed, many of Mr. Walters more egregious claims about cannabis appear to have been lifted straight from the 1936 propaganda film.

Contrary to Mr. Walters' allegations, marijuana is far less dangerous than alcohol or tobacco. Around 50,000 people die each year from alcohol poisoning. Similarly, more than 400,000 deaths each year are attributed to tobacco smoking. By comparison, marijuana is nontoxic and cannot cause death by overdose.

Pot's potential dependence liability and impact upon the brain are also far milder than Mr. Walters suggests. According to the U.S. Institute of Medicine, fewer than one in 10 marijuana smokers become regular users of the drug, and most voluntary cease their use after 34 years of age. By comparison, 15 percent of alcohol consumers and 32 percent of tobacco smokers exhibit symptoms of drug dependence.

Regarding marijuana's alleged impact on cognition, U.S. government-sponsored population studies conducted in Jamaica, Greece and Costa Rica found no significant cognitive differences between long-term smokers and non-smokers. Similarly, a 1999 study of 1,300 volunteers published in *The American Journal of Epidemiology* reported "no significant differences in cognitive decline between heavy users, light users, and nonusers of cannabis" over a 15-year period. Most recently, a meta-analysis of neuropsychological studies of long-term marijuana smokers by the U.S. National Institute on Drug Abuse reaffirmed this conclusion.

Perhaps most offensive of Mr. Walters aspersions are those he casts toward the medical use of marijuana by the seriously ill. The Drug Czar cynically asks the *Washington Post's* readers if America's health care system is "really being hobbled by a lack of smoked medicines?" He'd be better off asking our nation's doctors.

According to a 2001 national survey of U.S. physicians conducted for the American Society of Addiction Medicine, nearly half of all doctors with opinions support legalizing marijuana as a medicine. Moreover, no less than 80 state and national health care organizations - including the American Public Health Association and *The New England Journal of Medicine*—support immediate, legal patient access to medical cannabis. Contrary to Walters' ill-informed assertions, the medical community's support for medical marijuana is hardly based on "pseudo-science," but rather on the reports of thousands of patients and scores of scientific data affirming pot's therapeutic value.

Walters is correct in suggesting that marijuana, like other drugs, is not for kids. There are many activities that we permit adults to do, but forbid children, such as motorcycle riding, skydiving, signing contracts, getting married and drinking alcohol or smoking tobacco. However, we do not condone arresting adults who responsibly engage in these activities in order to dissuade our children from doing so. Nor can we justify arresting adult marijuana smokers, presently at the pace of some 734,000 per year, on the grounds of sending a message to children.

More than 76 million Americans, roughly one-third of the adult population, have smoked marijuana, and 18 to 20 million admit having done so in the past year. The vast majority of these people are upstanding, hardworking and productive citizens. They do not deserve to be treated like criminals.

Neither the marijuana user nor the drug itself constitutes a legitimate danger to public safety. Pot prohibition is a failed public policy that wastes billions of dollars of law enforcement resources that should be focused on violent crime—including terrorism—and needlessly destroys the lives and careers of hundreds of thousands of otherwise law abiding citizens each year. Indeed, if there exists any true "myth" regarding marijuana, it is that pot is more damaging to society than pot prohibition. By now, even Mr. Walters should know otherwise.

Sincerely,
R. Keith Stroup, Esq.
NORML Executive Director
Paul Armentano
NORML Senior Policy Analyst

[CONSERVATIVE COMPASSION]

DOPE FIENDS: A Tape Transcript

A. M. Rosenthal and Barry McCaffrey

From *Harper's Magazine*, November 2000

The following transcript is from a 1996 conversation between drug czar Barry R. McCaffrey and A. M. Rosenthal, then a *New York Times* columnist, just after California and Arizona passed referendums legalizing the medical use of marijuana. A tape recording of this conversation was an exhibit in the matter of Dr. Marcus Conant, et al. v. Barry R. McCaffrey, et al., a lawsuit that sought to block the government's stated intention to prosecute doctors who discussed with patients marijuana's potential benefits; on September 7, a federal judge ruled that such prosecutions would violate the First Amendment. According to his office, McCaffrey routinely recorded telephone conversations with journalists, often without their knowledge, to ensure that he was not misquoted.

A.M. ROSENTHAL: I'm calling because I know you have been watching this thing in California and Arizona as carefully as I should have, but, ah, it's really terribly worrisome. Maybe I'm overdoing it in my head, but—

BARRY R. MCCAFFREY: I think not.

ROSENTHAL: Okay. Let me ask you one or two things. We can speak on any basis you want.

MCCAFFREY: On the record.

ROSENTHAL: Yeah, because I really need somebody, I need a little help. I want to show the opposition to this. Where do we go from now? How would you describe this legislation in terms of impact on the drug war and so on? I don't want to put words in your mouth, but I'm trying to write a column in which I want to say that this thing has been done while the rest of us, too many of us, not including you, were asleep. That it shows every sign that in the next two years they will get ready to put this proposition on other ballots. And, uh, where do we go from here? First of all, what do we do about these, what happened in California and Arizona, as far as you're concerned? I know somewhere you said that federal law still applies. Tell me what you think, and I don't have to put words in your head.

MCCAFFREY: Well, we're enormously concerned about it. The way I heard about it the first month or two was the same way California voters and Arizona voters reacted to it: This doesn't sound like a very serious proposition. It's smoking dope to manage pain for older people with terminal cancer or young guys with AIDS, and so even though it sounds like bad medicine, why get too energized about it? That's sort of the way it came to me. And then there was—the second caution was—well, this is local politics, and they'll sort it out and none of them are very worried about it, so why should you be? And then when I had my lawyer pull it apart and we analyzed its probable impact and then talked to some serious people in the two states involved, we got enormously energized about the whole situation. And I got the president involved and—

ROSENTHAL: Did Clinton campaign against it?

MCCAFFREY: Both Clinton and Dole made statements, and Clinton obviously empowered all of us to get out there and try and educate the people. And I went and got three former presidents to sign a letter. We had Justice put out a legal opinion that didn't refer to the referendums but did refer to medical use of marijuana. And then we—

ROSENTHAL: You mean, saying it's not legal?

MCCAFFREY: Yeah, saying, look, we've been through this before, federal law and federal directives will remain unaffected by any referendum, and federal law will remain operative and dominant over any state law. So now, finally, the problem was getting the facts out in front of the people in California and Arizona, but, unfortunately, at that point, we had this bizarre situation where there was a lot of money, millions of dollars, pushing a referendum from out-of-state individuals, and not many of them. I think it was essentially six people who bankrolled the whole thing.

ROSENTHAL: And who were they?

MCCAFFREY: It's George Soros. It's a guy named Sterling, there's—Rockefeller was one of them.

ROSENTHAL: Which one?

MCCAFFREY: Golly, I can't keep them straight.

ROSENTHAL: The other day I wrote something, I mentioned Soros this guy is really gonna cause us—is causing trouble in this. He does all these things. He is supporting the prodrug foundations.

MCCAFFREY: I agree absolutely.

ROSENTHAL: All over the country.

MCCAFFREY: He's at the heart and soul of a lot of this. It's alleged he spent 15 million bucks plus—

ROSENTHAL: The heart and soul of what, the initiatives?

MCCAFFREY: Yeah, this is—We're now going to see this come up all over the country. And this is not paranoia on my part, this is a national legalization-of-drugs strategy. It's not paranoia on my part. In other words, I see this not as two medical initiatives dealing with the terminally ill; I see this as part of a national effort to legalize drugs, starting with marijuana, all over the United States.

ROSENTHAL: So do I.

MCCAFFREY: I think that's what's at stake in these two cases. It was absolutely cunning. It's worth a graduate-school paper to examine how they did it. They did polling, they determined what initiatives will work with the people, the voters in those states. The one in Arizona was even more byzantine than the one in California. California is a little bit Cheech and Chong, but the one in Arizona, if you read that initiative—

ROSENTHAL: Let me jump in for a little bit. You say the federal laws against the growing and use or possession of these things—marijuana—will still stand. Now what is it according to the proposition? As I gather, it is California law now that you can do it. Do they have to pass a specific law? I think this does it.

MCCAFFREY: Well, first of all, the jury is out. But I think what's going to happen in California is if you're growing, if you're sitting out in the middle of the national forest growing a hundred pot plants that are worth 10,000 bucks apiece, you're still gonna get arrested, and then you're gonna have to try and demonstrate that you were not in violation of existing California law and that you're covered in some way by this new initiative.

ROSENTHAL: You said the national park, but suppose someone is growing it in his backyard?

MCCAFFREY: Well, how about the balcony in an apartment building overlooking Los Angeles airport, 'cause you're gonna see that in about another three weeks, too.

ROSENTHAL: No question about it, they've got a victory on their hands and they're gonna use it. Of course they may decide to play it low key and—

MCCAFFREY: Well, Abe, the other thing I'd suggest to you, though, is legitimate doctors are not going to be using this. Some of them will be if they think there's money in it, but—

ROSENTHAL: But, Barry, in California, you don't need a prescription, a written prescription.

MCCAFFREY: You need a doctor to recommend it. And so, initially, are you going to go to a cancer doctor as a fourteen-year-old and get him to recommend marijuana? I think 85 percent of the people in California aren't going to smoke dope and aren't going to allow their kids to do it. And physicians aren't going to recommend it. I mean, it's just—it's counterintuitive to think that some intelligent woman or man who is a physician and trained in the healing arts is going to recommend smoking pot.

ROSENTHAL: Well, you're right, but—

MCCAFFREY: But some people are, and the real question is what are we going to do about them, and the answer is we don't know but for sure we're not getting rolled on this issue because this isn't medicine, this isn't science, this is legalization of drugs, and we think kids are at risk.

ROSENTHAL: Well, we got caught off base in California—

MCCAFFREY: Yes sir. Absolutely we did.

ROSENTHAL: And I think the best thing we can do is say we were caught off, those of us who were against it.

MCCAFFREY: I agree.

ROSENTHAL: And pull ourselves together.

MCCAFFREY: I agree, Abe. I've gone a long time in life not getting killed in combat because I pay attention to details. And you do what you're supposed to do, and if you do it regularly you don't get caught off guard. We don't want to go back to 1979, when we had 25 million Americans regularly using drugs, when we had a third of the armed forces using drugs and the NYPD using drugs and we had the faculty of universities using drugs.

ROSENTHAL: Are you talking about the seventies?

MCCAFFREY: Yeah, 1979 apparently was the peak year of drug abuse in America. And it didn't work out, and it left us with hundreds of thousands of people dead and billions of dollars—from 1990 through this year, we lost 100,000 dead and $300 billion from the abuse of illegal drugs in America.

ROSENTHAL: And what we've got to do, I mean, not we, but all of us, is convince people of the connection between the California initiative, which they still see as a pot initiative, and the 100,000 dead.

MCCAFFREY: Yeah, that's right.

ROSENTHAL: That's what we have to do.

MCCAFFREY: Yeah. You know the other thing we gotta say is, Do we want to promote a drugged, stoned America? Or do we want to promote one that's involved in athletics and academic achievement and sensitivity to other people and their problems? Or do we want to do Timothy O'Leary?

ROSENTHAL: We've got to get some way also to make it socially unacceptable. So how to do this except by pounding at them I don't know.

MCCAFFREY: Well, [inaudible].

ROSENTHAL: No, no. What? No, I mean for rich people—

MCCAFFREY: Yeah.

ROSENTHAL: —who will never wind up in the gutter

MCCAFFREY: Yeah, exactly.

ROSENTHAL: —who are fed, and that's what made Soros [inaudible]. It's socially unacceptable somehow for people to use their money in that way.

MCCAFFREY: Yeah, I agree. Well, you know, we've done it, we've started to do it with smoking cigarettes. We've started to do it with driving drunk on Saturday night—it's no longer a manly, kind of humorous thing to do; it's something you ought to be ashamed of. And if you're at a cocktail party in New York City now or in a military staff call, if you light up a cigarette you identify yourself as being a dull-witted lad or lass.

ROSENTHAL: Well, that's right, but how do we—I mean, as a society and the people who are anti-drugs—make it socially unacceptable not to smoke pot, but to give money to these causes?

MCCAFFREY: Yeah, I agree.

ROSENTHAL: It's terribly important.

MCCAFFREY: Yeah.

ROSENTHAL: And I think that is really something that you and the president ought to be doing.

MCCAFFREY: That's another idea, Abe. I have not heard that. I will take that aboard, that's a very good thought.

ROSENTHAL: If it hadn't been for Soros—

MCCAFFREY: Yep.

ROSENTHAL: —and a couple of other people that I run into at parties all over the place and everybody admires, blah, blah, blah—

MCCAFFREY: Yeah.

ROSENTHAL: —this would not have passed.

MCCAFFREY: Yeah, I agree.

ROSENTHAL: And we all know that.

MCCAFFREY: Yep, absolutely.

ROSENTHAL: And I think we have the right to say, you know, I wouldn't let a pornographer in my house, I wouldn't, I really will not allow—I'm just saying this to you—George Soros in my house.

MCCAFFREY: I absolutely agree. He ought to be ashamed of himself.

ROSENTHAL: Couldn't you say that people who give large amounts of money to these causes ought to be ashamed of themselves?

MCCAFFREY: Yeah, I just said it. Good for you.

ROSENTHAL: All right, and I'll use that. I think the problem is, I live in the city, and these guys, like the pornographers and whoever, get respect, are allowed to do what they want with their money, a lot of it tax-free, and at the same time the respectability is not demeaned.

MCCAFFREY: Yeah, I agree. I absolutely agree.

ROSENTHAL: I really have this deep-bone feeling that if somebody like the president or you or somebody said that people like Soros should be ashamed of themselves—I'm not going to put his name in because you didn't say so, but people who give large amounts of money ought to be ashamed of themselves.

MCCAFFREY: Yeah, I think that, yeah.

ROSENTHAL: I think it would have . . . I really believe that it would have an effect as much as any ad or anything, or more, a thousand times more.

MCCAFFREY: Yeah, I agree.

AMERICA'S ALTERED STATES: When Does Legal Relief of Pain Become Illegal Pursuit of Pleasure?

Joshua Wolf Shenk

From *Harper's Magazine*, May 1999

My soul was a burden, bruised and bleeding. It was tired of the man who carried it, but I found no place to set it down to rest. Neither the charm of the countryside nor the sweet scents of a garden could soothe it. It found no peace in song or laughter, none in the company of friends at table or in the pleasures of love, none even in books or poetry. . . . Where could my heart find refuge from itself? Where could I go, yet leave myself behind? —St. Augustine

To suffer and long for relief is a central experience of humanity. But the absence of pain or discomfort or what Pablo Neruda called "the infinite ache" is never enough. Relief is bound up with satisfaction, pleasure, happiness—the pursuit of which is declared a right in the manifesto of our republic. I sit here with two agents of that pursuit: on my right, a bottle from Duane Reade pharmacy; on my left, a bag of plant matter, bought last night for about the same sum in an East Village bar from a group of men who would have sold me different kinds of contraband if they hadn't sniffed cop in my curiosity and eagerness. This being Rudy Giuliani's New York, I had feared they were undercover. But my worst case scenario was a night or two in jail and theirs a fifteen-year minimum. As I exited the bar, I saw an empty police van idling, waiting to be filled with people like me but, mostly, people like them, who are there only because I am.

Fear and suspicion, secrecy and shame, the yearning for pleasure, and the wish to avoid men in blue uniforms. This is (in rough, incomplete terms) an emotional report from the front. The drug wars—which, having spanned more than eight decades, require the plural—are palpable in New York City. The mayor blends propaganda, brute force, and guerrilla tactics, dispatching undercover cops to call "smoke, smoke" and "bud, bud" and to arrest those who answer. In Washington Square Park, he erected ten video cameras that sweep the environs twenty-four hours a day. Surveillance is a larger theme of these wars, as is the notion that cherished freedoms are incidental. But it is telling that such an extreme manifestation of these ideas appears in a public park, one of the very few common spaces in this city not controlled by, and an altar to, corporate commerce.

Several times a month, I walk through that park to the pharmacy, where a doctor's slip is my passport to another world. Here, altering the mind and body with powders and plants is not only legal but even patriotic. Among the souls wandering these aisles, I feel I have kin. But I am equally at home, and equally ill at ease, among the outlaws. I cross back and forth with wide eyes.

What I see is this: From 1970 to 1998, the inflation-adjusted revenue of major pharmaceutical companies more than quadrupled to $81 billion, 24 percent of that from drugs affecting the central nervous system and sense organs. Sales of herbal medicines now exceed $4 billion a year. Meanwhile, the war on other drugs escalated dramatically. Since 1970 the federal antidrug budget has risen 3,700 percent and now exceeds $17 billion. More than one and a half million people are arrested on drug charges each year, and 400,000 are now in prison. These numbers are just a window onto an obvious truth: We take more drugs and reward those who supply them. We punish more people for taking drugs and especially punish those who supply them. On the surface, there is no conflict. One kind of drugs is medicine, righting wrongs, restoring the ill to a proper, natural state. These drugs have the sheen of corporate logos and men in white coats. They are kept in the room where we wash grime from our skin and do the same with our souls. Our conception of illegal drugs is a warped reflection of this picture. Offered up from the dirty underworld, they are hedonistic, not curative. They induce artificial pleasure, not health. They harm rather than help, enslave rather than liberate.

There is some truth in each of these extreme pictures. But with my dual citizenship, consciousness split and altered many times over, I come to say this: The drug wars and the drug boom are interrelated, of the same body. The hostility and veneration, the punishment and profits, these come from the same beliefs and the same mistakes.

I.

Before marijuana, cocaine, or ecstasy, before nitrous oxide or magic mushrooms, before I had tried any of these, I poked through the foil enclosing a single capsule of fluoxetine hydrochloride. My drug story begins at this point, at the end of a devastating first year of college. For years, I had wrapped myself in an illusion that my lifelong troubles—intense despair, loneliness, anxiety, a relentless inner soundtrack of self-criticism—would dissolve if I could only please the gatekeepers of the Ivy League. By the spring of freshman year, I had been skinned of this illusion and plunged into a deep darkness. From a phone booth in a library basement, I resumed contact with a psychiatrist I'd begun seeing in high school.

I told him how awful I felt, and, after a few sessions, he suggested I consider medication. By now our exchange is a familiar one. This was 1990, three years after Prozac introduced the country to a new class of antidepressants, called selective serotonin reuptake inhibitors. SSRIs were an impressive innovation chemically but a stunning innovation for the market, because, while no more effective than previous generations of antidepressants, SSRIs had fewer side effects and thus could be given to a much broader range of people. (At last count, 22 million Americans have used Prozac alone.) When my doctor suggested I take Prozac, it was with a casual tone. Although the idea of "altering my brain chemistry" unsettled me at first, I soon absorbed his attitude. When I returned home that summer, I asked him how such drugs worked. He drew a crude map of a synapse, or the junction between nerve cells. There is a neurotransmitter called serotonin, he told me, that is ordinarily released at one end of the synapse and, at the other end, absorbed by a sort of molecular pump. Prozac inhibits this pumping process and therefore increases serotonin's presence in the brain. "What we don't understand," he said, looking up from his pad, "is why increased levels of serotonin alleviate depression. But that's what seems to happen."

I didn't understand the importance of this moment until years later, after I had noticed many more sentences in which the distance between the name of a drug—Prozac, heroin, Ritalin, crack cocaine—and its effects had collapsed. For example, the phrase "Prozac eases depression," properly unpacked, actually represents this more complicated thought: "Prozac influences the serotonin patterns in the brain, which for some unknown reason is found to alleviate, more often than would a placebo, a collection of symptoms referred to as depression." What gets lost in abbreviation—Prozac cures! Heroin kills!—is that drugs work because the human body works, and they fail or hurt us because the body and spirit are vulnerable. When drugs spark miracles—prolonging the lives of those with HIV, say, or dulling the edges of a potentially deadly manic depression— we should be thankful.[1] But many of these processes are mysteries that might never yield to science. The psychiatric establishment, for example, still does not understand why serotonin affects mood. According to Michael Montagne of the Massachusetts College of Pharmacy, 42 percent of marketed drugs likewise have no proven mechanism of action. In *Listening to Prozac*, Peter Kramer quotes a pharmacologist explaining the problem this way: "If the human brain were simple enough for us to understand, we would be too simple to understand it." Yet pharmaceutical companies exude certainty. "Smooth and powerful depression relief," reads an ad for Effexor in a recent issue of the *American Journal of Psychiatry.* "Antidepressant efficacy that brings your patients back." In case this message is too subtle, the ad shows an ecstatic mother and child playing together, with a note written in crayon: "I got my mommy back."

The irony is that our faith in pharmaceuticals is based on a model of consciousness that science is slowly displacing. "Throughout history," chemist and religious scholar Daniel Perrine writes in *The Chemistry of Mind-Altering Drugs,* "the power that many psychoactive drugs have exerted over the behavior of human beings has been variously ascribed to gods or demons." In a sense, that continues. "We ascribe magical powers to substances," says Perrine, "as if the joy is inside the bottle. Our culture has no sacred realm, so we've assigned a sacred power to these drugs. This is what [Alfred North] Whitehead would call the 'fallacy of misplaced concreteness.' We say, 'The good is in that Prozac powder,' or 'The evil is in that cocaine powder.' But evil and good are not attributes of molecules."

This is a hard lesson to learn. In my gut, where it matters, I still haven't learned it. Back in 1990, I took the Prozac and, eventually, more than two dozen other medications: antidepressants, antipsychotics, antianxiety agents, and so on. The sample pills would be elegantly wrapped. Handing them to me, the doctors would explain the desired effect: this drug might quiet the voices in my head; this one might make me less depressed and less anxious; this combination might help my concentration and ease my repetitive, obsessive thoughts. Each time I swelled with hope. I've spent many years in therapy and have looked for redemption in literature, work, love. But nothing quite matches the expectancy of putting a capsule on my tongue and waiting to be remade.

But I was not remade. None of the promised benefits of the drugs came, and I suffered still. In 1993, I went to see Donald Klein, one of the top psychopharmacologists in the country. Klein's prestige, underscored by his precipitous fees, again set me off into fantasies of health. He peppered me with questions, listened thoughtfully. After an hour, he pushed his reading glasses onto his forehead and said, "Well, this is what I think you have." He opened the standard psychiatric reference text to a chapter on "disassociative disorders" and pointed to a sublisting called depersonalization disorder, "characterized by a persistent or recurrent feeling of being detached from one's mental processes or body."

I'm still not certain that this illness best describes my experience. I can't even describe myself as "clinically ill," because clinicians don't know what the hell to do with me. But Klein gave me an entirely new way of thinking about my problems, and a grim message. "Depersonalization is very difficult to treat," he said. So I was back where I started, with one exception. During our session, Klein had asked if I used marijuana. Once, I told him, but it didn't do much. After he had given me his diagnosis, he told me the reason he had asked: "A lot of people with depersonalization say they get relief from marijuana." At that time, I happened, for the first time in my life, to be surrounded by friends who liked to smoke pot. So in addition to taking drugs alone and waiting for a miracle, I looked for solace in my own small drug culture. And for a time, I got some. The basic function of antidepressants is to help people with battered inner lives participate in the world around them. This is what pot did for me. It helped me spend time with others, something I have yearned for but also feared; it sparked an eagerness to write and conjure ideas, some of which I found the morning after to be dreamy or naive, but some of which were the germ of something valuable. While high, I could enjoy life's simple pleasures in a way that I hadn't ever been able to and still find maddeningly difficult. Some might see this (and people watching me surely did) as silly and immature. But it's also a reason to keep living.

Sad to say, I quickly found pot's limitations. When my spirits are lifted, pot can help punctuate that. If I smoke while on a downward slope or while idling, I usually experience more depression or anxiety. Salvation, for me at least, is not within that smoked plant, or the granules of a pill, or any other substance. Like I said, it's a hard lesson to learn.

To the more sober-minded among us, it is a source of much consternation that drugs, alcohol, and cigarettes are so central to our collective social lives. It is hard, in fact, to think of a single social ritual that does not revolve around some consciousness-altering substance. ("Should we get together for coffee or drinks?") But drugs are much more than a social lubricant; they are also the centerpiece of many individual lives. When it comes to alcohol, or cigarettes, or any illicit substance, this is seen as a problem. With pharmaceuticals, it is usually considered healthy. Yet the dynamic is often the same.

It begins with a drug that satisfies a particular need or desire—maybe known to us, maybe not. So we have drinks, or a smoke, or swallow a few pills. And we get something from this, a whole lot or maybe just a bit. But we often don't realize that the feeling is inside, perhaps something that, with effort, could be experienced without the drugs or perhaps, as in the psychiatric equivalent of diabetes, something we will always need help with. Yet all too often we project upon the drug a power that resides elsewhere. Many believe this to be a failure of character. If so, it is a failure the whole culture is implicated in. A recent example came with the phrase "pure theatrical Viagra," widely used to describe a Broadway production starring Nicole Kidman. Notice what's happening: Sildenafil citrate is a substance that increases blood circulation and has the side effect of producing erections. As a medicine, it is intended to be used as an adjunct to sexual stimulation. As received by our culture, though, the drug becomes the desired effect, the "real thing" to which a naked woman onstage is compared.

Such exaltation of drugs is reinforced by the torrent of pharmaceutical ads that now stuff magazines and blanket the airwaves. Since 1994, drug makers have increased their direct-to-consumer advertising budget sevenfold, to $1.2 billion last year. Take the ad for Meridia, a weight-loss drug. Compared with other drug ads ("We're going to change lives," says a doctor pitching acne cream. "We're going to make a lot of people happy"), it is the essence of restraint. "You do your part," it says in an allusion to exercise and diet. "We'll do ours." The specific intent here is to convince people who are overweight (or believe themselves to be) that they should ask their doctor for Meridia.[2] Like the pitch for Baby Gap that announces "INSTANT KARMA" over a child wrapped in a $44 velvet jacket, drug ads suggest or explicitly say that we can solve our problems through magic-bullet consumption. As the old saying goes, "Better living through chemistry."

It's the job of advertisers to try every trick to sell their products. But that's the point: drugs are a commodity designed for profit and not necessarily the best route to health and happiness. The "self-help" shelves at pharmacies, the "expert-only" section behind the counter, these are promised to contain remedies for all ills. But the wizards behind the curtain are fallible human beings, just like us. Professor Montagne says that despite obvious financial incentives, "there really is an overwhelming belief among pharmacists that the last thing you should do for many problems is take a drug. They'll recommend something when you ask, but there's a good chance that when you're walking out the door they'll be saying, 'Aw, that guy doesn't need a laxative every day. He just needs to eat right. They don't need Tagamet. They just need to cut back on the spicy food.'" It is hard to get worked up about these examples, but they point to the broader pattern of drug worship. With illegal drugs, we see the same pattern, again through that warped mirror.

Not long after his second inauguration, President Clinton signed a bill earmarking $195 million for an antidrug ad campaign, the first installment of a $1 billion pledge. The ads, which began running last summer, all end with the words "Partnership for a Drug Free America" and "Office of National Drug Control Policy." It is fitting that the two entities are officially joined. The Partnership emerged in 1986, the year basketball star Len Bias died with cocaine in his system and President Reagan signed a bill creating, among many other new penalties, mandatory federal prison terms for possession of an illegal substance. This was the birth of the drug wars' latest phase, in which any drug use at all—not abuse or addiction or "drug-related crime"—became the enemy.[3] Soon the words "drug-free America" began to show up regularly, in the name of a White House conference as well as in legislation that declared it the "policy of the United States Government to create a Drug-Free America by 1995."

Although the work of the Partnership is spread over hundreds of ad firms, the driving force behind the organization is a man named James Burke, and he is a peculiar spokesman for a "drug-free" philosophy. Burke is the former CEO of Johnson & Johnson, the maker of Tylenol and other pain-relief products; Nicotrol, a nicotine-delivery device; Pepcid AC, an antacid; and various prescription medications. When he came to the Partnership, he brought with him a crucial grant of $3 million from the Robert Wood Johnson Foundation, a philanthropy tied to Johnson & Johnson stock. Having granted $24 million over the last ten years, RWJ is the Partnership's single largest funder, but the philanthropic arms of Merck, Bristol-Myers Squibb, and Hoffman-La Roche have also made sizable donations.

I resist the urge to use the word "hypocrisy," from the Greek *hypokrisis*, "acting of a part on the stage." I don't believe James Burke is acting. Rather, he embodies a contradiction so common that few people even notice it—the idea that altering the body and mind is morally wrong when done with some substances and salutary when done with others.

This contradiction, on close examination, resolves into coherence. Before the Partnership, Burke was in the business of burnishing the myth of the uber-drug, doing his best—as all marketers do—to make some external object the center of existence, displacing the complications of family, community, inner lives. Now, drawing on the same admakers, he does the same in reverse. (These admakers are happy to work pro bono, having been made rich by ads for pharmaceuticals, cigarettes, and alcohol. Until a few years ago, the Partnership also took money from these latter two industries.) The Partnership formula is to present a problem—urban violence, date rape, juvenile delinquency—and lay it at the feet of drugs. "Marijuana," says a remorseful-looking kid, "cost me a lot of things. I used to be a straight-A student, you know. I was liked by all the neighbors.

Never really caused any trouble. I was always a good kid growing up. Before I knew it, I was getting thrown out of my house."

This kid looks to be around seventeen. The Partnership couldn't tell me his real name or anything about him except that he was interviewed through a New York drug-treatment facility. I wanted to talk to him, because I wanted to ask: "Was it marijuana that cost you these things? Or was it your behavior while using marijuana? Was that behavior caused by, or did it merely coincide with, your marijuana use?"

These kinds of subtleties are crucial, but it isn't a mystery why they are usually glossed over. In Texas, federal prosecutors are seeking life sentences for dealers who supplied heroin to teenagers who subsequently died of overdose. Parents praised the authorities. "We just don't want other people to die," said one, who suggested drug tests for fourth-graders on up. Another said, "I kind of wish all this had happened a year ago so whoever was able to supply Jay that night was already in jail." The desire for justice, and to protect future generations, is certainly understandable. But it is striking to note how rarely, in a story of an overdose, the survivors ask the most important question. It is not: How do we rid illegal drugs from the earth?[4] Despite eighty years of criminal sanctions, stiffened to the point just short of summary executions, markets in this contraband flourish because supply meets demand. Had Jay's dealer been in jail that night, Jay surely would have been able to find someone else—and if not that night, then soon thereafter.

The real question—why do kids like Jay want to take heroin in the first place?—is consistently, aggressively avoided. Senator Orrin Hatch recently declared that "people who are pushing drugs on our kids . . . I think we ought to lock them up and throw away the keys." Implicit in this remark is the idea that kids only alter their consciousness because it is pushed upon them.

Blaming the alien invader—the dealer, the drug—provides some structure to chaos. Let's say you are a teenager and, in the course of establishing your own identity or quelling inner conflicts, you start smoking a lot of pot. You start running around with a "bad crowd." Your grades suffer. Friction with your parents crescendos, and they throw you out of the house. Later, you regret what you've done and you're offered a magic button, a way to condense and displace all your misdeeds. So, naturally, you blame everything on the drug. Something maddeningly complicated now has a single name. Psychologist Bruce Alexander points out that the same tendency exists among the seriously addicted. "If your life is really fucked up, you can get into heroin, and that's kind of a way of coping," he says. "You'll have friends to share something with. You'll have an identity. You'll have an explanation for all your troubles."

What works for individuals works for a society. ("Good People Go Bad in Iowa," read a 1996 *New York Times* headline, "And a Drug Is Being Blamed.") Why is the wealthiest society in history also one of the most fearful and cynical? What root of unhappiness and discontent spurs thousands of college students to join cults, millions of Americans to seek therapists, gurus, and spiritual advisers? Why has the rate of suicide for people fifteen to twenty-four tripled since 1960? Why would an eleven- and a thirteen-year-old take three rifles and seven hand-guns to their school, trigger the fire alarm, and shower gunfire on their school-mates and teachers? Stop searching for an answer. Drug Watch International, a drug "think tank" that regularly consults with drug czar Barry McCaffrey and testifies before Congress, answered the question in an April 1998 press release: "MARIJUANA USED BY JONESBORO KILLERS."[5]

II.

In 1912, Merck Pharmaceuticals in Germany synthesized a type of ampheta-mine, methylenedioxymethamphetamine, or MDMA. It remained largely unused until 1976, when a biochemist at the University of California, Alexander Shulgin, curious about reports from his students, produced and swallowed 120 milligrams of the compound. The result, he wrote soon afterward, was "an easily controlled altered state of consciousness with emotional and sensual overtones."

Shulgin's immediate thought was that the drug might be useful in psychotherapy the way LSD had been. In the two decades after its mind-altering properties were discovered in 1943 by a chemist for Sandoz Laboratories, LSD was widely used as an experimental treatment for alcoholism, depression, and various clinical neuroses. More than a thousand clinical papers discussed the use of LSD among an estimated 40,000 people, and research studies of the drug led to some extraordinary advances, including the discovery of the serotonin system. When LSD experiments were restricted in 1962 and again in 1965, Senator Robert Kennedy held a congressional hearing. "If they were worthwhile six months ago, why aren't they worthwhile now?" he asked officials of the Food and Drug Administration and the National Institute of Mental Health. "Perhaps to some extent we have lost sight of the fact that [LSD] can be very, very helpful in our society if used properly."

The answer to Kennedy's question was that LSD had leaked out of the uni-versities and clinics and into the hands of "recreational users." It had crossed the line that separates good drugs from bad. LSD was outlawed three years later. In

1970, when a new law devised five categories, or "schedules," of controlled substances, LSD was placed in Schedule I, along with heroin and marijuana. This is the designation for drugs with no accepted medical use and a "high potential for abuse." In 1986, MDMA would be added to that list of demon drugs. The question is: How does a substance get assigned to that category? What separates the good drugs from the bad?

In the nineteenth century, now-illegal substances were commonly used in medicine, tonics, and consumer products. (The Illinois asylum that housed Mary Todd Lincoln in the 1870s offered its patients morphine, cannabis, whiskey, beer, and ale. Sigmund Freud treated himself with cocaine and, for a time at least, praised it effusively, as did William McKinley and Thomas Edison.) A new era began with the federal Pure Food and Drug Act of 1906, which required the listing of ingredients in medical products. Then, the 1914 Harrison Narcotic Act, ostensibly a tax measure, asserted legal control over distributors and users of opium and cocaine.

On the surface, this might seem progressive, the story of a still-young nation establishing commercial and medical standards. And there was genuine uneasiness about drugs that were intoxicating or that produced dependence; with the disclosure required by the 1906 act, sales of patent medicines containing opium dropped by a third. But the movement for prohibition drew much of its power from a far less savory motive. "Cocaine," warned Theodore Roosevelt's drug adviser, "is often a direct incentive to the crime of rape by the Negroes."[6] As David Musto reports in The American Disease, the prohibitions of the early part of the century were all, in part, a reaction to inflamed fears of foreigners or minority groups. Opium was associated with the Chinese. In 1937, the Marihuana Tax Act targeted Mexican immigrants. "I wish I could show you what a small marijuana cigarette can do to one of our degenerate Spanish-speaking residents," a Colorado newspaper editor wrote to federal officials in 1936. Even the prohibition of alcohol was underlined by fears of immigrants and exaggerations of the effects of drinking. On the eve of its ban in 1919, a radio preacher told his audience, "The reign of tears is over. The slums will soon be a memory. We will turn our prisons into factories, our jails into storehouses and corncribs. Men will walk upright now, women will smile and the children will laugh. Hell will be forever for rent."

But the federal authorities, temperance advocates, and bigots had reached too far. Whereas alcohol (like coffee and tobacco) has been a demon drug in other cultures, in Western societies its use in medicine, recreation, and religious ceremonies stretches back thousands of years. Most Americans had personal experience with drink and could measure the benefits of Prohibition against the violence (by gangsters and by Prohibition agents, who, according to one estimate, killed 1,000 Americans between 1920 and 1930) and the deaths by "overdose."[7] After Franklin Roosevelt lifted Prohibition, subsequent generations knew that the drug, though often abused and often implicated in crimes, violence, and accidents, differs in its effects depending on the person using it. With outlawed drugs, no such reality check is available. People who use illegal drugs without great harm generally stay quiet.

Alcohol also can be legally used in medicines, such as Nyquil, or used medicinally in a casual way, say, to calm shattered nerves. Demon drugs, on the other hand, are prohibited or seriously limited even in cases of exceptional need. Forty percent of pain specialists admit that they undermedicate patients to avoid the suspicion of the Drug Enforcement Administration. Their fear is justified: every year about 100 doctors who prescribe narcotics lose their licenses, including, in 1996, Dr. William Hurwitz, a Virginia internist whose more than 200 patients were left with no one to treat them. One of these patients committed suicide, saying in a videotaped message, "Dr. Hurwitz isn't the only doctor that can help. He's the only doctor that will help." Chronic pain, mind you, doesn't mean dull throbbing. "I can't shower," one patient explained to *U.S. News & World Report*, "because the water feels like molten lava. Every time someone turns on a ceiling fan, it feels like razor blades are cutting through my legs." To ease such pain can require massive doses of narcotics. This is what Hurwitz prescribed. This is why he lost his license. At least narcotics are acknowledged as a legitimate medical tool. Marijuana is not, despite overwhelming evidence that smoking the cannabis plant is a powerful treatment for glaucoma and seizures, mollifies the effects of AIDS or cancer chemotherapy, and eases anxiety. The editors of *The New England Journal of Medicine*, the American Bar Association, the Institute of Medicine of the National Academy of Sciences, and the majority of voters in California and six other states (plus the District of Columbia) are among those who believe that these uses of marijuana are legitimate. So does the eminent geologist Stephen Jay Gould. He developed abdominal cancer in the 1980s and suffered such intense nausea from intravenous chemotherapy that he came to dread it with an "almost perverse intensity." "The treatment," he remembers, "seem[ed] worse than the disease itself." Gould was reluctant to smoke marijuana, which, as thousands of cancer patients have found, is a powerful antiemetic. When he did, he found it "the greatest boost I received in all my years of treatment." "It is beyond my comprehension," Gould concluded, "and I fancy myself able to comprehend a lot, including much nonsense, that any humane person would withhold such a beneficial substance from people in such great need simply because others use it for different purposes."

This distinction between "people in great need" and those with "different purposes" is crucial to the argument for the medical use of marijuana.[8] Like Gould, many who use marijuana for medical reasons dislike the "high." Many others don't even feel it. But it is a mistake to think that the reason these people can't legally use marijuana is simply that other people use it for purposes other than traditional medical need. Because the very idea of "medical need" is constantly shifting beneath our feet.

I do not have cancer or epilepsy, or a disabling mental disorder such as schizophrenia. The "other purposes" Gould refers to are, in many ways, mine. The qualities of my suffering are (to simplify) anxiety, numbness, and anhedonia. If these were relieved by a legal drug, in other words, if a pharmaceutical helped me relax, feel more alive, have fun, I would be firmly in the mainstream of American medicine. This is my strong preference. But when I returned to see Donald Klein this past summer, hoping that new medications might have emerged in the last five years, he told me that "there are lots of things to try but there's only marginal evidence that any of them would do any good." He also made it clear that I shouldn't get my hopes up. "What you have," he said, "is not a common condition, and it's almost impossible [for pharmaceutical companies] to do a systematic study, let alone make money, on a condition that's not common." And so, yes, I turn sometimes to marijuana and other illicit substances for the (limited) relief they offer. I don't merely feel justified in doing so; I feel entitled, particularly since, every year, the pharmaceutical industry rolls out new products for pleasure, vanity, convenience.

When Viagra emerged, it was not frowned upon by the authorities that lead the drug wars. Instead, President Clinton ordered Medicaid to cover the drug, and the Pentagon budgeted $50 million for fiscal 1999 to supply it to soldiers, veterans, and civilian employees. Pfizer hired Bob Dole to instruct the nation that "it may take a little courage" to use Viagra. This is a medicine whose sole purpose is to allow for sexual pleasure; it was embraced by the black market and is easily available from doctors, including some who perform "examinations" via a three-question form on the Internet. But Viagra's legitimacy was never questioned, because it treats a disease-erectile dysfunction. Before Viagra, when the only treatment options were less-effective pills and awkward injection-based therapies, this condition was referred to as impotence. The change in language is interesting. The "dys" sits on the front of dysfunction like a streak of dirt on a pane of glass. At a level more primal than cognitive, we want it removed. This is what we do with dysfunctions: we fix them. Impotence, on the other hand, meaning "weakness" or "helplessness," is something we all experience at one time or another. Applied to men "incapable of sexual intercourse, often because of an inability to achieve or sustain an erection," the word carries a sense of something unfortunate but part of living, and particularly of growing older.

Thus the advent of Viagra does not simply treat a disease. It changes our conception of disease. This paradigm shift is a common occurrence but is below our radar. Hair loss becomes a disease, not a fact of life. Acid indigestion becomes a disease, not a matter of eating poorly. If these examples seem to make light of the broadening of disease, the ascent of psychopharmaceuticals makes the issue urgent. Outside the realm of the tangibly physical, the power of drugs and drug-makers is far greater. What we now know as "anxiety disorder," for example, existed only in theory from Freud's time through World War II. In the early 1950s, a drug company polled doctors and found that most had no interest in a medication that treated anxiety. But by 1970, one woman in five and one man in thirteen were using a tranquilizer or sedative, and anxiety was a mainstay of psychiatry. The change could be directly attributed to two drugs, Miltown and Valium, which were released in 1955 and 1963, respectively. The successor to these drugs, Xanax, introduced in 1981, virtually created a disease itself. Donald Klein had already proposed the existence of something called "panic disorder," as opposed to generalized anxiety, some twenty years before. But his theory was widely refuted, and in practice panic anxiety was treated only in the context of a larger problem. Xanax changed that. "With a convenient, effective drug available," writes Peter Kramer, "doctors saw panic anxiety everywhere." Xanax has also become the litmus test for generalized anxiety disorder. "If Xanax doesn't work," instructs *The Essential Guide to Psychiatric Drugs*, "usually the original diagnosis was wrong."[9]

This is not to say that all specific disorders are arbitrary, just that there is a delicate line to be drawn. "The term 'disease'—and the border between health and disease—is a social construct," says Steven Hyman, director of the National Institute of Mental Health. "There are some things we would never argue about, like cancer. But do we call it a disease if you have a few foci of abnormal cells in your body, something that you could live with without any problem? There is a gray zone. With behavior and the brain, the gray zone is much larger." To Hyman's observation, it must be added that, whereas vague dissatisfactions make money for psychic hot lines and interior decorators, diseases make money for pharmaceutical companies. What Peter Kramer calls psychiatric diagnostic creep is not an accident of history but a movement engineered for profit.

We have only begun to grapple with the consequences. The example of Prozac has been chewed over, but it's worth chewing still more because it is so typical of a new generation of drugs, which are being used to treat debilitating conditions and also by people with far less serious problems. With Lauren Slater, author of the fine memoir *Prozac Diary*, we have a case anyone would regard as serious. Suffering from obsessive-compulsive disorder, severe depression, and anorexia, she had been hospitalized five times, attempted suicide twice, and cut herself with razors. Prescribed Prozac in 1988, she found the drug a reprieve from a lifetime sentence of serious illness—"a blessing, pure and simple," she writes. The patients described in Peter Kramer's *Listening to Prozac* are quite unlike Lauren Slater. They share, he writes, "something very much like 'neurosis,' psychoanalysis's umbrella term for the mildly disturbed, the near-normal, and those with very little wrong at all." The use of Prozac for these patients is not incidental; they make up a large portion, probably a wide majority, of people on the drug. (One good indication is that only 31 percent of antidepressant prescriptions are written by psychiatrists.)

Throughout his book, Kramer flirts with "unsettling" comparisons between Prozac and illegal drugs. Since Prozac can "lend social ease, command, even brilliance," for example, he wonders how its use for this purpose can "be distinguished from, say, the street use of amphetamine as a way of overcoming inhibitions and inspiring zest." The better comparison, I suggested in a conversation with Kramer, is between Prozac and MDMA. Both drugs work by increasing the presence of serotonin in the brain. (Whereas Prozac inhibits serotonin's reuptake, MDMA stimulates its release.) Both can be helpful to the seriously ill as well as to people with more common problems. Most of the objections to MDMA—that it distorts "real" personality, that it rids people of anxiety that may be personally or socially useful, that it induces more pleasure than is natural have also been marshaled against Prozac. Both these drugs challenge our definitions of normalcy and of the legitimate uses of a mind-altering substance. Yet Kramer rejects the comparison. "The distinction we make," he told me, "is between drugs that give pleasure directly and the drugs that give people the ability to function in society, which can indirectly lead to pleasure. If the medication can make you work well or parent well, and then through your work or parenting you get pleasure, that's fine. But if the drug gives you pleasure by taking it directly, that's not a legitimate use." (Viagra, because it allows men to experience sexual pleasure, falls on the side of legitimacy. But, Kramer said, a drug that directly induced an orgasm would not.)

The line between therapeutic and hedonistic pleasure, however, is awfully hard to draw. I think of a friend of mine who uses MDMA a few times a month. His is a textbook case of "recreational" use. He takes MDMA on weekends, in clubs, for fun. He is not ill and is not in psychotherapy. But he will live for the rest of his life in the shadow of a traumatic experience, which is that for more than two decades he hid his homosexuality. Some might say the drug is an unhealthy escape from "the real world," that the relaxation and intimacy he experiences are illusory. But these experiences give him a point of reference he can use in a "sober" state. His pleasure from the drug is entirely social-being and sharing and loving with other people. Is this hedonistic? "I found it astonishing," Kramer writes of Prozac, "that a pill could do in a matter of days what psychiatrists hope, and often fail, to accomplish by other means over a course of years: to restore to a person robbed of it in childhood the capacity to play."

Perhaps I would find restrictions on MDMA more reasonable if they at least carved out an exception for therapeutic use. Keep in mind, that's where this drug started. After Shulgin's experiment word spread, and thousands of doses were taken in a clinical setting. As with LSD, MDMA was seen not as a medicine but as a catalyst to be taken just a few times—or perhaps only once—in the presence of a therapist or "guide." The effects were impressive. Many users found their artifice and defenses stripped away and long-buried emotions rising to the surface. The drug also had the unusual effect of increasing empathy, which helped users trust their therapist—a crucial characteristic of effective healing—and also made it useful in couples therapy. In a collection of first-person accounts of therapeutic MDMA use, *Through the Gateway of the Heart*, published in 1985, a rape victim described working through her fears. Another woman described revelations about her son, her weight problems, and "why angry men are attracted to me."

I can hear the skeptics shuffling their feet, wanting data from double-blind controlled trials. But MDMA research never reached that stage. Mindful of what had happened with LSD, the therapists, scientists, and other adults experimenting with MDMA tried to keep it quiet. Inevitably, though, word spread, and a new mode of use sprang up at raves, in dance clubs, in dorm rooms. An astute distributor of the drug renamed it ecstasy to emphasize its pleasurable effects. ("'Empathy' would be more appropriate," he said later. "But how many people know what that means?")[10]

As the DEA moved to restrict MDMA, advocates of its medical use flooded the agency with testimony, pleading for a chance to subject the drug to methodical study. The agency's administrative-law judge, Francis Young, saw merit in this argument. In a ninety-page decision handed down in 1986, he recommended that the drug be placed in Schedule III, which would allow for it to be prescribed by doctors and tested further. Young cited its history of "currently accepted medical use in treatment in the United States" and argued that "the evidence of record does not establish that . . . MDMA has a 'high potential' for abuse."

DEA officials overruled Young and placed MDMA in Schedule I, with the assurance that its decision would be self-fulfilling. A Schedule I substance cannot be used clinically and can be studied only with great difficulty. So medical use is essentially forever impossible. That leaves illicit use, which, by one common definition, is the abuse for which Schedule I drugs have a "high potential." Since then, government-funded researchers have sought to document MDMA's dangers. Here we come to the truth about the line and how it is maintained. With rare exceptions, everything we know about legal drugs comes from research sponsored by the pharmaceutical industry. Naturally, this work emphasizes the benefits and downplays the accompanying risks. On the other hand, the National Institute on Drug Abuse, which funds more than 85 percent of the world's health research on illegal drugs, emphasizes the dangers and all but ignores potential benefits.

One recent NIDA-funded study on MDMA was widely reported last fall. Dr. George Ricaurte found, in fourteen men and women who had used MDMA 70 to 400 times in the previous six years, "long-lasting nerve cell damage in the brain." Specifically, Ricaurte found decreases in the number of serotonin-reuptake sites. The study begs three major questions. First, do its conclusions really reflect the experience of heavy MDMA users? British physician Karl Jansen reports that he referred MDMA users who had taken more than 1,000 doses and that "they were told by Ricaurte that they had a clean bill of health" but were excluded from his study. Second, should the brain changes Ricaurte found be called "damage," given that a number of psychiatric medications, Prozac and Zoloft among them, decrease the number of serotonin receptors by blockading them? As psychopharmacologist Julie Holland writes, "This could be interpreted as an adaptive response as opposed to a toxic or 'damaged' response." Third, do Ricaurte's findings have any bearing on the use of MDMA in therapy, which calls for a handful of doses over many months?

In this climate, it's hard to know. Charles Grob, a psychiatrist at Harbor-UCLA Medical Center in Los Angeles, has been trying to restart MDMA research for eight years. He received FDA approval to conduct Phase I trials on human volunteers, to see if MDMA is safe enough to be used as a medicine. But even with his impeccable credentials, the backing of a prestigious research hospital, and an extremely conservative protocol—involving terminal patients—Grob has faced a seemingly interminable wait for permission to begin Phase II, in which he would study efficacy. Grob's struggle explains why he has little company in the research community. "When you have a drug that's popular among young people," Grob says, "that's the kiss of death when it comes to exploring its potential utility in a medical context."

There is another "kiss of death": lack of interest from industry. I asked Lester Grinspoon, a professor of psychiatry at Harvard Medical School, who led the legal challenge to the DEA's scheduling decision, whether he had approached drug companies about supporting the effort. "We didn't even consider it," he said. "No drug company is going to be interested in a drug that's therapeutically useful only once or twice a year. That's a no-brainer for them." When you see the feel-good ads from the Pharmaceutical Research and Manufacturer's Association with the tag line "Leading the way in the search for cures," keep in mind that cures—conditions in which medication is no longer required—are not particularly high on the pharmaceutical companies' priority list.

Market potential isn't the only factor explaining the status of drugs, but its power shouldn't be underestimated. The principal psychoactive ingredient of marijuana, THC, is available in pill form and can be legally prescribed as Marinol. A "new" creation, it was patented by Unimed Pharmaceutical and is sold for about $15 per 10-mg pill. Marinol is considered by patients to be a poor substitute for marijuana, because doses cannot be titrated as precisely and because THC is only one of 460 known compounds in cannabis smoke, among other reasons. But Marinol's profit potential—necessary to justify the up-front research and testing, which can cost upward of $500 million per medication—brought it to market. Opponents of medical marijuana claim that they simply want all medicines to be approved by the FDA, but they know that drug companies have little incentive to overcome the regulatory and financial obstacles for a plant that can't be patented. The FDA is the tail, not the dog.

The market must be taken seriously as an explanation of drugs' status. The reason is that the explanations usually given fall so far short. Take the idea "Bad drugs induce violence." First, violence is demonstrably not a pharmacological effect of marijuana, heroin, and the psychedelics. Of cocaine, in some cases. (Of alcohol, in many.) But if it were violence we feared, then wouldn't we punish that act with the greatest severity? Drug sellers, even people marginally involved in a "conspiracy to distribute," consistently receive longer sentences than rapists and murderers.

Nor can the explanation be the danger of illegal drugs. Marijuana, though not harmless, has never been shown to have caused a single death. Heroin, in long-term "maintenance" use, is safer than habitual heavy drinking. Of course, illegal drugs can do the body great harm. All drugs have some risk, including many legal ones. Because of Viagra's novelty, the 130 deaths it has caused (as of last November) have received a fair amount of attention. But each year, anti-inflammatory agents such as Advil, Tylenol, and aspirin cause an estimated 7,000 deaths and 70,000 hospitalizations. Legal medications are the principal cause of between 45,000 and 200,000 American deaths each year, between 1- and 5.5 million hospitalizations. It is telling that we have only estimates. As Thomas J. Moore notes in *Prescription for Disaster*, the government calculates the annual deaths due to railway accidents and falls of less than one story, among hundreds of categories. But no federal agency collects information on deaths related to legal drugs. (The $30 million spent investigating the crash of TWA Flight 800, in which 230 people died, is six times larger than the FDA's budget for monitoring the safety of approved drugs.) Psychoactive drugs can be particularly toxic. In 1992, according to Moore, nearly 100,000 persons were diagnosed with "poisoning" by psychologically active drugs, 90 percent of the cases due to benzodiazepine tranquilizers and antidepressants. It is simply a myth that legal drugs have been proven "safe." According to one government estimate, 15 percent of children are on Ritalin. But the long-term effects of Ritalin—or antidepressants, which are also commonly prescribed—on kids isn't known. "I feel in between a rock and a hard place," says NIMH director Hyman. "I know that untreated depression is bad and that we better not just let kids be depressed. But by the same token we don't know what the effects of antidepressants are on the developing brain. . . . We should have humility and be a bit frightened."

These risks are striking, given that protecting children is the cornerstone of the drug wars. We forbid the use of medical marijuana, worrying that it will send a bad message. What message is sent by the long row of pills laid out by the

AMERICA'S ALTERED STATES   251

school nurse or by "educational" visits to high schools by drugmakers? But, you might object, these are medicines, and illegal drug use is purely hedonistic. What, then, about illegal drug use that clearly falls under the category of self-medication? One physician I know who treats women heroin users tells me that each of them suffered sexual abuse as children. According to University of Texas pharmacologist Kathryn Cunningham, 40 to 70 percent of cocaine users have pre-existing depressive conditions.

This is not to suggest that depressed people should use cocaine. The risks of dependence and compulsive use, and the roller-coaster experience of cocaine highs and lows, make for a toxic combination with intense suffering. Given these risks, not to mention the risk of arrest, why wouldn't a depressed person opt for legal treatment? The most obvious answers are economic (many cocaine users lack access to health care) and chemical. Cocaine is a formidable mood elevator and acts immediately, as opposed to the two to four weeks of most pre-scription antidepressants. Perhaps the most important factor, though, is cultural. Using a "pleasure drug" like cocaine does not signal weakness or vulnerability. Self-medication can be a way of avoiding the stigma of admitting to oneself and others that there is a problem to be treated.

Calling illegal drug use a disease is popular these days, and it is done, I believe, with a compassionate purpose: pushing treatment over incarceration. It also seems clear that drug abuse can be a distinct pathology. But isn't the "disease" whatever the drug users are trying to find relief from (or flee)? According to the Pharmaceutical Research and Manufacturer's Association, nineteen medications are in development for "substance use disorders." This includes six products for "smoking cessation" that contain nicotine. Are these treatments for a disease or competitors in the market for long-term nicotine maintenance?

Perhaps the most damning charge against illegal drugs is that they're addictive. Again, the real story is considerably more complicated. Many illegal drugs, like marijuana and cocaine, do not produce physical dependence. Some, like heroin, do. In any case, the most important factor in destructive use is the craving people experience—craving that leads them to continue a behavior despite serious adverse effects. Legal drugs preclude certain behaviors we associate with addiction, like stealing for dope money, but that doesn't mean people don't become addicted to them. By their own admissions, Betty Ford was addicted to Valium and William Rehnquist to the sleeping pill Placidyl, for nine years. Ritalin shares the addictive qualities of all the amphetamines. "For many people," says NIMH director Hyman, explaining why many psychiatrists will not prescribe one class of drugs, "stopping short-acting high-potency benzodi-azepines, such as Xanax, is sheer hell. As they try to stop they develop rebound anxiety symptoms (or insomnia) that seem worse than the original symptoms they were treating." Even antidepressants, although they certainly don't produce the intense craving of classic addiction, can be habit forming. Lauren Slater was first made well by one pill per day, then required more to feel the same effect, then found that even three would not return her to the miraculous health that she had at first experienced. This is called tolerance. She has also been unable to stop taking the drug without "breaking up." This is called depend-ence. " 'There are plenty of addicts who lead perfectly respectable lives,' " Slater's boyfriend tells her. To which she replies, "An addict. . . . You think so?' "

III.

In the late 1980s, in black communities, the Partnership for a Drug Free America placed billboards showing an outstretched hand filled with vials of crack cocaine. It read: "YO, SLAVE! The dealer is selling you something you don't want. . . . Addiction is slavery." The ad was obviously designed to resonate in the black neighborhoods most visibly affected by the wave of crack use. But its idea has a broader significance in a country for which independence of mind and spirit is a primary value.

In *Brave New World*, Aldous Huxley created the archetype of drug-as-enemy-of-freedom: soma. "A really efficient totalitarian state," he wrote in the book's fore-word, is one in which the "slaves . . . do not have to be coerced, because they love their servitude." Soma—"euphoric, narcotic, pleasantly hallucinant," with "all the advantages of Christianity and alcohol; none of their defects," and a way to "take a holiday from reality whenever you like, and come back without so much as a headache or a mythology"—is one of the key agents of that voluntary slavery.

In the spring of 1953, two decades after he published this book, Huxley offered himself as a guinea pig in the experiments of a British psychiatrist studying mescaline. What followed was a second masterpiece on drugs and man, *The Doors of Perception*. The title is from William Blake: "If the doors of perception were cleansed every thing would appear to man as it is, infinite—/For man has closed himself up, till he sees all things thro' narrow chinks of his cavern." Huxley found his mescaline experience to be "without question the most extraordinary and significant experience this side of the Beatific vision. . . . [I]t opens up a host of philosophical problems, throws intense light and raises all manner of questions in the field of aesthetics, religion, theory of knowledge."

Taken together, these two works frame the dual, contradictory nature of mind-altering substances: they can be agents of servitude or of freedom. Though we are deathly afraid of the first possibility, we are drawn like moths to the light of the second. "The urge to transcend self-conscious selfhood is," Huxley writes, "a principal appetite of the soul. When, for whatever reason, men and women fail to transcend themselves by means of worship, good works, and spiritual exercises, they are apt to resort to religion's chemical surrogates."

One might think, as mind diseases are broadened and the substances that alter consciousness take their place beside toothpaste and breakfast cereal, that users of other "surrogates" might receive more understanding and sympathy. You might think the executive taking Xanax before a speech, or the college student on BuSpar, or any of the recipients of 65 million annual antidepressant prescriptions, would have second thoughts about punishing the depressed user of cocaine, or even the person who is not seriously depressed, just, as the Prozac ad says, "feeling blue." In trying to imagine why the opposite has happened, I think of the people I know who use psychopharmaceuticals. Because I've always been up front about my experiences, friends often approach me when they're thinking of doing so. Every year there are more of them. And yet, in their hushed tones, I hear shame mixed with fear. I think we don't know quite what to make of our own brave new world. The more fixes that become available, the more we realize we're vulnerable. We solve some problems, but add new and perplexing ones.

In *The Odyssey*, when three of his crew are lured by the lotus-eaters and "lost all desire to send a message back, much less return," Odysseus responds decisively. "I brought them back . . . dragged them under the rowing benches, lashed them fast." "Already," writes David Lenson in *On Drugs*, "the high is unspeakable, and already the official response is arrest and restraint." The pattern is set: since people lose their freedom from drugs, we take their freedom to keep them from drugs.[11] Odysseus's frantic response, though, seems more than just a practical measure. Perhaps he fears his own desire to retire amidst the lotus-eaters. Perhaps he fears what underlies that desire. If we even feel the lure of drugs, we acknowledge that we are not satisfied by what is good and productive and healthy. And that is a frightening thought. "The War on Drugs has been with us," writes Lenson, "for as long as we have despised the part of ourselves that wants to get high."

As Lenson points out, "It is a peculiar feature of history, that peoples with strong historical, physical, and cultural affinities tend to detest each other with the most venom." In the American drug wars, too, animosity runs in both directions. Many users of illegal drugs—particularly kids—do so not just because they like the feeling but because it sets them apart from "straight" society, allows them (without any effort or thought) to join a culture of dissent. On the other side, "straight society" sees a hated version of itself in the drug users. This is not just the 11 percent of Americans using psychotropic medications, or the 6 million who admit to "nonmedical" use of legal drugs, but anyone who fears and desires pleasure, who fears and desires loss of control, who fears and desires chemically enhanced living.

Straight society has remarkable power: it can arrest the enemy, seize assets without judicial review, withdraw public housing or assistance. But the real power of prohibition is that it creates the forbidden world of danger and hedonism that the straights want to distinguish themselves from. A black market spawns violence, thievery, and illnesses—all can be blamed on the demon drugs. For a reminder, we need only go to the movies (in which drug dealers are the stock villains). Or watch "Cops," in which, one by one, the bedraggled junkies, fearsome crack dealers, and hapless dope smokers are led away in chains. For anyone who is secretly ashamed, or confused, about the explosion in legal drug-taking, here is reassurance: The people in handcuffs are the bad ones. Anything the rest of us do is saintly by comparison.

We are like Robert Louis Stevenson's Dr. Jekyll, longing that we might be divided in two, that "the unjust might go his way . . . and the just could walk steadfastly and securely on his upward path, doing the good things in which he found his pleasure, and no longer exposed to disgrace and penitence by the hands of this extraneous evil." In his laboratory, Jekyll creates the "foul soul" of Edward Hyde, whose presence heightens the reputation of the esteemed doctor. But Jekyll's dream cannot last. Just before his suicide, he confesses to having become "a creature eaten up and emptied by fever, languidly weak both in body and mind, and solely occupied by one thought: the horror of my other self." To react to an unpleasant truth by separating from it is a fundamental human instinct. Usually, though, what is denied only grows in injurious power. We believe that lashing at the illegal drug user will purify us. We try to separate the "evil" from the "good" of drugs, what we love and what we fear about them, to enforce a drug-free America with handcuffs and jail cells while legal drugs grow in popularity and variety. But we cannot separate the inseparable. We know the truth about ourselves. It is time to begin living with that horror, and that blessing.

NOTES

1. Although I am critical of the exaltation of drugs, it must be noted that a crisis runs in the opposite direction. Only a small minority of people with schizophrenia, bipolar disorder, and major depression—for which medications can be very helpful—receive treatment of any kind.

2. Fifty-five percent of American adults, or 97 million people, are overweight or obese. It is no surprise, then, that at least forty-five companies have weight-loss drugs in development. But many of these drugs are creatures more of marketing than of pharmacology. Meridia is an SSRI, like Prozac. Similarly, Zyban, a Glaxo Wellcome product for smoking cessation, is chemically identical to the antidepressant Wellbutrin. Admakers exclude this information because they want their products to seem like targeted cures—not vaguely understood remedies like the "tonics" of yesteryear.

3. Declared Nancy Reagan, "If you're a casual drug user, you're an accomplice to murder." Los Angeles police chief Daryl Gates told the Senate that "casual drug users should be taken out and shot." And so on.

4. Many people believe that this is still possible, among them House Speaker Dennis Hastert, who last year coauthored a plan to "help create a drug-free America by the year 2002." In 1995, Hastert sponsored a bill allowing herbal remedies to bypass FDA regulations, thus helping to satisfy Americans' incessant desire for improvement and consciousness alteration.

5. The release describes Andrew Golden and Mitchell Johnson as "reputed marijuana smokers." No reference to Golden and pot could be found in the Nexis database. The *Washington Post* reports that Johnson "said he smoked marijuana. None of his classmates believed him."

6. Such propaganda was crucial in convincing the South to allow the Harrison Act's unprecedented extension of federal power. It would be comforting to view this as a sad moment in history, but a prohibition with racist origins continues to have a racist effect: Blacks account for 12 percent of the U.S. population and 15 percent of regular drug users. But they make up 35 percent of arrests for drug possession and 60 percent of the people in state prison on drug offenses.

7. Overdoses always increase in a black market, because drugs are of unknown purity and often include contaminants. Although drug use declined between 1978 and 1994, overdose deaths increased by 400 percent.

8. A popular argument against medical marijuana is that it is a ruse for the "real" goal of unrestricted use, but this argument is itself a ruse. We put aside disagreements over immigration to allow amnesty for victims of political torture. We—at least most of

us—put aside disagreements over abortion in cases of rape. Medical marijuana use for the seriously ill has the same unambiguous claim to legitimacy. Yet sick people face arrest and punishment. In 1997, there were 606,519 arrests for marijuana possession and 88,682 arrests for sale/manufacture; in the latter category fell an Oklahoma man with severe rheumatoid arthritis who received ninety-three years in prison for growing marijuana in his basement. The prosecutor had told the jury that, in sentencing, they should "pick a number and add two or three zeros to it."

9. Defining diseases around medication pleases drug companies as well as HMOs. From 1988 to 1997, as general health-care benefits declined 7 percent, mental-health benefits fell 54 percent. Substituting pills for psychotherapy helps cut costs.

10. With a street name like Ecstasy, it is hard to take MDMA seriously as a medicine, especially compared with words like painkillers, or antidepressants, which signify the elimination of a problem as opposed to the creation of pleasure. But the faux-Latin pharmaceutical names are also designed to suggest the drugs' wonders. David Wood, who used to run the firm that came up with the name Prozac, explains it this way: "It's short and aggressive, the 'Pro' is positive, and the Z indicates efficacy." One of Wood's employees elaborated on good drug names: "Sounds such as 'ah,' or 'ay,' which require that the mouth be open, evoke a feeling of expansiveness and openness." As in Meridia, Viagra, Propecia.

11. In the 1992 campaign, Bill Clinton said, "I don't think my brother would be alive today if it wasn't for the criminal justice system." Roger served sixteen months in Arkansas State Prison for conspiracy to distribute cocaine. Had he been convicted three years later, he would have faced a five-year mandatory minimum sentence, without the possibility of parole. If he had had a prior felony or had sold the same amount of cocaine in crack form, he would have automatically received ten years.

THE WAR ON (SOME) DRUGS

Stephen Jay Gould

From *Harper's Magazine*, April 1990. A longer version of the article appeared in *Dissent*, Winter 1990.

Categories often exert a tyranny over our perceptions and judgments. An old joke—perhaps it even happened—from the bad old days of McCarthyism tells of a leftist rally in Philadelphia, viciously broken up by police. A passerby gets caught in the melee and, as the cops are beating him, he pleads, "Stop, stop, I'm an anticommunist." "I don't care what kind of communist you are," says the cop, as he continues pummeling.

We seem driven to think in dichotomies. Protagoras, according to Diogenes, asserted that "there are two sides to every question, exactly opposite to each other." We set up our categories, often by arbitrary division based on tiny differences; then, mistaking names for moral principles, and using banners and slogans as substitutes for reason, we vow to live or die for one or the other side of a false dichotomy. The situation is lamentable enough when the boundaries are profound and natural; if cows declared war on chickens, we might deplore the barnyard carnage, but at least the divisions would be deep, and membership by birth could not be disputed. But when humans struggle with other humans, the boundaries are almost always fluid and largely arbitrary (or at least a curious result of very recent historical contingencies.)

Our current drug crisis is a tragedy born of a phony system of classification. For reasons that are little more than accidents of history, we have divided a group of nonfood substances into two categories: items purchasable for supposed pleasure (such as alcohol) and illicit drugs. The categories were once reversed. Opiates were legal in America before the Harrison Narcotics Act of 1914; and members of the Women's Christian Temperance Union, who campaigned against alcohol during the day, drank their valued "women's tonics" at night, products laced with laudanum (tincture of opium).

I could abide—though I would still oppose—our current intransigence if we applied the principle of total interdiction to all harmful drugs. But how can we possibly defend our current policy based on a dichotomy that encourages us to view one class of substances as a preeminent scourge while the two most dangerous and life-destroying substances by far, alcohol and tobacco, form a second class advertised in neon on every street corner in urban America? And why, moreover, should heroin be viewed with horror while chemical cognates that are no different from heroin than lemonade is from iced tea perform work of enormous compassion by relieving the pain of terminal cancer patients in their last days?

Consider just a few recent items rooted in our false classification.

1. A *New York Times* editorial describes methadone as a drug that "blocks the craving for heroin." You might as well say that a Coke blocks the craving for a Pepsi. Methadone and heroin are both opiates, but methadone is legal as a controlled substitute for heroin (fine by me; I think they both should be controlled and decriminalized). We permit methadone because some favorable features lead to easier control (oral administration, longer action, and a less intense high), but methadone is a chemical cousin to heroin.

2. Representative Charles Rangel (Dem., N.Y.) implacable foe of legalisation, spurns all talk about his subject as the chatter of eggheads. In 1988, in a *New York Times* op-ed piece, he wrote, "Let's take this legislation issue and put it where it belongs—amid idle chit-chat as cocktail glasses knock together at social events." Don't you get it, Mr. Rangel? The stuff in the glasses is as bad as the stuff on the streets. But our classifications permit a majority of Americans to live well enough with one while forcing a minority to murder and die for the other.

3. Former surgeon general C. Everett Koop, who was hired by Reagan to be an ideologue and decided to be a doctor instead, accurately branded nicotine as no less addictive than heroin and cocaine. Representative Terry Bruce (Dem., Ill.) challenged this assertion by arguing that smokers are not "breaking into liquor stores late at night to get money to buy a pack of cigarettes." Koop properly replied that the only difference resides in social definition as legal or illegal: "You take cigarettes off the streets and people will be breaking into liquor stores. I think one of the things that many people confuse is the behavior of cocaine and heroin addicts when they are deprived of these drugs. That's the difference between a licit and an illicit drug. Tobacco is perfectly legal. You can get it whenever you want to satisfy the craving.

We do not ponder our methods of classification with sufficient scrutiny—and have never done so. Taxonomy, or the study of classification, occupies a low status among the sciences because most people view the activity as a kind of glorified bookkeeping dedicated to pasting objects into preassigned spaces in nature's stamp album. This judgment rests on the false premise that our categories are given by nature and ascertained by simple, direct observation. Nature is full of facts—and they are not distributed isotropically, so nature does provide some hints about divisions.

But our classifications are human impositions, or at least culturally based decisions on what to stress among a plethora of viable alternatives. Classifications are therefore theories of order, not simple records of nature. More important, since classifications are actively imposed, not passively imbibed, they shape our thoughts and deeds in ways that we scarcely perceive because we view our categories as "obvious" and "natural."

Some classifications channel our thinking into fruitful directions because they properly capture the causes of order; others lead us to tragic and vicious errors (the older taxonomies of human races, for example) because they sink their roots in prejudice and mayhem. Too rarely, in our political criticism, do we look to false taxonomies, particularly to improper dichotomies, as the basis for inadequate analysis.

Our drug crisis is largely the product of such a false dichotomy. At the moment, hundreds of thousands of drug users live in tortured limbo, driven to crime, exposed to AIDS, and doomed (at least statistically speaking) to early death. Millions of others suffer palpably from the deeds of the addicted—experiencing violence, robbery, or simple urban fear that steals the joy from life. Billions of dollars go down the rathole to enrich the entrepreneurs or to try to stem the plague by necessarily ineffective interdiction. The politics of several nations in our hemisphere are corrupted, the cultures of whole peoples severely compromised.

William Jennings Bryan once argued that we were about to crucify mankind on a cross of gold. Are we not now significantly lowering the quality of life for everyone, and causing thousands of deaths directly, by basing our drug policy on something even worse—a false and senseless classification?

NO RELIEF IN SIGHT

Jacob Sullum

An earlier version of this article appeared in *Reason Magazine,* January 1997.

David Covillion finally got relief from his pain with the help of Jack Kevorkian. The pain came from neck and back injuries Covillion had suffered in April 1987, when his station wagon was broadsided by a school bus at an intersection in Hillside, New Jersey. The crash compounded damage already caused by an on-the-job injury and a bicycle accident. Covillion, a former police officer living in upstate New York, underwent surgery that fall, but it only made the pain worse. Along with a muscle relaxant and an anti-inflammatory drug, his doctor prescribed Percocet, a combination of acetaminophen and the narcotic oxycodone, for the pain.

The doctor was uneasy about the Percocet prescriptions. In New York, as in eight other states, physicians have to write prescriptions for Schedule II drugs — a category that includes most narcotics — on special multiple-copy forms. The doctor keeps one copy, the patient takes the original to the pharmacy, and another copy goes to the state. After a year or so, Covillion recalled in an interview, his doctor started saying, "I've got to get you off these drugs. It's raising red flags." Covillion continued to demand painkiller, and eventually the doctor accused him of harassment and terminated their relationship.

"Then the nightmare really began," Covillion said. "As I ran out of medication, I was confined to my bed totally, because it hurt to move. . . . At times I'd have liked to just take an ax and chop my arm right off, because the pain got so bad, but I would have had to take half of my neck with it." He started going from doctor to doctor. Many said they did not write narcotic prescriptions. Others would initially prescribe pain medication for him, but soon they would get nervous. "I'd find a doctor who would treat me for a little while," he said. "Then he'd make up an excuse to get rid of me." Eventually, Covillion went through all the doctors in the phone book. That's when he decided to call Kevorkian.

The retired Michigan pathologist, who had helped dozens of patients end their lives, was reluctant to add Covillion to the list. At Kevorkian's insistence, Covillion sought help from various pain treatment centers, without success. He called Kevorkian back and told him: "I'm done. I have no more energy now. I just don't have the fight. If you don't want to help me, then I'll do it here myself." Kevorkian urged him to try one more possibility: the National Chronic Pain Outreach Association, which referred him to Dr. William E. Hurwitz, an internist in Washington, D.C., who serves as the group's president.

The day he called Hurwitz, Covillion was planning his death. "I had everything laid out," he said. "I got a few hoses and made it so it would be a tight fit around the exhaust pipe of my car. I taped them up to one of those giant leaf bags, and I put a little hole in the end of the bag. All I had to do was start the car up, and it would have filled the bag right up, pushed whatever air was in there out, and it would have filled the bag up with carbon monoxide. Same thing as what Dr. Kevorkian uses. And then I had a snorkel, and I made it so I could run a hose from the bag full of gas and hook it up to that snorkel, and all I had to do was put it in my mouth, close my eyes, and go to sleep. And that would have been it. I would have been gone that Friday."

But on Thursday afternoon, Covillion talked to Hurwitz, who promised to help and asked him to send his medical records by Federal Express. After reviewing the records, Hurwitz saw Covillion at his office in Washington and began treating him. "The last three years I've been all right," he said in a July interview. "I have a life." Yet Covillion was worried that his life would be taken away once again. On May 14 the Virginia Board of Medicine had suspended Hurwitz's license, charging him with excessive prescribing and inadequate supervision of his patients. At the time Hurwitz was treating about 220 people for chronic pain. Some had been injured in accidents, failed surgery, or both; others had degenerative conditions or severe headaches. Most lived outside the Washington area and had come to Hurwitz because, like Covillion, they could not find anyone nearby to help them.

In July, after the case was covered by the *Washington Post* and CBS News, the Pennsylvania pharmaceutical warehouse that had been supplying Covillion with painkillers stopped filling Hurwitz's prescriptions, even though he was still licensed to practice in D.C. The pharmacist who informed Covillion of this decision (in a telephone conversation that Covillion recorded) suggested that Hurwitz had prescribed "excessively high amounts." At the same time, he recommended that Covillion "find another doctor" to continue the prescriptions. Covillion's reply was angry and anguished: "There is no other doctor!"

Hurwitz may not be the only physician in the country who is willing to prescribe narcotics for chronic pain, but there are few enough that patients travel hundreds of miles to see them. "I call it the Painful Underground Railroad," says Dr. Harvey L. Rose, a Carmichael, California, family practitioner who, like Hurwitz, once battled state regulators who accused him of excessive prescribing. "These are people who are hurting, who have to go out of state in order to find a doctor. We still get calls from all over the country: 'My doctor won't give me any pain medicine.' Or, 'My doctor died, and the new doctor won't touch me.' These people are desperate."

In medical journals and textbooks, the cause of this desperation has a name: opiophobia. Doctors are leery of the drugs derived from opium and the synthetics that resemble them, substances like morphine and codeine, hydromorphone (Dilaudid) and meperidine (Demerol). They are leery despite the fact that, compared to other pharmaceuticals, opioids are remarkably safe: The most serious side effect of long-term use is usually constipation, whereas over-the-counter analgesics can cause stomach, kidney, and liver damage. They are leery because opioids have a double identity: They can be used to get relief or to get high, to ease physical pain or to soothe emotional distress.

Doctors are afraid of the drugs themselves, of their potency and addictiveness. And they are afraid of what might happen if they prescribe opioids to the wrong people, for the wrong reasons, or in the wrong quantities. Attracting the attention of state regulators or the Drug Enforcement Administration could mean anything from inconvenience and embarrassment to loss of their licenses and livelihoods. In the legal and cultural climate created by the eight-decade war on drugs, these two fears reinforce each other: Beliefs about the hazards of narcotics justify efforts to prevent diversion of opioids, while those efforts help sustain the beliefs. The result is untold suffering.

Because pain is hard to verify objectively, the conflict between drug control and pain relief is inevitable. It can be alleviated through regulatory reform, but it can never be eliminated. A system that completely prevented nonmedical use of prescription drugs would also leave millions of patients in agony. Conversely, a system that enabled every patient with treatable pain to get relief would also allow some fakers to obtain narcotics for their own use or for sale to others. In deciding how to resolve this dilemma, it's important to keep in mind that people who use prescription drugs to get high do so voluntarily, while patients who suffer because of inadequate pain treatment have no choice in the matter.

Clinicians and researchers have long remarked on the link between opiophobia and undertreatment of pain. In a 1966 pharmacology textbook, the psychiatrist Jerome H. Jaffe, who later became Richard Nixon's drug czar, emphasized that *"no patient should ever wish for death because of his physician's reluctance to use adequate amounts of potent narcotics."* This admonition suggests that undertreatment of pain was common, an impression confirmed in the early 1970s by two psychiatrists at Montefiore Hospital and Medical Center in New York. Assigned to handle "difficult" patients, Richard M. Marks and Edward J. Sachar discovered a very good reason why so many continued to complain even after being treated with narcotics: They were still in pain. "To our surprise," they wrote in the February 1973 *Annals of Internal Medicine,* "instead of the primary issue being personality problems in the patient, in virtually every case it was found that the patient was not being adequately treated with analgesics and, further, the house staff for various reasons was hesitant to prescribe more."

Marks and Sachar's surveys of patients and doctors found "a general pattern of undertreatment of pain with narcotic analgesics, leading to widespread and significant distress." In part they blamed "excessive and unrealistic concern about the danger of addiction," which doctors erroneously equated with tolerance (the need for higher doses to achieve the same effect) and physical dependence (indicated by withdrawal symptoms). Marks and Sachar emphasized the distinction between a patient who seeks a drug for pain relief and an addict who seeks a drug for its euphoric effects: The patient can readily give up the drug once the pain is gone, whereas the addict depends on it to deal with daily life. Marks and Sachar estimated that less than 1 percent of patients treated with narcotics in a hospital become addicts. Although they urged better training in pain treatment, they concluded with a prescient warning: "For many physicians these drugs may have a special emotional significance that interferes with their rational use."

Subsequent studies confirmed that patients treated with narcotics rarely become addicts. In 1980 researchers at Boston University Medical Center reported that they had reviewed the records of 11,882 hospital patients treated with narcotics and found "only four cases of reasonably well- documented addiction in patients who had no history of addiction." A 1982 study of 10,000 burn victims who had received narcotic injections, most of them for weeks or months, found no cases of drug abuse that could be attributed to pain treatment. In a 1986 study of 38 chronic pain patients who were treated with opioids for years, only two became addicted, and both had histories of drug abuse.

Despite such reassuring findings, many patients continued to suffer because of their doctors' opiophobia. In December, 1987, the *New York Times* ran a story with the headline, "Physicians Said to Persist in Undertreating Pain and Ignoring the Evidence." Russell Portenoy, director of analgesic studies at Memorial Sloan-Kettering Cancer Center, told the *Times,* "The undertreatment of pain in hospitals is absolutely medieval. . . .The problem persists because physicians share the widespread social attitudes that these drugs are unacceptable." He added that "many physicians fear sanctions against themselves if they prescribe the drugs more liberally." The article cited a recent survey in which 203 out of 353 patients at a Chicago hospital said they had experienced "unbearable" pain during their stay. More than half were in pain at the time of the survey, and 8 percent called the pain "excruciating" or "horrible." Most of the patients said nurses had not even asked them about their pain. The same study found that nurses were dispensing, on average, just one-fourth the amount of painkiller authorized by physicians.

The ordeal of Henry James, which began and ended the same year the *New York Times* article appeared, illustrates this stingier-than-thou tendency. James, a 74-year-old with prostate cancer that had spread to his leg and spine, was admitted to Guardian Care of Ahoskie, a North Carolina nursing home, in February 1987. Like many patients in the late stages of cancer, James was in severe pain, and his doctor had prescribed 150 milligrams of morphine every three or four hours, "as needed." The nursing staff thought that was far too much. They started cutting back his doses, substituting headache medicine and placebos. He received 240 doses in January but only 41 in February. The nursing supervisor, Rebecca Carter, told James and his family that she didn't want him to become an addict. She also said that if he took too much pain medication early on, it wouldn't work anymore when he really needed it.

James died after four months of agony. His family sued Guardian Care, and at the trial pain experts testified that the amount of medication Carter and her staff dispensed was grossly inadequate. They also noted that narcotic doses can be increased indefinitely to compensate for tolerance, so Carter's concern that the medicine would stop working was "ridiculous." In November 1990 the jury ordered the nursing home to pay James's estate $15 million, including $7.5 million in punitive damages. After the verdict, an unrepentant Carter told the *Los Angeles Times* "nothing whatsoever has changed. . . .We still give drugs the way we always have."

Outside of Guardian Care, however, things were starting to change by the mid-'80s. As critics drew attention to the torture inflicted by undertreatment, the use of painkillers began rising substantially. Between 1979 and 1985, for example, consumption of oxycodone and hydromorphone rose 40 percent and 67 percent, respectively, according to DEA figures. The National Institute on Drug Abuse acknowledged the problem of opiophobia. In 1989 NIDA Director

Charles Schuster confessed, "We have been so effective in warning the medical establishment and the public in general about the inappropriate use of opiates that we have endowed these drugs with a mysterious power to enslave that is overrated." A 1993 article in NIDA's newsletter said "these drugs are rarely abused when used for medical purposes" and lamented that "thousands of patients suffer needlessly." In 1992 and 1994 the U.S. Department of Health and Human Services issued guidelines urging more aggressive treatment of postoperative pain and cancer pain, respectively. The 1994 guidelines said 90 percent of cancer pain could be controlled with available methods. On the same day that HHS released the guidelines, *The New England Journal of Medicine* published a national study estimating that 42 percent of cancer outpatients do not receive adequate pain treatment.

It is startling to realize that, as the twentieth century drew to a close, the idea of giving patients enough medication to relieve their pain was just catching on. One reason for the slow progress is that advocates of better pain treatment have been fighting deeply rooted prejudices. Dr. Sidney Schnoll, a pain and addiction specialist who chairs the Division of Substance Abuse Medicine at the Medical College of Virginia, cites the impact of anti-drug propaganda "telling us that there's an addict on every corner, under every stone. So of course people are fearful. I find that my own patients are often unwilling. I have to convince them to take the medications I'm prescribing them." Dr. Kathleen M. Foley, chief of the pain service at Memorial Sloan-Kettering Cancer Center, says the problem is especially vexing in the case of children. "Parents are so afraid of addicting their kids that they do not want to treat them," she says. "They say, 'The pain's not so bad,' or, 'We don't want him to be sleepy,' or, 'We don't want to make him an addict.' They say to the kid, 'Be tough.' But they're very torn and confused. They're afraid of the drugs, because every parent has heard Nancy Reagan say, 'Say no to drugs.' So they're saying, 'My God! Drug addiction could be worse than my child's cancer.' "

By perpetuating such attitudes, the war on drugs obstructs pain relief. Through efforts to prevent narcotics from falling into the wrong hands, it has a more direct effect. A 1987 DEA report cites declines of 30 to 55 percent in the use of Schedule II drugs within two years after the adoption of multiple-copy prescription programs in various states during the 1960s and 1970s. "I think it's a testament to the percentage of misprescribing and criminal prescribing that goes on," says Gene Haislip, the DEA's director of diversion control. "I don't think there's any evidence that they're discouraging appropriate medical use. We think there's some evidence to suggest they're discouraging *in*appropriate prescribing, but I don't have any reason to think they really have an impact on legitimate practitioners." Haislip likens compliance with a multiple-copy prescription program to filing an income tax return. "We don't decide not to make money because we have to report it," he says. "And I don't think doctors are deciding, 'Well, this patient isn't going to get medical treatment that's appropriate because somewhere somebody may read something and ask me some questions.'"

The tax code, of course, has a big impact on the way people make (or don't make) money. And despite Haislip's reassurances, there is substantial evidence that prescription monitoring has a chilling effect on the practice of medicine. To begin with, a large percentage of doctors in multiple-copy states—in California, almost half—do not even request the special forms, which suggests that "legitimate practitioners" are deterred by the hassle and scrutiny involved. "When I was in Illinois," says Sidney Schnoll, "there were physicians who just didn't want to carry triplicate forms. Sometimes they would call me up and say, 'You have triplicates, don't you? Can you write a prescription for so-and-so?' That's not good medicine."

Furthermore, it hardly seems plausible that frivolous or fraudulent prescriptions could account for a third to a half of a state's licit narcotic use, as Haislip suggests. The limited research on this question does not support that view. A 1984 study reported in the *American Journal of Hospital Pharmacy* found that Schedule II prescriptions at a major Texas hospital dropped more than 60 percent the year after the state began requiring triplicate forms for such drugs. At the same time, prescriptions of analgesics not covered by the program rose. A 1991 study reported in the *Journal of the American Medical Association* found a similar pattern in New York state, which added benzodiazepines, a class of sedatives that includes Valium, to the drugs covered by its monitoring program in 1989. Prescriptions for benzodiazepines dropped substantially in New York, while use of several other sedatives rose, even as consumption of those drugs fell in the rest of the country. The researchers noted that "the alternative sedative-hypnotic medications are less effective, more likely to be abused, and more dangerous in overdose than benzodiazepines." These studies suggest that multiple-copy prescription programs lead physicians to replace monitored drugs with less appropriate alternatives.

This sort of behavior is reinforced every time a conscientious doctor gets hassled by the authorities because someone thought his prescriptions looked suspicious. In 1987 two state drug agents visited the office of Ronald Blum, associate director of New York University's Kaplan Comprehensive Cancer Center. "They showed me their badges and guns, and read me my rights," he told the *Journal of NIH Research*. It turned out that Blum had filled out some narcotic prescription forms incorrectly. The Department of Health charged him with three administrative violations, including failure to report his cancer patients to the state as habitual drug users. A year and a half later, after Blum had spent $10,000 in legal fees, the state finally dropped the charges. In 1987 the DEA investigated Portland, Oregon, oncologist Albert Brady because he was prescribing high doses of Dilaudid to a cancer patient in a nursing home. Although the DEA concluded that Brady was not supplying drugs to the black market, it notified the state Board of Medical Examiners, which fined him $5,000 for overprescribing and suspended his license for a month. It does not take many incidents like these to "have an impact on legitimate practitioners." Brady told the *Journal of NIH Research* that his two partners "changed their practice overnight and became reluctant to prescribe sufficient doses of painkillers."

As the Brady case illustrates, even in states that do not require special forms for certain drugs, physicians have to worry about attracting the attention of state licensing boards. A 1991 survey of ninety physicians reported in the *Wisconsin Medical Journal* found that most were concerned enough about regulatory scrutiny to prescribe lower doses, indicate smaller amounts, allow fewer refills, or select a different drug than they otherwise would have. Given the attitudes of many regulators, such caution is understandable. In 1992 the University of Wisconsin Pain Research Group surveyed state medical board members throughout the country. The results, as reported in the newsletter of the American Pain Society, were striking: "Only 75% of medical board members were confident that prescribing opioids for chronic cancer pain was both legal and acceptable medical practice. . . . If the patient's chronic pain did not involve a malignancy, only 12% were confident that the practice was both legal and medically acceptable." Since these are the people who define the limits of appropriate medicine, their beliefs are bound to affect the treatment of pain.

Dr. C. Stratton Hill, a professor of medicine at the M.D. Anderson Cancer Center in Houston, became interested in the impact of regulatory expectations on medical practice about a decade and a half ago. "Patients with obvious cancer pain were given doses that were not adequate," he says. "So I began looking at why physicians were reluctant to prescribe opioids in appropriate amounts, and I realized that the bottom line was that they were afraid of sanctions by regulatory agencies."

Hill and other physicians lobbied for what came to be known as the Intractable Pain Treatment Act, which the Texas legislature approved in 1989. Essentially, the law said doctors would not be punished for prescribing narcotics to patients suffering from pain that could not be relieved through other means. But this assurance "did not make any difference in what the doctor did," Hill says, "because there was no commonly understood standard of practice. The doctor could still be charged and have to defend himself, and that cost money. Maybe the doctor would win, but that would be $25,000 later."

In 1995 Hill and his colleagues convinced the state Board of Medical Examiners to adopt rules clarifying the vague provisions of the state Medical Practice Act under which doctors were most commonly charged. Under the new rules, a doctor who prescribes a drug in good faith for a legitimate medical purpose (including pain relief) is not subject to sanctions, provided he observes certain safeguards and keeps careful records. Hill thinks the new policy may be having an impact. The year after the rules were issued, seventeen doctors were charged under the relevant sections, compared to thirty-seven the year before.

Hill's work in Texas helped inspire similar efforts in California, where Harvey Rose emerged from his battle with regulators—which took $140,000 in legal fees and five years to resolve—determined to help other doctors avoid similar conflicts. In 1990 the state legislature adopted an Intractable Pain Treatment Act modeled after the Texas statute, and in 1994 the Medical Board of California issued guidelines intended to reassure wary doctors. Although California's current approach is decidedly more enlightened than the policies of other states, Rose says "doctors are still fearful. They just don't want to deal with patients like this, because they're afraid it's too difficult. They're never sure if they're getting enough records and covering their butts enough. It's much easier just to say, 'No, I'm sorry. I don't take care of your kind.' "

That was essentially the response encountered by Cynthia A. Snyder, a nurse who recently described her own search for pain relief in the *Journal of Law, Medicine, and Ethics*. After a cerebral aneurysm and brain surgery in 1983, Snyder suffered from seizures, memory loss, and "terrible, unrelenting pain." But she soon learned that "I lacked the 'proper diagnosis' to control my pain. I did not have terminal cancer." Like many other patients in the same situation, Snyder found that her desperation for relief was viewed with suspicion. "Several times," she writes, "I was openly accused of being an 'addict' and of falsely reporting chronic pain just to obtain prescription drugs. . . . Finally, I found myself begging, as though I were a criminal." After five years of suffering, she found a physician willing to prescribe regular doses of codeine. "Within two weeks, I felt reborn!" she recalls. "I began writing again. My doctorate was completed, and once more I began to teach part-time. *My hope was restored, and my life was no longer crippled by constant severe pain.*"

Eventually, Snyder reports, "the precise neuropathology of the pain was discovered." But that was years after her brain surgery. When she was searching for a doctor to help her, she could not offer any definitive evidence of her pain. There were records of the aneurysm and the operation, but only her complaint testified to her ongoing suffering. This is often the case with intractable pain. How do you prove the existence of migraine headaches or back pain, not to mention controversial conditions such as fibromyalgia and chronic fatigue syndrome? A doctor can take a patient's history, inquire about symptoms, and perform an exam. He can consider the patient's character and reputation. But in the end, he is only surmising that the pain is real. Ultimately, he has to take the patient at his word, knowing that misplaced trust could mean professional ruin.

Ask William Hurwitz. The doctor who offered David Covillion an alternative to a Kevorkian-style death lost his license in August, as did Jerome A. Danoff, the pharmacist who filled prescriptions for many of Hurwitz's patients. The investigation began in May 1995, when agents of the DEA and the Virginia Department of Health Professions visited Danoff's store because a wholesaler had reported unusually large orders of narcotics. Hurwitz asked his patients to sign waivers of confidentiality and opened up his records to the investigators. A year later, when relatives of two patients who had died in January 1996 complained to the Virginia Board of Medicine, the board suspended Hurwitz's license, charging him with misprescribing not only for those patients but for twenty-eight others.

It's doubtful that the deaths resulted from Hurwitz's negligence. One patient, a Tennessee man with a head injury that impaired his sense of smell, died after eating rotten chicken fajitas and vomiting all weekend. Hurwitz believes he died of intestinal hemorrhaging caused by food poisoning, but the medical examiner, after finding a lot of empty Dilaudid bottles, concluded that the man had died of an overdose, a theory that was not supported by a blood test. On the other hand, needle tracks indicated that the man had been dissolving his painkiller and injecting it, contrary to Hurwitz's instructions, and his girlfriend said he had been taking excessive doses of a muscle relaxant. In the other case, which involved a Florida woman suffering from facial pain after failed jaw surgery, toxicology tests showed that she had taken oxycodone and morphine in much higher doses than Hurwitz had prescribed. He believes her death was a suicide, and the patient's mother, who defends him, concurs. Her ex-husband thinks his daughter died of an accidental overdose and blames Hurwitz.

The investigators found one former patient who complained that Hurwitz had given him too many pills and too little information about their side effects. But none of his current patients had anything bad to say about him. Many traveled long distances to show their support at his hearing before the Board of Medicine, and more than fifty testified on his behalf. Hurwitz's motives were not in doubt, and the hearing focused largely on the amounts of medication he had prescribed. His patients were taking anywhere from 10 to 200 pills a day.

Hurwitz explained that some patients are especially resistant to narcotics to begin with, and all develop tolerance. He insisted that the number of pills is not the issue, since a patient who would otherwise be incapacitated by pain can function well on doses of narcotics that would kill the average person. In fact, Virginia has an Intractable Pain Treatment Act that allows doctors to prescribe narcotics "in excess of the recommended dosage upon certifying the medical necessity." Dr. Mitchell Max, director of the Pain Research Clinic at the National Institutes of Health, testified: "I see nothing wrong with the doses, the amount, the number of pills per se. . . . He is just taking regimens that work in cancer patients that everyone agrees on, and using them in people who had life-impairing, or even life-threatening, levels of pain. . . . We routinely give doses up to ten times that size in patients with cancer."

The state questioned the thoroughness of Hurwitz's examinations, documentation, and monitoring. Hurwitz says most of his pain patients came to him with well-established problems, and "my main purpose in doing the diagnosis was to make sure that the patients were who they said they were. If they said they had back surgery, I wanted to see a back scar. If they said they had no leg, I wanted to look at the stump. So my physical exam was really limited to confirmatory findings that would illustrate the complaints and make sure they weren't conning me." As for monitoring, he saw patients who lived in the area once a month, but those who lived hundreds of miles away might visit his office only once or twice a year. The visits were supplemented by a monthly written report and telephone calls.

"The average practitioner does have reservations about prescribing long-term opiates," testified Dr. Stephen P. Long, director of acute pain services at the Medical College of Virginia Hospitals. "I would have performed a more thorough physical exam. I would like to have seen more detailed documentation."

On the other hand, Dr. James Campbell, director of the Blaustein Pain Treatment Center at Johns Hopkins University, said Hurwitz "is doing heroic things for his patients. I think what he is doing involves enormous sacrifice. There are a lot of bad doctors out there, but he is not one of them."

On August 10, after the longest hearing in its history, the Virginia Board of Medicine found Hurwitz guilty of inadequate screening, excessive prescribing, and deficient monitoring. It revoked his license, saying it would be restored after three months if he agreed to take courses in narcotic prescription, pharmacology, psychiatry, addiction, medical record keeping, and pain management. Even then, he would be forbidden to prescribe narcotics for a year. Hurwitz has registered for the courses, but he has also filed an appeal in Arlington Circuit Court. After the Virginia ruling, the D.C. Board of Medicine suspended Hurwitz's license. Unable to practice, he had to give up his office. About the same time, the Virginia Board of Pharmacy revoked Jerome Danoff's license for two years and fined him $10,000. He also planned to appeal.

Meanwhile, Hurwitz's patients were left high and dry. "I'm flabbergasted," he told the Washington Post after his Virginia license was revoked. "The Board of Medicine has told my patients, 'Drop dead.' " Said Laura D. Cooper, a patient with multiple sclerosis: "The board has made no provision for the patients. If I can't get medicine, I'm going to die the next time I get sick, and that's not histrionics. Some of us are candidates for suicide right now." Cooper, an attorney, has filed a federal class-action suit against the Virginia Board of Medicine, the Department of Health Professions, and the DEA on behalf of herself and Hurwitz's other pain patients.

David Covillion is not a party to the suit. He killed himself on September 11.

WHITHER MEDICAL MARIJUANA

Lester Grinspoon, M.D.

The modern renaissance of medicinal cannabis began in the early 1970s, when several young patients who were being treated with the recently developed cancer chemotherapies discovered that marijuana was much more effective than conventional medicines for the relief of the intense and prolonged nausea and vomiting induced by some of these agents.[1] Word spread rapidly over the cancer treatment grapevine. By mid-decade, the capacity of marijuana to lower intraocular pressure had been observed, and patients suffering from glaucoma began to experiment with it.[2] As the AIDS epidemic gathered momentum, many patients who suffered HIV-associated weight loss learned that marijuana was the most effective and least toxic treatment for this life-threatening symptom. These three new medical uses of cannabis have led to wider folk experimentation. Soon the use of marijuana in the symptomatic treatment of convulsive disorders, migraine, insomnia, and dysmenorrhea had been rediscovered.

We have now identified more than thirty symptoms and syndromes for which patients have found cannabis useful,[3] and others will undoubtedly be discovered. Many patients regard it as more effective than conventional medicines, with fewer or less disturbing side effects. Consider the pain of osteoarthritis, which was often treated in the nineteenthth century with tincture of cannabis. Aspirin, the first of the non-steroidal antiinflammatory drugs (NSAIDs), rapidly displaced cannabis as the treatment of choice for this and many other kinds of mild to moderate pain. But NSAIDs now claim more than 7,000 lives annually in the United States alone; cannabis, by contrast, has never killed anyone using it for the relief of pain or any other purpose.[4] It is not surprising that many patients now treat their osteoarthritis with cannabis, asserting that it provides a better quality of pain relief than NSAIDs and also elevates their spirits.

The number of Americans who understand the medical uses of cannabis has grown greatly in the last few years. The passage of initiatives or legislation allowing some restricted legal use of cannabis as a medicine in ten states is the most striking political manifestation of this growing interest. The state laws have led to a battle with federal authorities who, until recently, proclaimed medical marijuana to be a hoax. Under public pressure to acknowledge the medical potential of marijuana, the White House Office of National Drug Policy, authorized a review by the Institute of Medicine of the National Academy of Science which was published in March of 1999.[5]

The report acknowledged the medical value of marijuana, but grudgingly. One of its most important shortcomings was a failure to put into perspective the vast anecdotal evidence of marijuana's striking medicinal versatility and limited toxicity. The report states that smoking is too dangerous a form of delivery, but this conclusion is based on an exaggerated evaluation of the toxicity of the smoke. The report's Recommendation Six would allow patients with what it calls "debilitating symptoms (such as intractable pain or vomiting)" to use smoked marijuana for only six months, and then only after all other approved medicines have failed. The treatment would have to be monitored with "an oversight strategy comparable to an institutional review board process."[6] This would make legal use of medical cannabis impossible in practice. The IOM would have patients who find cannabis helpful when taken by inhalation wait for years until a means of delivering smoke-free cannabinoids is developed. But there are now available devices that take advantage of the fact that cannabinoids vaporize at temperatures below the ignition point of dried cannabis plant material.

The authors of the IOM report discuss marijuana as if it were a drug like thalidomide, with well-established serious toxicity (phocomelia) and limited clinical usefulness (leprosy). This is inappropriate for a drug with a long history, limited toxicity, unusual versatility, and easy availability. But at least the report confirms that even government officials no longer doubt that cannabis has medical uses. Inevitably, cannabinoids will eventually be allowed to compete with other medicines in the treatment of a variety of symptoms and conditions; the only uncertainty involves the form in which they will be delivered.

When I first considered this issue in the early 1970s, I assumed that cannabis as medicine would be identical to the marijuana that is used for other purposes (the dried flowering tops of female Cannabis indica plants); its toxicity is minimal, its dosage is easily titrated and, once freed of the prohibition tariff, it will be inexpensive. I thought the main problem was its classification in Schedule I of the Comprehensive Drug Abuse and Control Act of 1970, which describes it as having a high potential for abuse, no accepted medical use in the United States, and lack of accepted safety for use under medical supervision. At that time I naively believed that a change to Schedule II would overcome a major obstacle to its legal availability as a medicine. I had already come to believe that the greatest harm in recreational use of marijuana came not from the drug itself but from the effects of prohibition. But I saw that as a separate issue; I believed that, like opiates and cocaine, cannabis could be used medically while remaining outlawed for other purposes. I thought that once it was transferred to Schedule II, clinical research on marijuana would be pursued eagerly. A quarter of a century later, I have begun to doubt this. It would be highly desirable if marijuana could be approved as a legitimate medicine within the present federal regulatory system, but it now seems to me unlikely.

Today, transferring marijuana to Schedule II (high potential for abuse, limited medical use) would not be enough to make it available as a prescription drug. Such drugs must undergo rigorous, expensive, and time-consuming tests before they are approved by the FDA. This system is designed to regulate the commercial distribution of drug company products and protect the public against false or misleading claims about their efficacy and safety. The drug is generally a single synthetic chemical that a pharmaceutical company has developed and patented. The company submits an application to the FDA and tests it first for safety in animals and then for clinical safety and efficacy. The company must present evidence from double-blind controlled studies showing that the drug is more effective than a placebo and as effective as available drugs. Case reports, expert opinion, and clinical experience are not considered sufficient. The cost of this evaluation exceeds $200 million per drug.

It is unlikely that whole smoked marijuana should or will ever be developed as an officially recognized medicine via this route. Thousands of years of use have demonstrated its medical value; the extensive government-supported effort of the last three decades to establish a sufficient level of toxicity to support the harsh prohibition has instead provided a record of safety that is more compelling than that of most approved medicines. The modern FDA protocol is not necessary to establish a risk-benefit estimate for a drug with such a history. To impose this protocol on cannabis would be like making the same demand of aspirin, which was accepted as a medicine more than sixty years before the advent of the double-blind controlled study. Many years of experience have shown us that aspirin has many uses and limited toxicity, yet today it could not be marshalled through the FDA approval process. The patent has long since expired, and with it the incentive to underwrite the enormous cost of this modern seal of approval. Cannabis too is unpatentable, so the only source of funding for a "start-from-scratch" approval would be the government, which is, to put it mildly, unlikely to be helpful. Other reasons for doubting that marijuana would ever be officially approved are today's anti-smoking climate and, most important, the widespread use of cannabis for purposes disapproved by the government.

To see the importance of this obstacle, consider the effects of granting marijuana legitimacy as a medicine while prohibiting it for any other use. How would the appropriate "labeled" uses be determined and how would "off-label" uses be proscribed? Then there is the question of who will provide the cannabis. The federal government now provides marijuana from its farm in Mississippi to seven patients under a now-discontinued Compassionate IND program. But surely the government could not or would not produce marijuana for many thousands of patients receiving prescriptions, any more than it does for other prescription drugs. If production is contracted out, will the farmers have to enclose their fields with security fences and protect them with security guards? How would the marijuana be distributed? If through pharmacies, how would they provide secure facilities capable of keeping fresh supplies? Would the price of pharmaceutical marijuana have to be controlled: not too high, lest patients be tempted to buy it on the street or grow their own; not too low, lest people with marginal or fictitious "medical" conditions besiege their doctors for prescriptions? What about the parallel problems with potency? When urine tests are demanded for workers, how would those who use marijuana legally as a medicine be distinguished from those who use it for other purposes?

To realize the full potential of cannabis as a medicine in the setting of the present prohibition system, we would have to address all these problems and more. A delivery system that successfully navigated this minefield would be cumbersome, inefficient, and bureaucratically top-heavy. Government and medical licensing boards would insist on tight restrictions, challenging physicians as though cannabis were a dangerous drug every time it was used for any new patient or purpose. There would be constant conflict with one of two outcomes: patients would not get all the benefits they should, or they would get the benefits by abandoning the legal system for the black market or their own gardens and closets.

A solution now being proposed, notably in the IOM Report, is what might be called the "pharmaceuticalization" of cannabis: prescription of isolated individual cannabinoids, synthetic cannabinoids, and cannabinoid analogs. The IOM Report states that "if there is any future for marijuana as a medicine, it lies in its isolated components, the cannabinoids, and their synthetic derivatives." It goes on: "Therefore, the purpose of clinical trials of smoked marijuana would not be to develop marijuana as a licensed drug, but such trials could be a first step towards the development of rapid-onset, non-smoked cannabinoid delivery systems."[7] Some cannabinoids and analogs may have advantages over whole smoked or ingested marijuana in limited circumstances. For example, cannabidiol may be more effective as an anti-anxiety medicine and an anticonvulsant when it is not taken along with THC, which sometimes generates anxiety. Other cannabinoids and analogs may occasionally prove more useful than marijuana because they can be administered intravenously. For example, 15 to 20 percent of patients lose consciousness after suffering a thrombotic or embolic stroke, and some people who suffer brain syndrome after a severe blow to the head become unconscious. The new analog dexanabinol (HU-211) has been shown to protect brain cells from damage by glutamate excitotoxicity in these circumstances, and it will be possible to give it intravenously to an unconscious person.[8] Presumably other analogs may offer related advantages. Some of these commercial products may also lack the psychoactive effects which make marijuana useful to some for nonmedical purposes. Therefore they will not be defined as "abusable" drugs subject to the constraints of the Comprehensive Drug Abuse and Control Act. Nasal sprays, nebulizers, skin patches, pills, and suppositories can be used to avoid exposure of the lungs to the particulate matter in marijuana smoke.

The question is whether these developments will make marijuana itself medically obsolete. Surely many of these new products would be useful and safe enough for commercial development. It is uncertain, however, whether pharmaceutical companies will find them worth the enormous development costs. Some may be (for example, a cannabinoid inverse agonist that reduces appetite might be highly lucrative), but for most specific symptoms, analogs or combinations of analogs are unlikely to be more useful than natural cannabis. Nor are they likely to have a significantly wider spectrum of therapeutic uses, since the natural product contains the compounds (and synergistic combinations of compounds) from which they are derived. THC and cannabidiol, as well as dexanabinol, protect brain cells after a stroke or traumatic injury. Synthetic tetrahydrocannabinol (dronabinol or Marinol) has been available for years, but patients generally find whole smoked marijuana to be more effective.

The cannabinoids in whole marijuana can be separated from the burnt plant products by vaporization devices that will be inexpensive when manufactured in large numbers. Inhalation is a highly effective means of delivery, and faster means will not be available for analogs (except in a few situations such as parenteral injection in a patient who is unconscious or suffering from pulmonary impairment). Furthermore, any new analog will have to have an acceptable therapeutic ratio. The therapeutic ratio of marijuana is not known because it has never caused an overdose death, but it is estimated on the basis of extrapolation from animal data to be 20,000 to 40,000. The therapeutic ratio of a new analog is unlikely to be higher than that; in fact, new analogs may be less safe than smoked marijuana because it will be physically possible to ingest more of them. And there is the problem of classification under the Comprehensive Drug Abuse and Control Act for analogs with psychoactive effects. The more restrictive the classification of a drug, the less likely drug companies are to develop it and physicians to prescribe it. Recognizing this economic fact of life, Unimed, the manufacturer of Marinol, has recently succeeding in getting it reclassified from Schedule II to Schedule III. Nevertheless, many physicians will continue to avoid prescribing it for fear of the drug enforcement authorities.

A somewhat different approach to the pharmaceuticalization of cannabis is being taken by a British company, G. W. Pharmaceuticals. Recognizing the great usefulness of naturally occurring cannabinoids, this firm is developing a seed bank of cannabis strains with particular value in the treatment of various symptoms and disorders. They are also attempting to develop products and delivery systems which will skirt the two primary concerns about the use of marijuana as a medicine: the smoke and the psychoactive effects (the "high").

To avoid the need for smoking, G. W. Pharmaceuticals is exploring the possibility of delivering cannabis extracts sublingually or via nebulizers. The company expects its products to be effective therapeutically at doses too low to produce the psychoactive effects sought by recreational and other users. My clinical experience leads me to question whether this is possible in most or even many cases. Furthermore, the issue is complicated by tolerance. Recreational users soon discover that the more often they use marijuana, the less "high" they feel. A patient who smokes cannabis frequently for the relief of, say, chronic pain or elevated intraocular pressure will not experience a "high" at all. Furthermore, as a clinician who has considerable experience with medical cannabis use, I have to question whether the psychoactive effect is necessarily undesirable. Many patients suffering from serious chronic illnesses say that cannabis generally improves their spirits. If they note psychoactive effects at all, they speak of a slight mood elevation — certainly nothing unwanted or incapacitating.

In principle, administration of cannabis extracts via a nebulizer has the same advantages as smoked marijuana — rapid onset and easy titratability of the effect. But the design of the G. W. Pharmaceutical nebulizer negates this advantage.

The device has electronic controls that monitor the dose and halt delivery if the patient tries to take more than the physician or pharmacist has set it to deliver. The proposal to use this cumbersome and expensive device apparently reflects a fear that patients cannot accurately titrate the amount or a concern that they might take more than they need and experience some degree of "high" (always assuming, doubtfully, that the two can easily be separated, especially when cannabis is used infrequently). Because these products will be considerably more expensive than natural marijuana, they will succeed only if patients and physicians take the health risks of smoking very seriously and feel that it is necessary to avoid any hint of a psychoactive effect.

In the end, the commercial success of any cannabinoid product will depend on how vigorously the prohibition against marijuana is enforced. It is safe to predict that new analogs and extracts will cost much more than whole smoked or ingested marijuana even at the inflated prices imposed by the prohibition tariff. I doubt that pharmaceutical companies would be interested in developing cannabinoid products if they had to compete with natural marijuana on a level playing field. The most common reason for using Marinol is the illegality of marijuana, and many patients choose to ignore the law for reasons of efficacy and price. The number of arrests on marijuana charges has been steadily increasing and has now reached more than 730,000 annually, yet patients continue to use smoked cannabis as a medicine. I wonder whether any level of enforcement would compel enough compliance with the law to embolden drug companies to commit the many millions of dollars it would take to develop new cannabinoid products. Unimed is able to profit from the exorbitantly priced dronabinol (Marinol) only because the United States government underwrote much of the cost of development. Pharmaceutical companies will undoubtedly develop useful cannabinoid products, some of which may not be subject to the constraints of the Comprehensive Drug Abuse and Control Act. But this pharmaceuticalization will never displace natural marijuana for most medical purposes.

Thus two powerful forces are now colliding: the growing acceptance of medical cannabis and the proscription against any use of marijuana, medical or nonmedical. There are no signs that we are moving away from absolute prohibition to a regulatory system that would allow responsible use of marijuana. As a result, we are going to have two distribution systems for medical cannabis: the conventional model of pharmacy-filled prescriptions for FDA-approved medicines, and a model closer to the distribution of alternative and herbal medicines. The only difference, an enormous one, will be the continued illegality of whole smoked or ingested cannabis. In any case, increasing medical use by either distribution pathway will inevitably make growing numbers of people familiar with cannabis and its derivatives. As they learn that its harmfulness has been greatly exaggerated and its usefulness underestimated, the pressure will increase for drastic change in the way we as a society deal with this drug.

NOTES

1. L. Grinspoon and J. B. Bakalar. *Marihuana, the Forbidden Medicine*, Revised and Expanded Edition. New Haven: Yale University Press, 1997, pp. 25-27.

2. R. S. Hepler and I. M. Frank. Marihuana Smoking and Intraocular Pressure. *Journal of the American Medical Association*, Vol. 217 (1971), p. 1392.

3. L. Grinspoon and J. B. Bakalar. *Marihuana, the Forbidden Medicine*, Revised and Expanded Edition. New Haven: Yale University Press, 1997.

4. S. Girkipal, D. R. Ramey, D. Morfeld, G. Singh, H. T. Hatoum, and J. F. Fries. Gastrointestinal Tract Complications of Nonsteroidal Anti-inflammatory Drug Treatment in Rheumatoid Arthritis. *Archives of Internal Medicine*, Vol. 156 (July 22, 1996), pp. 1530-1536.

5. *Marijuana and Medicine: Assessing the Science Base*. J. E. Joy, S. J. Watson, Jr., and J. A. Benson, Jr., Editors. Institute of Medicine, Washington, D.C.: National Academy Press (1999).

6. *Ibid*, pp. 7-8.

7. *Ibid*, p. 11.

8. R. R. Leker, E. Shohami, O. Abramsky, and H. Ovadia. Dexanabinol; A Novel Neuroprotective Drug in Experimental Focal Cerebral Ischemia. *Journal of Neurological Science*, Vol. 162, No. 2 (January 15, 1999), pp. 114-119; E. Shohami, M. Novikov, and R. Bass. Long-term Effect of HU-211, a Novel Non-competitive NMDA Antagonist, on Motor and Memory Functions after Closed Head Injury in the Rat. *Brain Research*, Vol. 674, No. 1 (March 13, 1995), pp. 55-62.

About the Contributors

Mike Gray is an award-winning journalist, screenwriter, and film producer. He is the author of *Drug Crazy: How We Got Into This Mess and How We Can Get Out*, the result of six years of research and writing on U.S. drug policy. Mr. Gray is Chairman of Common Sense for Drug Policy (www.csdp.org).

T.D. Allman is a renowned war correspondent and author of two books: *Miami: City of the Future and Unmanifest Destiny* and *Mayhem and Illusion in American Foreign Policy*. Mr. Allman was the foreign correspondent for *Vanity Fair* and a staff writer for the *New Yorker*. His articles have appeared in *Rolling Stone, National Geographic Magazine* and the historical anthology, *Reporting Vietnam*.

Paul Armentano is a senior policy analyst for NORML and The NORML Foundation. His writing has appeared in numerous newspapers, magazines, and anthologies, including Policy Papers prepared for the 11th International Conference on Drug Policy Reform (Drug Policy Foundation Press, 1997), *Drug Abuse: Opposing Viewpoints, and You Are Being Lied To.*

Russ Baker is an investigative reporter whose work has appeared in *The Nation, Columbia Journalism Review, Esquire* and the *Philadelphia Inquirer* among others. He has reported for *60 Minutes*, Fox News, NPR's *All Things Considered*, CBS Radio, and is currently directing and producing his first documentary film.

Philippe Bourgois is a Professor and Chair of the Department of Anthropology, History and Social Medicine at the University of California, San Francisco. He is the author of numerous articles on substance abuse, *Ethnicity at Work* and the award-winning *In Search of Respect: Selling Crack in El Barrio*.

Charles Bowden is a journalist whose work frequently appears in *Harper's, Esquire, GQ* and other publications. He is the author of several books including *Blood Orchid: An Unnatural History of America* and *Blues for Cannibals: The Notes from Underground*. Mr. Bowden is a contributing editor of *Harper's*.

Graham Boyd is the founder and director of the ACLU Drug Policy Litigation Project. He is a national expert on drug policy and speaks frequently for the media. Currently, Graham also serves as the President of A Better Way Foundation, dedicated to promoting drug policy reform.

W. F. Buckley, Jr. is syndicated columnist, author and founder of *National Review*. He has been a presidential appointee to the U.S. Information Agency, the United Nations, and the National Security Council.

Matthew Brzezinski is a staff writer for the *Wall Street Journal* and a frequent contributor to the *New York Times*. He is the author of *Casino Moscow: A Tale of Greed and Adventure on Capitalism's Wildest Frontier.*

Jim Dwyer is a two-time Pulitzer winning columnist. He is the author of *Subway Lives, Two Seconds Under the World* and the co-author of the acclaimed *Actual Innocence: Five Days to Execution, and other Dispatches from the Wrongfully Convicted.*

Alexandra Eyle is a freelance journalist and editor for *ReconsiDer*, the Forum on Drug Policy's quarterly publication. She regularly contributes to *Syracuse University Magazine.*

Maurice Frank is an Associated Press writer and contributes to many publications including the *Guardian* (London) and *Mother Jones*. He is based in Germany.

Milton Friedman is a professor emeritus of the University of Chicago and a vocal critic of government infringements on the freedom of the individual. He won the 1976 Nobel Prize in Economics.

Lester Grinspoon is Professor of Psychiatry emeritus at Harvard Medical School, and the author of over 180 publications including 12 books. His first book, *Marihuana Reconsidered*, originally published in 1971 by Harvard University Press, was recently republished as a classic. Mr. Grinspoon's latest book, *Marihuana, the Forbidden Medicine*, published by Yale University Press in 1993, has now been translated into ten languages.

Stephen Jay Gould was one of the world's foremost evolutionary biologists. He campaigned for the medicinal use of marijuana after contracting a rare form of abdominal cancer. He died in May of 2002.

Charles S. Grob, M.D., is a medical doctor and Professor of Psychiatry and Pediatrics at the UCLA School of Medicine. He is also Director of the Division of Child and Adolescent Psychiatry at Harbor/UCLA Medical Center, Torrance, California.

Christopher Hitchens is a contributing editor for *Vanity Fair* and columnist for *The Nation*. He has also contributed to dozens of international periodicals, including *Harper's*, the *New York Review of Books,* and the *Guardian* (UK). Mr. Hitchens has written several books, including *The Trial of Henry Kissinger* and most recently, *Why Orwell Matters.*

Jack Hitt has written for numerous publications including the *New York Times Magazine, Salon* and *Harper's Magazine*. He is the author of *Off The Road: A Modern Day Walk Down the Pilgrim's Route into Spain,* and a co-author of *The Perfect*

Murder: Five Great Mystery Writers Create the Perfect Crime. He is a contributing editor of *Harper's.*

Russ Kick is the editor of *Alternewswire.* He is he author of *Psychotropedia* and *Hot Off the Net.*

Dave Kopel is the Research Director of the Independence Institute, and associate policy analyst at the Cato Institute. He writes for many publications including the *National Review* online, the *Rocky Mountain News/Denver Post* and is a contributing editor of *Liberty* magazine.

General Barry McCaffrey, the drug czar, is an international affairs expert and former director of the White House Office of Drug Control Policy.

Joseph McNamara, a former police chief, has been a consultant for the United States Department of Justice, State Department and the Federal Bureau of Investigation. He has written five books including three best-selling detective novels and a respected crime prevention text.

Ethan A. Nadelmann founded the Lindesmith Center, a drug policy and research institute, in 1994. Nadelmann's writings on drug policy have appeared in *Science, Rolling Stone, National Review, Foreign Policy, Foreign Affairs* and *American Heritage.* He is currently the Executive Director of the Lindesmith Center-Drug Policy Foundation.

P. J. O'Rourke is the best-selling author of nine books including *Holidays From Hell and Eat the Rich.* He has written for such diverse publications as *Car and Driver, Playboy, The New Republic,* the *New York Times Book Review,* and *Rolling Stone.*

Craig Reinarman is a professor of Sociology at the University of California, Santa Cruz. He is co-editor of *Crack in America: Demon, Drugs and Social Justice* and author of *American States of Mind: Political Beliefs and Behavior Among Private and Public Workers.*

Marsha Rosenbaum earned her Ph.D. in medical sociology at the University of California at San Francisco in 1979. She is the co-author of several books on the effects of illegal drug use including: *Women on Heroin, Pursuit of Ecstasy: The MDMA Experience* and *Pregnant Women on Drugs: Combating Stereotypes and Stigma.*

A.M. Rosenthal is an Op-Ed columnist for the *New York Daily News* and the former Executive Editor of the *New York Times.* He is a Pulitzer Prize winner and the recipient of several Overseas Press Club Awards.

Kurt Schmoke, appointed by President Jimmy Carter to the White House domestic policy staff, also served as the U.S. Attorney for the District of Maryland and is a former mayor of Baltimore, Maryland. He founded the Baltimore Community Development Financing Corporation in 1988.

Joshua Wolf Shenk is contributing editor of *Washington Monthly* and a writing instructor at the New School. His forthcoming book is entitled *The Melancholy of Abraham Lincoln*.

Adam J. Smith regularly reports on the drug trade and drug policy as a staff writer for the *Generator 21* website and for other publications including the *Guardian*. He is the Associate Director of the Drug Reform Coordination Network.

Oliver Stone is a writer, actor, producer and an Oscar award-winning director whose credits include *Born on the Fourth of July, JFK*, and *Any Given Sunday*.

Keith Stroup is the founder and executive director of the National Organization for the Reform of Marijuana Laws, NORML. Mr. Stroup is one of America's chief proponents of marijuana law reform, and his opinion has been solicited for debates featured in the *New York Times* and on CNN's *Crossfire*.

Jacob Sullum is a syndicated newspaper columnist and senior editor of *Reason Magazine*. He is the author of *For Your Own Good: The Anti-Smoking Crusade and the Tyranny of Public Health*.

Robert W. Sweet is a Senior Judge for the Southern District of New York. In the late 1980s he led dozens of federal judges in refusing to hear drug cases as a protest regressive mandatory minimum sentencing guidelines.

Maia Szalavitz is the co-author of *Recovery Options: The Complete Guide, How You and Your Loved Ones Can Understand and Treat Alcohol and Other Drug Problems*. Her articles have appeared in the *American Prospect*, the *Village Voice, Alternet*, and *Salon*.

William Triplett is a freelance writer.

John P. Walters heads the White House Office of National Drug Control Policy, coordinating all aspects of federal drug programs and spending.

Tim Wells is a teacher and a freelance writer. His articles have appeared in *Playboy*, the *Washington Post Magazine*, and *Washington Lawyer Magazine*.

Rowena Young is Chief Executive of the School for Social Entrepreneurs in the UK, and was formerly Development Director at Kaleidoscope, the UK's leading one-stop drug rehabilitation center.

Resources

ACLU Drug Policy Litigation Project (www.aclu.org/drugpolicy) Conducts the only national litigation program addressing civil rights and civil liberties violations arising from the war on drugs. The DPLP has litigated cases in federal courts dealing with drug testing, government benefits policies, harm reduction, medical marijuana, racial justice, religious freedom, and voting rights. The DPLP also provides legal support to drug reform efforts at the local, state and national levels.

Cannabis Action Network (www.cannabisaction.net) The website for the pro-marijuana legalization organization's national headquarters.

Cato Institute (www.cato.org) A Washington DC-based think-tank whose site features studies on drug policy.

Common Sense for Drug Policy (www.csdp.org) A non-profit organization, dedicated to expanding discussion on drug policy by resonating the voices of those raising questions about existing law and educating the public about alternatives to current policies.

D.A.R.E. (www.dare-america.com) The official website for the D.A.R.E. program purposed to discourage children from drug use through classroom instruction.

DRCNet Online Library of Drug Policy (www.druglibrary.org/) A listing of drug policy information resources and libraries.

Drug Enforcement Administration (www.dea.gov) The U.S. government's anti-drug law enforcement agency.

Drug Policy Alliance (www.drugpolicy.org) Formerly the Lindesmith Center Drug Policy Foundation, this organization works to "broaden the public debate on drug policy and to promote realistic alternatives to the war on drugs based on science, compassion, public health and human rights."

Drug Sense (www.drugsense.org) A non-profit organization that seeks to educate the public and media about the negative effects of drug prohibition.

DrugWatch International (www.DrugWatch.org) A volunteer, non-profit drug information network that promotes a drug-free society.

Foreign Policy Center (www.fpc.org.uk) A United Kingdom-based think-tank created by Prime Minister Tony Blair and Secretary of State for Foreign and Commonwealth Affairs, Robin Cook. The site includes reports and news on drug policy and other issues.

Hemp.net (www.hemp.net) A site containing recent marijuana-related news, scientific reports and related email addresses.

Law Enforcement Against Prohibition (www.leap.cc) An organization of current and former law enforcement officials that campaigns for the regulation of drugs instead of their prohibition.

Marijuana.org (www.marijuana.org) A medical marijuana resource website from the patients who wrote Proposition 215, which petitions for the legalization of medicinal marijuana use and dissemination.

Marijuana Policy Project (www.mpp.org) A site focused on removing the criminal penalties for marijuana use and legalizing the medicinal use of the substance.

Medical Marijuana Website (www.rxmarijuana.com) A website devoted to the exchange of information about the use of marijuana as a medicine compiled by members of the faculty of the Harvard Medical School who have been studying marijuana for many years.

Mothers Against Misuse and Abuse (www.mamas.org) A non-profit organization committed to fighting marijuana prohibition and teaching America's youth about the health and social consequences of marijuana use.

National Center for Policy Analysis (www.ncpa.org/) A non-profit, non-partisan organization whose mission is to "seek innovative private-sector solutions to public policy problems."

National Clearinghouse on Drugs and Alcohol (www.health.org) An information service from the Center for Substance Abuse Prevention claiming to be the world's largest resource of current information and materials concerning substance abuse.

National Criminal Justice Research Service (www.ncjrs.org) A federally funded resource site offering justice and substance abuse information.

National Drug Court Institute (www.ndci.org) The website for the National Association of Drug Court Professionals which includes research, evaluations and relevant commentary on drug regulation and penalties for illegal drug use and dissemination in the United States.

National Drug Strategy Network (www.ndsn.org) An impartial source on drug policy information.

National Institute of Drug Abuse (www.drugabuse.gov) An organization dedicated to reducing drug abuse and addiction through science.

National Institute of Health (www.nih.gov) The U.S. government's leading scientific anti-drug agency.

National Organization for the Reform of Marijuana Laws (NORML) (www.norml.org/) A Washington, DC-based public interest lobby that represents the interests of responsible marijuana smokers in America. NORML supports the elimination of all penalties for the responsible use of marijuana by adults, and the creation of a legally regulated market where consumers could purchase their marijuana from a safe and secure environment.

November Coalition (www.november.org) A non-profit, grassroots organization committed to reforming drug policy-specifically the harsh penalties dealt to perpetrators of drug-related crimes.

Office of National Drug Control Policy (www.whitehousedrugpolicy.gov) The official website of the White House's department on drug policy in the United States.

Partnership for a Drug Free America (www.drugfreeamerica.org) A coalition of communications professionals dedicated to helping teens and children reject drug abuse.

Science of Medical Marijuana (www.medmjscience.org/) A website dedicated to proving the medicinal importance of marijuana through scientific data.

Partnership for Responsible Drug Information (www.prdi.org) An organization which provides information on, and encourages the discussion of, drug policy.

RAND's Drug Policy Research Center (www.rand.org/centers/dprc) An organization dedicated to providing community leaders and public officials with information to more effectively deal with drug problems.

Students for Sensible Drug Policy (www.ssdp.org) A student organization dedicated to educating youth on the harms of the current "war on drugs."

United Nations Office for Drug Control and Crime Prevention

(www.undcp.org) An organization which fights globally against illicit drugs and international crime.

Uses of Marijuana Project Web Site (www.marijuana-uses.com) A website that solicits readers accounts of cannabis enhancement which will ultimately become the basis for a book.

Permissions